The Final Days of Jesus

Detailing the final days of Jesus's life on earth is a theological, literary, archaeological, historical and geographical conundrum which requires many different interpretive skills to understand what really happened and how we know what we think we know about those final days. Many recent authors have tried to write about these moments that are so significant for many around the world. Mark D. Smith's training in the material culture and in the study of the classical world makes *The Final Days of Jesus: The Thrill of Defeat, The Agony of Victory* the closest to giving us a full rendering of what happened and why.

Professor Richard Freund,
Maurice Greenberg Professor of Jewish History and
Director of the Maurice Greenberg Center for Judaic Studies
at the University of Hartford

Mark Smith has brought vividly to life the politics that swirled around the arrest and trial of Jesus. Using insight and the latest archaeological findings, Smith explores the inter-dependence of the Roman governor Pilate and the house of the high priest Caiaphas, calling into question the standard narrative of Jesus's trial before the Sanhedrin. A thoughtful perspective, from which readers of all faiths will benefit.

H.A. Drake,
author of *A Century of Miracles*

The Final Days of Jesus

The Thrill of Defeat,
The Agony of Victory

A Classical Historian Explores Jesus's
Arrest, Trial, and Execution

Mark D. Smith

The Lutterworth Press

The Lutterworth Press
P.O. Box 60
Cambridge
CB1 2NT
United Kingdom

www.lutterworth.com
publishing@lutterworth.com

ISBN: 978 0 7188 9510 5

British Library Cataloguing in Publication Data
A record is available from the British Library

First Published, 2018

For Debi:

My partner, my comfort, my mirror,

My most incisive critic,

My best friend,

My lover,

My wife.

Contents

List of Illustrations and Tables

Illustrations

Tables

In Principio:[1]
Preface

This book finds its genesis in three formative encounters. The first was a graduate course I took from an orthodox rabbi on Judaism in the time of Jesus. That course not only painted a fuller and more nuanced portrait of the period than I had ever considered, but it also provided me with a thoughtful encounter with the Sanhedrin, especially the many ways in which its behaviour in the New Testament accounts of the trials of Jesus was inconsistent with Jewish law. That course also helped to sensitise me to the long and terrible history of Christian anti-Semitism that has grown out of the claim that the Jews were responsible for killing Jesus. The rabbi doubtless said many more sophisticated things than I can remember, for it was a long time ago, but he gave me the profound gift of a stubborn and fertile question.

The second was my initial encounter with the Jesus Seminar. Many years ago, I attended the lectures of a colleague, a New Testament scholar and affiliate of the Jesus Seminar, who was teaching a course on the historical Jesus. His required readings included Marcus Borg, John Dominic Crossan, and E.P. Sanders, among others. It was there that I first encountered seriously the so-called 'Third Quest' for the historical Jesus. I also learned of its advances over the first two quests, many of which seemed quite sensible, such as paying attention to historical evidence beyond the pages of the New Testament and thinking carefully about one's methodology for evaluating evidence. Under my colleague's tutelage, I came to grapple with the Seminar's procedures, assumptions, criteria, and provocative conclusions. In particular, I was struck by Crossan's argument that it is unlikely that Jesus was ever buried after the Romans crucified him, for, he asserted, denial of burial was part of the standard punishment the Romans meted out to those they executed. As a Roman historian, I could understand where he got

---

1. *In principio* are the first words of Genesis and the Gospel of John in the Latin Vulgate translation: 'In the beginning. . . .'

these ideas, but I also wondered what a careful scrutiny of the evidence for Roman executions might reveal. On the whole, I was impressed, but I was struck also by a niggling sense of disconnect between the study of the historical Jesus and the study of other historical subjects in the ancient world.

It took the better part of two decades for me to find the opportunity to connect the dots between these two encounters. I began by studying capital punishment in the Roman Empire, which led ineluctably to that most infamous of Roman executions, and backwards from there to the rest of the research that forms the foundation of this book.

The third encounter will explain the subtitle. When I was young, my family had a weekly ritual: we would gather round the television to watch ABC's *Wide World of Sports*. Every Saturday afternoon, the inimitable voice of Jim McKay greeted us: 'Spanning the globe to bring you the constant variety of sport, the thrill of victory, the agony of defeat. . . .' Those words and the accompanying music always raised the heartrate. I can't remember the pictures associated with the thrill of victory, but I'll never forget the agony of defeat: an ill-starred ski jumper, falling off the side of the ramp and bouncing like a rag doll down the icy slope. That ski jumper, I later learned, was Vinko Bogataj of Slovenia. He was actually quite a good jumper, except on March 21, 1970 when he suffered that terrible accident. Little did he know that he was destined to repeat that feat every Saturday afternoon for the next twenty-eight years. As an athlete and a student of history, I've thought a good deal about the thrill of victory and the agony of defeat but the story of the final days of Jesus seems to invert the premise, showing us instead the thrill of defeat, and the agony of victory.[1]

---

1. I owe this phrasing to Dr Timothy Weber.

I

Historia:[1]
Evidence and Classical History

As the sun sank into the *mare nostrum*, as the Romans called the Mediterranean Sea, 14 Nissan on the Hebrew calendar had arrived. It was the beginning of the much-anticipated Passover feast of the year AD 33.[2] In one of the best-loved customs of the historic Passover Seder, it is the responsibility of the youngest child to inaugurate the festivities by asking, 'Why is this night different from all other nights?'[3] While it is the Passover celebration, ritual, and meal that makes this night different from all other nights of the year, the Passover of AD 33 differed from all other Passovers. On this Passover, the inexorable current of history had drawn together three individuals in Jerusalem who, in a single day, would change the course of Western civilisation.

One of the individuals was a minor Roman who by dint of family connections and military service had risen to become the marginally competent governor of an obscure Roman province: Judaea. Were it not for the events of that Passover, the name Pontius Pilatus would probably be known only among a handful of specialised scholars. The second individual was a self-made man from a minor priestly family who had risen to the position of high priest of Israel from AD 6 to 15. His family

---

1. *'Historia'* is a Latin transliteration from the Greek, meaning 'inquiry' or 'investigation'. Herodotus, the Greek 'Father of History,' used this term in the preface to his great historical investigation of the conflict between Greeks and Persians.
2. Scholars of religion, concerned with the sectarian nature of the BC/AD dating system, have substituted BCE/CE, while the dates remain the same. I here employ BC/AD, not for sectarian reasons, but because that is common practice in professional publications in history. I do so, however, with some misgivings. In the classroom, I use both designations interchangeably. Detailed analysis of the chronology here assumed may be found in Appendix I.
3. From *Mishnah* tractate *Pesachim* 10.4.

connections, dedication, and rare knack for diplomacy had brought his family to wealth and prominence. His name was Chanin ben Seth, better known in the New Testament as Annas. The third individual was an obscure itinerant Jewish teacher from the tiny Galilean village of Nazareth, far removed from the urban bustle of Jerusalem. As a pilgrim, he too had come to the Holy City for this night unlike all other nights. His name, in the Hebrew of the time, was Yeshu ha-Notsri or Yeshua ben Yoseph, Jesus of Nazareth or Jesus son of Joseph, who was a builder by trade.

This Passover differed from all other Passovers because of the extraordinary convergence of the history of the Roman Empire and the history of the Jewish people around these three men. Their motives, perspectives, actions, interactions, and inactions over the course of a single day would cut a new channel for the flow of history. Because of the magnitude of the changes wrought on this day, immense quantities of ink have been spilt on the subject. Why, then, another book on the last days of Jesus? Because, I hope, this book differs from other books. It comes from the pen of a classical historian and from the perspective of ancient Roman culture, both of which promise a different, richer, more nuanced understanding of the people and issues at play that make the Passover of AD 33 so compelling and endlessly fascinating.

So I invite you to join me on a journey of exploration, a study-tour, of sorts, to breathe the dusty air, to walk the limestone-paved streets, to marvel at the exquisite homes of the Upper City, to dip in a ritual bath, to behold the wonder of the Temple precinct as you pay the Temple tax and offer the reluctant, unblemished lamb, to smell the smoke of incense and sacrifice, to hear the trumpet's call, to witness the trial of the millennium, to feel the tension and the pain, to grapple with the stakes for an individual, for a family, for a community of faith, and for an empire. Only by immersing ourselves in the world of first-century Judaea will we understand why this Passover differed from any other. I invite you to travel back with me to that year in Jerusalem.

Before we depart, however, I suspect you will want to know something about your guide. I am a classical historian who specialises in the Roman Empire. I am neither a theologian nor a New Testament specialist, though I do explore these fields to a degree in light of their larger context, offering courses in all areas of classical history, culture, languages and religion, including the study of Jesus in archaeology and history. I am also a student of classical coinage (numismatics) and archaeology by avocation, for I have found these fields essential to my research and teaching. In addition, I have long had the honour of serving as one of the co-directors of the Bethsaida Excavations Project in Israel. My research has focused on late antiquity, classical Greece, and the early Roman Empire. My perspective and qualifications are therefore unusual for someone writing a book on the historical Jesus, with all of the attendant benefits and liabilities.

There has long been an uncomfortable though respectful division of labour between historians and biblical scholars. While biblical scholars, at least on occasion, have worked on the turf of ancient historians, historians have seldom returned the compliment.[1] Historians understand that the study of the Bible is a crowded and technical field; they have tended to keep their distance and depend on the expertise of biblical scholars to provide them with generalised conclusions and interpretations they can utilise as they explore pastures that seem greener for having been less trampled upon. From my perspective, this respectful division of labour is unfortunate. Historians benefit from the detailed literary and contextual analysis for which biblical scholars are rightly lauded and biblical scholars would likewise benefit from the perspectives and methodologies that historians have long applied to every area of the ancient world *except* the Bible.

In its own modest way, this book is an attempt to overcome this divide and provide a classical historian's perspective on at least one aspect of historical Jesus studies. This is a work of Roman history by a historian of the Roman Empire. It is not a work of theology or exegesis, though it cannot ignore those fields entirely. I aim to apply the same methods and the same sort of contextual analysis of the evidence that ancient historians employ when studying any other subject. I am able to pursue this goal as a broad practitioner who has spent his entire career developing such methods and doing such analyses on subjects ranging from Constantius I to Eusebius to Josephus to Pliny the Elder. The methods and types of analysis employed in this study are common to all my research and, indeed, to the entire field of ancient history (though of course historians have plenty of arguments about such matters, as does any other group of scholars).

This book is intended to reach a broad audience, both popular and scholarly. The central chapters are intended to provide analysis and narrative reconstruction of the different players and events surrounding

---

1. There are, however, a few ancient historians who have sought to overcome this division of labour, such as A.N. Sherwin-White, F. Millar, J. Russell, and M. Goodman. Some recent work by social historians has also spanned the divide to a degree.

the last days of Jesus.[1] The language of these chapters is intentionally popular. I have kept footnotes to a minimum and limited them to explanations and the ancient evidence, what historians call 'primary sources', in the belief that all audiences want to have some sense of the evidentiary foundation underlying historical claims. I have chosen, however, to minimise the footnoting of 'secondary sources' – that is, works of modern scholarship – on the assumption that scholars will not need them and others will not want them. To compensate for that absence, I have included a bibliography of the secondary sources I have found most valuable and consider most worthy of further exploration.[2] Two appendices provide the kind of detailed evidence and analysis that lies behind the more popular chapters. At a few points in the main text, I will engage in an unusually detailed examination of an issue. When I do so, I will forewarn the reader.

History is often defined as 'the study of the past', though such a definition is misleading. History is the analysis of evidence concerning the past in context. Historians know nothing without evidence. Nevertheless, while evidence is essential, it does not speak for itself. It requires analysis, and not just any analysis will do. Historical evidence needs to be analysed in context – in the context of its time, place, language, culture, and genre.

I must also acknowledge the biggest issue that confronts anyone who would study the classical world. Ancient history is the exploration of complex puzzles: the one thousand piece variety. The central problem that all ancient historians encounter is that we never have a thousand pieces available to us. Usually, if we're lucky, we have more like a hundred pieces, some of which are broken, worn, or faded, for most of the evidence that once existed and which we would dearly love to examine has been lost to the dust of antiquity. This reality is what makes the task of ancient

---

1. When I use the term 'reconstruction', I do not mean to suggest a pseudo-scientific enlightenment mentality. Rather, I use the term to refer informally to the process of putting evidence to the question, and seeking, by means of careful analysis and interpretation of a broad range of sources, to put the pieces together into the most probable historical narrative that accounts for all the extant evidence.

2. The works of a few scholars have been particularly helpful for this study, and my debt to them is evident throughout this book: Helen K. Bond, E. Mary Smallwood, Shimon Gibson, Raymond E. Brown, Craig Evans, N.T. Wright, Robert H. Gundry, A.N. Sherwin-White, Fergus Millar, H.A. Drake, J.D. Crossan, M. Hengel, Rami Arav, and M. Goodman. See the bibliography for further details.

historians so challenging and so endlessly captivating. It takes great care and skill to make sense of a one thousand piece puzzle with nine hundred pieces missing. It also takes creativity. As a result, the historian's task is never done. Add one piece, move another, or turn the puzzle and look at it from a different angle, and our understanding deepens, becoming richer, more colourful, and more vital. Ancient history is therefore a creative and dynamic enterprise, and one that is immensely rewarding. It is also humbling. There is always the hope (or fear!) that we will find new puzzle-pieces (one of the reasons I love archaeology), and that new questions will yield new perspectives. Conclusions in ancient history are seldom final, which is why I believe that the respectful division of labour should be resisted. I am indebted to my friends and colleagues in theology, religious studies, and biblical studies. In some small way, I hope this study begins to repay that debt.

Since this is a book of Roman history, we must start where all historians start – with the most foundational of all historical questions: what is the nature of the evidence? At this point, you have a decision to make. Because historians know nothing without evidence, it is wise to have a firm understanding of the nature of the evidence before delving into the analysis and narrative. On the other hand, grappling with the nature of the evidence entails some detailed discussion of ancient writings, dates, sources and methodology, and some readers may find such material daunting. I would recommend that when you finish this introduction, you continue on to Chapter II to gain a grounding in the evidence. If, on the other hand, you wish to forego that challenge for the moment, you have my permission to skip Chapter II and proceed to Chapter III for the beginning of the analysis and the narrative. You will not get lost, but your understanding will be enriched if you spend some time getting to know the most important authors who inform our understanding of the people and events that surround the last days of Jesus. If you choose to jump ahead, Chapter II will always be waiting for you should you learn the wisdom of Augustus: *festina lente,* 'make haste slowly'.

We are now prepared to analyse the evidence. The arrangement of this analysis is fairly straightforward. While Chapter II grapples with evidence and methodology, Chapters III and IV will introduce our primary three subjects: Pilate, Annas, and Caiaphas. Their background, context, perspectives, and agendas are crucial to a nuanced understanding of the final days of Jesus. Once we have a sound understanding of the major players, we will proceed to ask why Jesus was arrested and taken to the home of the high priest for questioning, who was there, and what they hoped to accomplish. From there, we will move to the tribunal of Pilate for the trial of the millennium, which we will need to understand both in terms of Roman law and of the personal circumstances and agendas of the major players. After we have dealt with Jesus's condemnation, we will explore the machinery of Roman capital punishment, Roman and Jewish burial practices, and where and how Jesus was buried.

II
Ad Fontes:[1]
Sources, Analysis and what Classical Historians Do

If classical history consists largely of the analysis of complex puzzles with most of the pieces missing, then we will do well to think carefully about the precious few pieces we have available to us. To make sense of the puzzle of the last days of Jesus, we need to examine the nature of those pieces and consider some methods for putting them together in a manner that fits the historical context.

The pieces of the puzzle are what historians call 'primary sources', that is, evidence of any sort from the time and place under examination.[2] The evidence available to us is both unwritten and written. The unwritten evidence includes discoveries via excavations (archaeology). Inscriptions (epigraphy) and coins (numismatics) discovered through excavations combine elements of written and unwritten evidence. The written evidence comprises primarily the surviving texts of Philo, Josephus, Tacitus, Suetonius, Dio Cassius, Rabbinic literature, and the New Testament. Specific archaeological, epigraphical, and numismatic evidence appears in the chapters where it is germane to our inquiry. For now, let us examine the primary pieces of written evidence.

---

1. *Ad fontes* was a favourite theme among scholars of the Italian Renaissance. It literally means '[back] to the sources', capturing the passion of learned humanists who sought to explore the wisdom and beauty of classical antiquity.
2. 'Secondary sources' are produced later in time and are dependent on primary sources. Philo is a primary source; this book is a secondary source. This distinction becomes convoluted when considering a source like Josephus, a primary source for events from his own period, but a secondary source, dependent on other primary sources, when writing about Jewish history that occurred before his time.

Philo Judaeus (c. 20 BC-AD 50): Philo Judaeus, a contemporary of Jesus, Annas, Caiaphas, and Pilate, was a highly influential Jewish scholar, philosopher, and commentator from Alexandria, Egypt. Philo is important for our purposes due to two of his works: *On Flaccus* and *Embassy*. *On Flaccus* gives us a helpful picture of Jewish-Roman relations in the Roman province of Egypt, including the terrible abuses and persecution of the Jews under Flaccus, the prefect of Egypt. *Embassy*, addressed to the Emperor Claudius, is the account of a group of Jews led by Philo, who had travelled to Rome to lodge a protest before Claudius's predecessor, the Emperor Caligula. Their protest centred on two grievances: the persecution of Jews in Alexandria, and Caligula's decree that his statue should be set up in the guise of Apollo in the Holy of Holies in the Temple of Jerusalem. In *Embassy*, Philo provides the only evidence for Pilate's Affair of the Shields.[1]

Both of these works share a common perspective. In *On Flaccus*, Philo details the abuses of Flaccus, complaining that it had long been the custom of Roman governors to prevent such violence. In former years, prefects and emperors had treated Jews with respect and deference, even granting them a degree of autonomy under a council of Jewish elders. From Philo's perspective, not only did Flaccus fail to fulfil his traditional role as keeper of the peace and purveyor of Roman justice, but he exchanged protection for pogrom, exacerbating the persecution by crucifying Jewish elders in the theatre while celebrating the birthday of Augustus. Philo expects his audience to be repulsed by Flaccus's violence and violations of Roman mores.

The heart of Philo's argument in *Embassy* is similar: that Claudius should learn from Caligula's errors, emulating instead the statesmanship of Augustus and Tiberius. They understood the importance of respecting local traditions and the religious freedom that Roman law and government had long granted to Jews. Philo hearkens back to the reign of Tiberius and his relationship with Pontius Pilate, focussing on the Affair of the Shields. These shields, which Pilate set up in his palace courtyard in Jerusalem, bore inscriptions that some Jews considered offensive. This act resulted in a modest Jewish protest, a letter of complaint sent to Rome, and a stern rebuke from Tiberius to Pilate. In the pages of Philo's *Embassy*, Pilate serves as something of a foil. For Philo, a good emperor like Tiberius favours the Jews, even in little things, and takes his governor to task when the latter

---

1. See Chapter III for detailed discussion.

does not. Tiberius's rebuke of Pilate serves to make Tiberius a positive example. By contrast, Caligula's grievous offence against the Jews demonstrates how far he has removed himself from the venerability of his predecessors.

In addition to this one incident, Philo makes several derogatory comments about Pilate which need to be understood in their rhetorical context. Philo suggests that Pilate was a man of 'inflexible, stubborn, and cruel disposition', whose administration was characterised by violence, corruption, abusive behaviour, needless executions, and savage ferocity.[1] The language Philo employs for Pilate closely parallels his descriptions of Flaccus's misrule in Alexandria. Moreover, the aim of Philo's criticism is less to describe the governor than to depict Tiberius in the best possible light as an example of proper Roman statesmanship for Claudius. Tiberius did things right, Philo argues, by taking Pilate to task and ensuring that local Jewish sensibilities were honoured by Roman government. Because of this rhetorical context, it is difficult to know how much Philo actually knew about the administration of Pilate or how seriously to take his characterisation of the man when his specific vocabulary closely parallels Philo's stereotypical critique of any leader he dislikes. Another possible purpose of Philo's negative references to Pilate in his *Embassy* may be to urge Claudius to return Judaea to Herodian rule under Herod Agrippa, to whom Philo was related by marriage.

As a contemporary of Jesus and Pilate, Philo is one of our earliest sources of first-generation evidence about Jewish-Roman relations.[2] His

---

1. *Embassy* 299-305.
2. When applied to historical evidence, I employ the term 'first generation' in a particular sense – to refer to a source that was written within the lifetime of at least some people who were alive at the time of the events discussed in the source. While life expectancy was considerably shorter in antiquity than in modernity, the difference is to a large degree based on infant and child mortality. Bear in mind that we have no census data, so any calculation of life expectancy is an extrapolation from little evidence. While a high proportion of the population died by the age of ten (some suggest up to fifty percent), anyone who survived childhood must have had a very strong immune system. Once a person reached adulthood, death at a ripe old age was not uncommon, assuming one did not die in battle or childbirth. When we hear estimates of life expectancy pointing to one's thirties, this number represents an average age of death, not an average age of adult death. If life expectancy was around thirty, and some fifty percent of children died by the age of ten, then the average age of adult death must have been somewhere well above thirty. People who reached their fortieth birthday were not considered senior citizens, just reasonably

rhetorical strategies, biases, and penchant for sensationalist language do not detract from the value of the evidence he provides, though we must account for them in our analysis.[1]

Flavius Josephus (c. AD 37-98): Josephus was an elite Jewish priest, general, apologist, and historian, who was born near the time Jesus was executed. In the early stages of the Jewish Revolt of 66-73, Josephus led Jewish forces against Rome until he was captured by the general

---

mature. Life expectancy probably differed considerably among men and women, slaves and free, and likely varied depending on one's social status, but we have little evidence available to test such claims. Most of what we know about the age of adult death comes from inscriptions in cemeteries and literary sources; that is, mostly from the upper classes. For our purposes, that narrow lens is sufficient, for it was the upper classes who were most literate and therefore the most likely to read a written text. A few examples will suffice to demonstrate how long potential readers would live. In the Roman Republic, minimum age for election to the consulship was forty-one or forty-two. Julius Caesar was assassinated at the age of fifty-six; Socrates was executed at seventy; Augustus, though ill much of his life, expired at age seventy-seven; Eusebius lived to about eighty; Sophocles died at ninety or ninety-one; St. Anthony, the desert father, may well have lived over a hundred years. Closer to the subject at hand, Herod the Great died at age sixty-nine; Josephus, Philo, Yohanan ben Zakkai, and Caiaphas, at about sixty; Tiberius at seventy-nine; Rabbi Akiva somewhere between eighty-five and ninety-five. Claudius was assassinated at age sixty-four. Annas, given the fact that he had a son who was old enough to be appointed high priest in AD 16, would have been in his late sixties, if not his early seventies, at the time of the trial of Jesus. It is thus reasonable that a source written within about sixty to sixty-five years of the events it describes would be read by at least some people who experienced the events themselves. That probability drops off thereafter, as do those who experienced the events. I therefore employ the term 'first-generation source' to describe texts that were written within about sixty-five years of the events they discuss. Relative to the lifetime of Jesus, both the later writings of Josephus and the Gospel of John, usually dated to the 90s, would qualify as later first-generation sources. For discussion of how Greeks, Romans, and Jews viewed the elders in their midst, see M. Goodman, *Rome and Jerusalem: The Clash of Ancient Civilizations* (New York: Vantage, 2007), 344ff.

1. For further discussion on Philo, see H.K. Bond, *Pontius Pilate in History and Interpretation.* (Cambridge: Cambridge University Press, 1998); K. Schenck, *A Brief Guide to Philo* (Louisville: Westminster John Knox, 2005); P. Van der Horst, *Philo's Flaccus: The First Pogrom* (Atlanta: Society for Biblical Literature, 2003).

and future emperor Vespasian (69-79). Thereafter, Josephus predicted that Vespasian would become emperor – a prediction that may have saved Josephus's life. In time, Vespasian and his son Titus came to view Josephus as a valuable resource, kept him in tow, and eventually brought him to Rome, where they put him up in a family villa and patronised his career as a writer. It was under the sponsorship of the imperial family, therefore, that Josephus wrote *The Jewish War*, *Antiquities of the Jews*, *Against Apion*, and his autobiographical *Life*, all in the last decades of the first century. He penned his first work, *The Jewish War*, about the late 70s. Because of his personal experience, Josephus had a unique vantage point from which to appreciate both Jewish and Roman cultural perspectives. For these same reasons, his writings have been variously appreciated, utilised, distrusted or vilified ever since. Josephus shares to a large degree the perspective of Philo that Rome had a long history as a largely tolerant and at times benevolent presence in Jewish life. For much of Roman history, Jews were accorded a significant degree of regional autonomy and deference and their religious sensibilities were respected. In light of this relatively favourable perspective on Roman governance, Josephus, like Philo, presents any Roman abuses of power as aberrations. Josephus places the blame for conflict between Jews and Romans both on incompetent or hot-headed Roman governors who violated long-standing Roman policy and on Jewish Zealots spoiling for a fight.[1]

As a Jewish priest and aristocrat, Josephus brings an unusual perspective to bear on everything he writes. As a result, he is a particularly helpful source for understanding the values and perspectives of the high priestly family of Annas since, to a large degree, he shares their view of the world. On the other hand, the perspective of Josephus is far removed from the bulk of the contemporary Jewish population.

Josephus is our sole source for three important events in the career of Pilate: the Affair of the Standards, the Aqueduct Riot, and the violent crackdown on the Samaritans that ultimately ended his career as prefect of Judaea. Josephus also makes two references to Jesus in his *Antiquities*. One consists merely of a brief mention of the name

---

1. Goodman also argues persuasively that Josephus provides ample evidence demonstrating the combination of problems caused by factionalism and the failure of the ruling class of Judaea to provide effective leadership in the midst of growing crisis (*Ruling Class of Judaea: The Origins of the Jewish Revolt against Rome A.D. 66-70* [Cambridge: Cambridge University Press, 1987]). Josephus himself belonged to this ruling class.

of Jesus in Josephus's account of the execution of James the Just.[1] The second is the famous *Testimonium Flavianum*, the 'Flavian Testimony' about the life of Jesus. Here is the passage, which occurs in the context of Josephus's longer discussion of the career of Pontius Pilate:

> About this time there lived Jesus, a wise man, if indeed one ought to call him a man. For he was one who performed surprising deeds and was a teacher of the kind of people who accept the truth gladly. He won over many Jews and many Greeks. He was the Messiah. When Pilate, upon hearing him accused by men of the highest standing among us, had condemned him to be crucified, those who had at first come to love him did not abandon their affection for him. On the third day he appeared to them restored to life, for the prophets of God had prophesied these and countless other marvellous things about him. And the tribe of the Christians, named after him, has still to this day not disappeared.[2]

Most scholars agree that at least some of this text has undergone what textual critics call interpolation. It appears that some Christian scribe made creative additions to the text of Josephus in the early stages manuscript copying, though there remains some disagreement over how much of this passage retains Josephus's original language. Most agree, however, that the central sentence, which mentions Pilate and 'men of the highest standing among us', accords well with Josephus's grammar and vocabulary elsewhere, and therefore probably represents Josephan authorship.[3] If this is correct, Josephus provides substantial corroboration of other sources concerning the trial and execution of Jesus.

The Pilate who emerges from the pages of Josephus is arrogant, stubborn, and contemptuous towards his subjects and their customs, gravely underestimating their courage and the strength of their religious convictions. Josephus is in no better position than Philo to understand the motives of Pilate, but his portrayal of Pilate's actions is exceedingly important for our purposes. As with Philo, the actions of Pilate in Josephus also serve as a foil for his rhetorical agenda and biases. What Pilate did or thought was far less important for Josephus than how Jews responded. In the Affair of the Standards, Josephus has a perfect example of successful non-violent Jewish resistance to unreasonable behaviour from a Roman ruler. At the beginning of his administration, Pilate's soldiers brought

---

1. *Antiquities* 20.200.
2. *Antiquities* 18.63-4. All translations are my own unless otherwise indicated.
3. Cf. *Jewish War* 6.300-305.

into Jerusalem military standards featuring 'graven images', which were prohibited by Jewish law. Jews protested and, ultimately, Pilate relented, moving that particular contingent of soldiers out of Jerusalem. With the Aqueduct Riot, however, Josephus provides a counter-example: the unsuccessful and deadly results of violent resistance. In this case, Pilate built an aqueduct using funds from the Temple treasury in Jerusalem. Some Jews staged a violent protest and Pilate's efforts at crowd control resulted in a number of injuries and deaths.[1] Theologically speaking, for Josephus, God blesses passive resistance but rejects violent rebellion. As with Philo, the rhetorical and theological biases and agendas of Josephus do not detract from his value as evidence, but they must be taken into consideration. While Josephus was writing significantly later than Philo, he is still a crucial first-generation source for Jewish-Roman relations, Roman provincial administration, and the prefecture of Pontius Pilate.[2]

Tacitus (c. AD 56-120): Writing in the early second century, the Roman historian Tacitus is one of our most important sources for understanding the early emperors of Rome, especially Tiberius and his relationship with Sejanus, his praetorian prefect. Tacitus, therefore, helps us understand the details of Roman administration as well as the family issues and power struggles that shaped the career of Pilate, who appears only once in his pages. Tacitus, who anachronistically refers to Pilate as 'Procurator', makes this singular reference in the context of his infamous explanation of Nero's response to the fire of Rome in 64. To deflect a widespread rumour that Nero himself had set the fire:

> Nero invented scapegoats – and punished with every refinement the notoriously depraved Christians (as they were popularly called). Their originator, Christ, had been executed in Tiberius's reign by Pontius Pilatus, the Procurator of Judaea. But in spite of this temporary setback the deadly superstition had broken out afresh, not only in Judaea (where the mischief had started), but even in Rome.[3]

Even though Tacitus is not a first-generation source and tells us little about Jewish-Roman relations until later in the century, he does provide a detailed, elitist senatorial perspective on the early empire. He also

---

1. For detailed discussion of both the Affair of the Shields and the Aqueduct Riot, see Chapter III.
2. For further discussion, see H. Bond, *Pontius Pilate in History and Interpretation* (Cambridge: Cambridge University Press, 1998); S. Mason, *Josephus and the New Testament* (Peabody: Hendrickson, 2003).
3. *Annals* 15.44.

provides helpful evidence about Roman provincial administration in his *Annals, Histories,* and *Agricola,* the latter of which details the career of his father-in-law, who served as governor of Britannia. Tacitus also corroborates at points the earlier evidence from Josephus, Philo, and the New Testament.

Suetonius (c. AD 69-140): Like Tacitus, Suetonius wrote from an elite, senatorial perspective in the early second century. He is therefore not a first-generation source either, but his *Lives* of Caesar, Augustus, and Tiberius help to fill gaps and to corroborate evidence from Tacitus concerning the administration of the early empire. Suetonius has an unfortunate tendency to revel in malicious gossip whose substance we cannot corroborate. At times this tendency mars what is otherwise helpful, if heavily biased, evidence.

Cassius Dio (c. AD 163-235): Cassius Dio (also called Dio Cassius or just Dio), a Greek from Bithynia, wrote his mammoth *Roman History* mostly in the early third century. Of the eighty original books, ranging from the Trojan War to Dio's own day, only those dealing with the late republic and the early empire have survived more or less intact. For our purposes, Dio provides helpful information and occasional corroboration concerning the reigns of Augustus and Tiberius, all from a provincial perspective.

Rabbinic Literature: Rabbinic literature makes some references to the families of earlier high priests, including that of Annas and Caiaphas. In addition, it offers some evidence concerning the high priesthood and Sanhedrin of Jerusalem. We should exercise due caution, however, when drawing on Rabbinic literature to understand issues in the early first century, for while it doubtless preserves many authentic traditions from that period, it is difficult to date individual sections, and all of it was written down many generations after the events took place (*Mishnah* c. 200, *Tosefta* c. 300, *Jerusalem Talmud* c. 400, *Babylonian Talmud* c. 500). Anachronisms and idealisations abound, in which later traditions and ideas are retrojected back into earlier centuries, or the past is treated uncritically. The line between authentic tradition and anachronism is often impossible to detect.[1]

The Gospel of Peter: Eusebius of Caesarea twice refers to the existence of a Gospel attributed to Peter which in his day (c. AD 300) was considered spurious.[2] In another context, Eusebius quotes Serapion,

---

1. For discussion of the challenges with using rabbinic literature as historical evidence for events of the first century, see Sanders, *Judaism Practice and Belief 63 BCE-66 CE* (London: SCM, 1992), 458-72.

2. That is, Eusebius believed that this text was not written by Peter and was not written in the age of the Apostles. There were several such late Gospels

Bishop of Antioch (c. 200), who also mentions a *Gospel of Peter.*[1] None of these references quotes any text from the Gospel. In 1886, excavators at a Christian cemetery at Akhmîm, Egypt, found a fragment of a Gospel in a coffin. Many have identified this Gospel with the *Gospel of Peter* mentioned by Eusebius, though this identification is by no means certain. Years later, three papyri, two from Oxyrinchus and one from Fayyum, were tentatively identified with that same Gospel.[2] Even if these identifications are all correct, they indicate, as most scholars have concluded, that the *Gospel of Peter* was likely written c. 150-190. The text from Akhmîm depends significantly on the four canonical Gospels of the New Testament. Attempts to argue that the *Gospel of Peter* contains fragments of a primitive 'Cross Gospel' have failed to win scholarly assent. While there is some possibility that the *Gospel of Peter* contains some primitive traditions, its dependence on the Gospels of the New Testament, combined with a lack of confirming evidence among early Christian writers, renders even that doubtful. The primary value of the *Gospel of Peter* for our inquiry is to provide corroboration of earlier materials.

The New Testament: Much of the evidence available to us that deals with the last days of Jesus comes from the Gospels in the New Testament: Matthew, Mark, Luke, and John.[3] We need to understand the date of their composition and their relationship to one another if we are to utilise them with proper care. Immense scholarly effort has been expended on this topic, so here I will offer only a brief introduction from a classical historian's perspective.

The date of the writing of the Gospels is important for our inquiry. Nowhere is the unfortunate division of labour between historical Jesus scholars and ancient historians more evident. It is commonplace in the pages of historical Jesus research for interpreters to complain about how late the Gospels are as sources. This complaint is rather curious from the perspective of the ancient historian, for we inhabit a scholarly world in which first-generation evidence is rare and priceless. We are most grateful if we have available a single first-generation source, let alone more than one. The Gospels are, relative to the material regularly utilised

ascribed to Apostles in existence by the time of Eusebius. *Church History* 3.3.1-4; 3.25.6.

1. *Church History* 6.12.3-6.
2. *Oxyrinchus Papyrus* 2949; 4009; *Papyrus Vindobensis* G.2325.
3. Paul also provides corroboration for many aspects of the passion of Jesus. For further discussion, see D. Allison, *Constructing Jesus: Memory, Imagination, and History* (Grand Rapids: Baker, 2010), 392-423.

by ancient historians, very early sources, and the fact there are four is a form of riches rare in our profession. They are also, of course, biased documents, each with its own agenda – a characteristic shared by all the written evidence we have already considered. Our analysis will need to consider the evidence and account for biases and agendas with care.

How early are the Gospels of the New Testament? That is a complicated topic, the full exploration of which is beyond the scope of this study, but a summary is in order. Let us grant, as most scholars do, that Mark was the first of the four Gospels to be written. Matthew and Luke followed, both of them borrowing liberally and creatively from Mark, as well as contributing their own material. Most also agree that the Gospel of John is largely independent of the other three 'synoptic Gospels' and written some time later.[1] Thus far, there will be little controversy over these claims. If these common assumptions are correct (and they are not without problems), then the dating of the first three is an interdependent question centring on when the first, Mark, was written. It is common to date the Gospel of Mark shortly after the sack of Jerusalem in 70. If that is accurate, then it follows that the authors of Matthew and Luke would need time to get their hands on Mark and compose their own Gospels, with the result that they are commonly dated somewhere in the 80s. Some argue for even later dates. While many would agree with this reconstruction, from the perspective of the ancient historian, this scheme of dating is problematic, for it depends on relatively weak evidence, while not sufficiently considering more substantial evidence.

Many scholars date Mark after the destruction of the Temple because of this passage:

> As he came out of the Temple, one of his disciples said to him, 'Look, Teacher, what large stones and what large buildings!' Then Jesus asked him, 'Do you see these great buildings? Not one stone will be left here upon another; all will be thrown down.'[2]

---

1. 'Synoptic Gospels' refers to Matthew, Mark, and Luke because of their close literary similarities. Most scholars also believe that Matthew and Luke had access to an earlier source: Q, though that question is not germane to our inquiry, given our focus on the trial and execution of Jesus. Some scholars suggest that John may have had access to, even if he did not depend on, one or more of the synoptic Gospels.
2. Mark 13.1-2. All quotations from the Bible are from the NRSV unless otherwise indicated.

The common argument is that this specific prediction of Jesus could have been made only after the Temple had actually been destroyed; it is *vaticinium ex eventu*, a prediction of what has in fact already happened. That is one possible interpretation, but it assumes that a prediction of the destruction of the Jewish Temple would be unimaginable in the time of Jesus, an assumption not grounded in evidence. The Temple had already been destroyed once by the Babylonians; Pompey had entered it; Crassus had forcibly removed its treasury; and Judaea had suffered its share of turbulence. That Jesus lived in such a historical context renders this common assumption anything but compelling. It is not at all surprising that someone who did not hold the status quo in high regard would predict its future demise at some unspecified time in the future. There is nothing specific about this prediction, either in detail or in terms of time, that would point to an event already past. One can easily imagine a Philo or a Yehuda of Gamla making such a prediction from a very different perspective: if abuses of power and rebellious rhetoric continued unchecked, it would be only a matter of time before Jerusalem lay in ashes and the Temple was destroyed.[1] It did not require supernatural prescience to suggest that the deteriorating state of affairs in Roman-controlled Jerusalem would likely not stand the test of time. In fact, we have a good example of just that from a few years later (in the AD 60s), at what Josephus calls a time of peace and prosperity: another Jesus, son of Ananias, predicted the destruction of Jerusalem, and in particular, the sanctuary.[2] The common interpretation of Mark's text as an *ex eventu* prediction is thus a possible but not at all a necessary inference.[3] From a historian's perspective, dating the Gospel of Mark post-70 is possible but somewhat dubious.

Much stronger evidence to the contrary comes from Luke–Acts (both written by the same author), in particular, the ending of the Acts of the Apostles. According to the narrative structure of that text, Paul was arrested, imprisoned for some time in Caesarea, and then shipped off to Rome for a hearing before the emperor himself.

1. Yehuda of Gamla (Judas of Galilee), according to Josephus, rebelled against Rome at the time of the Roman census of AD 6. For further discussion, see Chapter III and Appendix I.
2. *Jewish War* 6.300-305.
3. One might also expect that an *ex eventu* prophecy would make specific reference to the more spectacular events surrounding the destruction of the Temple, especially the fire which consumed it, described strikingly by Josephus.

The narrative pace of the last several chapters of the text slows down, and the content becomes rich in local detail. In the final chapter of the book, Paul is awaiting his hearing, under house arrest in Rome, receiving kindly treatment at the hands of his guards, and freely entertaining visitors. The last two verses are startling in their tone and simplicity:

> He lived there two whole years at his own expense and welcomed all who came to him, proclaiming the kingdom of God and teaching about the Lord Jesus Christ with all boldness and without hindrance.[1]

Many scholars have found this ending confusing if not troubling. One might think from the end of this text that much is good with the world. Paul is being treated well by the Roman authorities, he is about to get his hearing before the emperor, and there is a good chance he will be exonerated (as later Christian tradition affirms). All of that makes sense, and it fits well with one of the themes of Luke-Acts, which is the portrayal of Christians as good, loyal citizens and subjects who do not pose a threat to Rome. The problem is that the emperor at the time, who would eventually hear Paul's appeal, was Nero. Paul was not waiting to visit with the benevolent Augustus; he was waiting to encounter one of the most vicious persecutors of Christians in history. The crux of the matter is the date, for Nero launched his persecution of Christians only after the great fire of Rome in 64. If Acts was written before 64, its ending makes perfect sense, for Christians had no reason to fear him. If, however, Acts were written after 64, the ending becomes confusing, if not actively misleading. In response to these singular facts, many have argued that the ending of Acts was created for literary effect – to leave the reader with a reinforcing sense that respectful accommodation between Rome and Christians is possible, that conflict is not inevitable. Perhaps, if the book was completed by 63. But if the book was written any time after 64, such a literary effect would be self-defeating. From the time Nero began his persecution of Roman Christians, he haunted the pages of Christian writings for centuries beyond his death.[2] He served as the model of the evil ruler, the paradigm for all future persecutors; fear that he would rise from the dead was widespread. The closest parallel in the modern world would likely be Hitler.

---

1. Acts 28.30-31.
2. The New Testament book of Revelation is a case in point.

Change the context to Nazi Germany and the problem might become clearer.[1] Imagine writing a story whose purpose is, in part, to show how Jews and Nazis can develop respectful accommodation. Then end that story with the Jewish hero in prison, well-treated by his German guards, awaiting a hearing before Hitler. If this story were written in the early 1920s, shortly after Hitler's release from prison, a reader might, in a stretch, conceivably grant the possibility that the hearing before Hitler could go well and accommodation between Jews and Hitler could be possible.[2] If, however, this same story were written after the Holocaust became public knowledge, or even after Kristallnacht, the ending would be self-defeating; the very idea of a Jew facing a hearing before Hitler would be charged with anxieties and memories of pillaging, riots, ghettos and gas chambers in the minds of readers. No such book was written, and for good reason. While no analogy is perfect, this one does suggest why it is very probable that Acts was composed before 64 and almost inconceivable that it was written after. The best explanation of the ending of Acts, therefore, is that the author wrote up to his present time and then concluded no later than 63.

If Acts was written at the latest in 63, because it is the second volume of Luke-Acts, Luke must have been written at least a little earlier.[3] If

---

1. While there is no meaningful comparison between the Neronian persecution of Christians and the Holocaust, Nero did take on, in the early Christian mind, a symbolic status in some ways analogous to that of Hitler.
2. Readers of *Mein Kampf* would certainly doubt such an assertion, but that is precisely the point. Because, in retrospect, we know about *Mein Kampf,* and we know what happened later, it is difficult for us to imagine there ever being a possibility of positive relations between Jews and Hitler. The same would be true of any Christian reading a text after 64 involving Nero. If, however, we were living in the early 1920s and had little knowledge of Hitler and no knowledge at all of *Mein Kampf,* it would not be nearly so difficult to imagine such a possibility. Our imaginations are forever blinkered only a few years later.
3. A possible objection arises from Luke 21.20. There Luke redacts Mark's 'abomination of desolation' (13.14) into 'Jerusalem surrounded by armies' (cf. Luke 19.43). Might not that redaction be evidence that Luke was writing after the Roman siege of Jerusalem in 70? That is a possible but by no means a necessary inference, for there are other ways to account for Luke's detailed language. This whole discourse begins with a reference to the future destruction of the Temple. When the Babylonians destroyed the first Temple, it was the result of a military siege. It is quite natural to think that a future destruction would also result from Jerusalem being surrounded by armies. Moreover, Hebrew prophets had used similar language to

the author of Luke had a copy of Mark when composing his Gospel, then Mark must have been written early enough to have been copied and disseminated to the extent that it fell into the hands of the later Gospel writer. All of this places the composition of Mark in the late 50s or early 60s; that is, about twenty-five years after the execution of Jesus.[1]

Like Luke, Matthew could have been written any time after the late 50s, but now we can turn the argument about the destruction of the Temple on its head: Matthew quotes that same prediction from Mark almost verbatim.[2] One might expect that if Matthew were written after 70, he might have added some detail based on his *post eventum* knowledge. If he's simply borrowing directly from Mark, that suggests that the Temple was still standing when Matthew was written. This last is, admittedly, not a strong argument, but it is no weaker than the argument usually adduced for dating Mark after 70. Those who date Matthew post-70 also point to Matthew 22.7, suggesting that the burning of the city by the troops of an enraged king is a reflection of the sack of Jerusalem. Those who argue for a pre-70 date turn to 17.24-27, suggesting that this story about the Temple tax would be irrelevant had

---

foreshadow other destructions of Jerusalem, such as Isaiah 29.3; 37.33; Ezekiel 4.1-4, including detailed references to siege ramps, battering rams, and circumvallation walls. As we have already seen, after Jesus was executed, another Jesus also predicted the destruction of the Temple. A prediction that Jerusalem would be surrounded by armies and that the Temple would be destroyed thus hardly requires supernatural prescience or personal experience of Titus's siege. A simpler and more consistent explanation of Luke's redaction of Mark's 'abomination of desolation' is that Luke was following his usual practice of translating technical Jewish terms into terms his broader audience would understand. To the extent that Luke was following his standard procedure, this particular reference may have no bearing on the date of composition and the text as a whole poses no problems for an earlier date.

1. Patristic sources are mostly consistent with this assessment. See, for example: Papias, as quoted in Eusebius of Caesarea, *Church History* 3.39.15; Eusebius of Caesarea, *Chronicon* 183 (Helm); Clement of Alexandria as quoted in Eusebius, *Church History* 6.14.5-7; cf. 2.14.6; 2.17.1; Jerome, *On Illustrious Men* 8. Some have argued that Mark was only written after Peter died, but this rests on unnecessarily forced translations of Eusebius, *Church History* 3.39.15, 5.8.1-5, and Irenaeus, *Against Heresies* 3.1.1. For detailed discussion, see R.H. Gundry, *Mark: A Commentary on His Apology for the Cross* (Grand Rapids: Eerdmans, 1993), 1026-45.
2. Matthew 24.2.

Matthew been written after the destruction of the Temple. Because none of these arguments is conclusive, Matthew could have been written any time between the 60s and the 80s.

The date of the Gospel of John rests on even weaker evidence, which need not detain us here. Some have argued for an early date based on the Jewish flavour of the book and its lack of reference to the Temple's destruction, but most scholars suggest a date in the 90s. We know that it cannot have been written much later than 90 because of the John Rylands Papyrus. This may be the oldest known manuscript of the New Testament, dating from early in the second century. The existence of the John Rylands Papyrus, discovered in Egypt, requires the Gospel of John to be written, copied, and disseminated across much of the Roman Empire before about 120. Appropriately for this study, it contains a portion of text from John 18, the narrative of the trial of Jesus before Pilate. A date much later than 90 thus becomes increasingly untenable.

For purposes of the present analysis, I will assume that Mark was probably written in the late 50s or early 60s, Luke before 63, Matthew in the 60s to 80s, and John in the 80s to 90s. While each of these dates is subject to dispute, and this short overview is insufficient to address many of the technical challenges, we can have some confidence that all Gospels of the New Testament are first-generation sources, written during the lifetime of at least some people who were alive at the time of Jesus's execution. These sources are quite early compared to the evidence ancient historians usually encounter.[1]

The date of these writings is of particular significance for our inquiry because the destruction of the Jewish Temple in 70 represents not only a watershed in Jewish history, but a turning point in the relationship between Jews and Christians. Before then, and especially before 64, it was advantageous for Christians to be considered merely another sect of Judaism, particularly when dealing with Roman authorities, for there was the venerability of antiquity and legal protection to be had under the

---

1. It is important to note that my analysis of the final days of Jesus does not depend on early dates for the Gospels of the New Testament. While these dates are the most probable based on my consideration of the evidence, more 'orthodox' dates for the composition of the Gospels between the 70s and 90s would have little bearing on our understanding of Jesus's trial and execution, so long as these texts were written within the lifetime of at least some who experienced the events under consideration. Classical historians do not commonly have the luxury of any first-generation sources on which to base their analyses. The availability of at least four for our analysis is both rare and precious.

Jewish umbrella. Once out from under that umbrella, Christians were at risk of being considered a novel religion, which would cause them to lose the legal protections Rome had provided to Jews. When Jews revolted against Rome, however, there was no longer protection to be found under the guise of Judaism. Christians began increasingly to part ways from their parent faith. Moreover, in time, Gentile Christians began to outnumber Jewish Christians. After 70, there is far more probability that anti-Jewish sentiment and the desire to differentiate themselves would begin to inform various Christian communities, sentiments that may be reflected in later Gospels. Before 70, however, such sentiments were rare and unlikely to affect the earlier Gospels.

The Gospels of the New Testament are not only early but also represent multiple strands of evidence. Their interrelationships are complex and require some introduction. Because we have four first-generation sources, we have the opportunity to revel in our evidentiary riches. We can compare these sources with one another to see where they agree, where they conflict, and where their individual biases and agendas lead them in different directions. That is a welcome luxury, but one which raises its own challenges. Multiple lines of evidence create opportunity for corroboration, one of the most potent tools of historical analysis. But not all corroborations are created equal. For example, there is no evidence that Josephus drew from Philo when writing about Pilate. Evidence from Josephus which corroborates that of Philo is thus very strong, and the probability of the event under investigation increases considerably. Similarly, the Gospels of Mark and John seem to represent distinct lines of tradition; therefore, when one corroborates the other, the result is a substantial increase in probability. The Gospels of Mark and Luke, however, have a different kind of relationship, since the author of Luke likely had a copy of Mark when composing his Gospel. When Luke corroborates a claim that appears in Mark, therefore, it is a weaker form of corroboration. The author of Luke did make the choice to include some material from Mark, so in some sense he agrees with it, or at least does not disagree with it, but the nature of the corroboration increases the probability of the event only modestly.

In his important recent study, R. Bauckham has argued that the Gospels of the New Testament rely heavily on eyewitness testimony as the preferred form of ancient historiography. Those eyewitnesses in turn, so long as they lived, travelled, and communicated among early Christian communities, provided a source of information as well as a reasonable check on creative retellings of Jesus stories. These stories, then, formed the core of the literary composition of the Gospels, whose authors edited and shaped these testimonia to suit their particular objectives. If Bauckham is right, then any corroboration among the Gospels would point to a high degree of probability.[1]

This discussion of the Gospels as historical evidence should not cause us to forget that each Gospel is a literary creation in its own right. With the Gospels as much as with Philo or Josephus, each text has its own perspectives, objectives and biases. Mark's fairly straightforward narrative emphasises an 'apology for the cross'.[2] Recognising that crucifixion was viewed as a shameful way to die in the Roman world, Mark's narrative is shaped to reassure his readers that Jesus did not die as a shameful criminal. Rather he predicted his death in some detail, thus demonstrating that the cross was merely a part of a larger divine strategy. Matthew depicts Jesus as a new and greater Moses, as well as the long-awaited Messiah.[3] Moreover, Matthew is concerned with providing support for a Christian community that was probably facing persecution and therefore emphasises Jesus as the fulfilment of Hebrew prophecy and the rightful heir to the line of David. Matthew is utterly uninterested in matters of chronology and geography. Luke's Gospel, meanwhile, is written with the larger world in mind, stressing the universal nature of the ministry of Jesus. His emphasis on women, the poor, Samaritans, and others who get little ink in the other Gospels demonstrates his concern to portray the broad reach and relevance of Jesus. The addition of the book of Acts as a second volume extends that universality. Luke's theology emphasises the role of the Holy Spirit in the Church and the responsibility of Christians to live as peaceful and law-abiding subjects of the Roman Empire. In addition to his theological concerns, Luke is a researcher at heart, as he articulates in the first page of his Gospel. He is unusual among ancient authors in his scrupulous attention to details that most other writers ignore. He goes to great lengths in his attempt to provide chronological synchronicity with the greater Roman world. He cares a great deal about chronology, geography, and the niceties of Roman provincial administration, even undertaking the research required to discover the proper and

---

1. R. Bauckham, *Jesus and the Eyewitnesses: The Gospels as Eyewitness Testimony* (Grand Rapids: Eerdmans, 2006). I find his central arguments compelling and concur that evidence from early Christian sources such as Papias and Irenaeus should be taken much more seriously than is common in Biblical Studies circles.
2. Gundry, *Mark.*
3. D.C. Allison, *The New Moses: A Matthaean Typology* (Minneapolis: Fortress, 1993).

distinctive title for each Roman governor in Thessalonica, Malta, and Philippi.[1] Where we can check him, the evidence he provides for Roman chronology, geography, and governance fits coherently with other sources (and I have checked him thoroughly).[2]

Finally, John emphasises Jesus as the Son of God, and the importance of belief in him. Many scholars believe that his Gospel seems to be written in a supplementary fashion to the synoptics, but at times he departs from that role. His portrayal of the words of Jesus is also quite different from the other Gospels.

In the broadest strokes, all these generalisations simply represent the omnipresent reality of all ancient written sources: Every literary text has its own agenda and its own biases, and it is the job of the historian to understand them and take them into account when analysing the evidence. Biased sources do present challenges, but these challenges are anything but unusual and they do not present insuperable difficulties. Whether theological, moral, personal, ideological, or cultural, biases do not detract from the value of the texts as historical evidence, though they should certainly shape how we interpret the evidence. Indeed, we can learn a great deal of importance from the biases themselves. The fact that Suetonius and Josephus and Philo are all biased against Caligula does not necessarily mean that the many negative things they say about Caligula are fabrications. There is nothing to suggest that they invented,

---

1. With respect to geography, I refer primarily to the Roman Empire as it appears in Acts. Luke's geographical handling of the life of Jesus leaves something to be desired.

2. Sherwin-White, a classical historian, demonstrated this point long ago (*Roman Society and Roman Law in the New Testament* [Oxford: Oxford University Press, 1963]). It is remarkable that many reputable scholars have not done such checking, with the result that Luke's unusual concern for chronological, geographical, and political detail is often impugned. See Appendix I for more detailed discussion, especially with reference to the census of Quirinius. There is, however, one passage that is problematic: the reference to 'Theudas' in the speech attributed to Gamaliel in Acts 5.36. Josephus mentions a magician of some note by the name of Theudas who cannot fit into this chronological context, since Josephus places him around AD 44 (*Antiquities* 20.97-98). If Luke is referring to this same Theudas, this reference is anachronistic. It is possible, however, that he is referring to another otherwise unknown Theudas who led an earlier rebellion. There were plenty of small rebel leaders surrounding the death of Herod the Great. Unfortunately, the name of Theudas is not terribly common. Here is one of those places where we would dearly wish to have another puzzle piece, but the benefit of the doubt, given his record, must remain with Luke.

for example, Caligula's order to place his statue in the Temple in Jerusalem. On the other hand, the scurrilous gossip about Caligula they report, which is unsubstantiated and not corroborated, is more likely to be embellished. Similarly, the theological and literary agendas and biases of the Gospels do not detract from their value as historical sources, but they must be taken into account when analysing the texts.

All of this discussion represents an oversimplification of an enormously complex field, but it is enough to allow us to begin to analyse the evidence.

In the end, it is always the goal of historians to put the evidence to the question, to determine to the best of our ability what probably happened and why, in a manner that does justice to all the evidence available from the historical context – all the while recognising that any narrative reconstruction is subject to the nature of the evidence, the perspective of the analyst, and the nature of the question under investigation. Because most of the pieces of any ancient puzzle are missing, we must acknowledge at the outset that the level of probability of any reconstruction is modest.

Now that we have examined some of the more important pieces of our puzzle, we must consider how we can put them together so that they make sense together in context. We therefore turn our attention to the issue of historical methodology.

What Classical Historians Do

Classical historians have, over centuries of painstaking investigation, developed methods for thinking through complex puzzles and dealing with a dearth of evidence. We long ago gave up the idea that we could 'prove' anything. Our goals are more modest, and we would do well to abandon the idea of certainty at the outset. Rather, our task is to think in terms of probability.

Classical historians, most fundamentally, interrogate ancient sources. Either a source provides no evidence to answer a question, or it provides some. Improbability, whatever that might mean, is not a concept utilised by historians. It might be easiest to picture a continuum of probability ranging from 0 to 10, where 0 represents no probability and 10 represents the highest possible level of probability – near certainty.

| 0 | 5 | 10 |

A probability level of 0 means that we have nothing to talk about, for historians know nothing without evidence. A probability level of 10 would be exceedingly rare, and occurs nowhere in the field of ancient history. Since, when dealing with antiquity, we almost always encounter more gaps than evidence, the probability level of any historical analyses or reconstructions will usually range around 4-6 on our scale. When classical historians analyse the lives of prominent ancient figures like Tiberius or Pericles, everything we say about them is a reconstruction based on the limited availability of biased evidence and, therefore, characterised by modest probability. This is the simple reality for all classical historians. It is relatively rare that we have available a single piece of first-generation evidence, let alone multiple sources. Often our evidence is fragmentary, slanted, and distant from the time of the events or people to which it refers.[1]

Some historical Jesus scholars treat their quest like a criminal case in the American legal system. The 'burden of proof' falls upon anyone who would attempt to find any historical content in the Gospels or any other sources concerning the life of Jesus. Unless Jesus can be 'proven' to have done or said something beyond a reasonable doubt, he probably did not do or say it.[2] Classical historians, however, think more along the lines of civil cases in which claims are substantiated by a preponderance of the evidence – evidence that makes it slightly more likely that an event happened than not. Very little evidence from the ancient world would rise to the 'beyond a reasonable doubt' standard, while much would reach the level of preponderance. I am not fond of legal analogies with history, but this one can facilitate at least some understanding of the disciplinary difficulties. Classical historians are scrupulous and critical, but not highly sceptical, in the classical sense of that term. They take a relatively generous approach to evidence

---

1. For a thoughtful analysis of the nature of the evidence for the ancient historian and the problem of the lack of primary sources, see M.I. Finley, *Ancient History: Evidence and Models* (New York: Penguin, 1985).
2. R.W. Funk and R.W. Hoover, *The Five Gospels* (New York: Macmillan, 1993), 1-38. This treatment of assumptions and methods represents the convictions of the highly influential Jesus Seminar, now absorbed into the Westar Institute. Such assumptions inform the voting mechanisms that lie at the basis of the colour-coding of the *Five Gospels*. Red represents words that Jesus 'unequivocally' or 'undoubtedly' said, or at least something very like them. Pink represents words Jesus probably or might have said. Grey represents words that Jesus probably did not say and black represents words he did not say.

and do their analyses and reconstructions with the full knowledge of the limitations of their evidence and therefore the modest level of probability they can hope to attain. We never prove anything, but we do put the evidence to the question, probing and cross-examining it from multiple angles, hoping to make sense of the puzzle before us to the highest level of probability feasible.

With this understanding, the first question of any classical historian is: 'What is the nature of the evidence?' Under that head many sub-questions emerge, such as who wrote the source? What was her or his perspective, status, objective(s), bias(es), agenda(s)? Who benefits from this source? What was this person in a position to know? When was the text written? Where? Under what circumstances? For what intended audience? What is the literary genre and why choose that genre? What was happening in the world around this author that might inform our understanding? Answers to questions such as these help us analyse and interpret the evidence in its context while accounting for its uniqueness. Once we get a handle on such questions, we must recognise that certain answers increase or decrease the probability of our conclusions. I will here present some basic operating principles that all historians share when analysing sources. In particular, we will discuss five: proximity, corroboration, consistency, *cui bono* ('to whose good'), and authorial intent.

1. Proximity. To put it simply, earlier evidence is usually better. The closer in time and place a source is to the people and events it describes, the more its potential probability. Close proximity leaves little time for memories to fade or for legendary accretions to develop. In particular, there is a significant watershed between first-generation sources, written during the lifetime of at least some who knew the person or experienced the event in question, and sources from subsequent generations. One needs only to compare the Gospel of Mark with the *Infancy Gospel of Thomas* to understand the difference. Contrary to the assumptions of many historical Jesus scholars, it is most difficult for legendary accretions to develop in first-generation sources. They can develop but they take time, well beyond the first generation.[1] During the first

---

1. For fuller discussion, see Sherwin-White, 186-93. Of course, proximity, even in the first generation, does not guarantee consistency among sources. On the contrary, inconsistencies among first-generation sources are not uncommon, but they grow out of differences in perspective, genre, intent, redaction, or bias, not wholesale fabrication. First-generation sources do on occasion make theological claims about such things as the origins or destiny or significance of their subjects, but these are quite different from legendary

generation, eyewitnesses to events are still alive and, at least potentially, actively talking about the things they saw, heard, or remembered. While memories can fade or become distorted over time, the living presence of such individuals serves as a powerful check on fabrication.[1]

There is also, with first-generation sources, the possibility of falsifiable evidence. For evidence to be falsifiable, the event in question must be public, and some of those who witnessed the event must still be alive. Any claims about this public event by a first-generation source are subject to the immediate review of those who were there. Any author making claims contrary to the public memory of those who experienced the event in question would be committing reputational suicide. Falsifiable evidence, while quite rare in the ancient world, provides an extremely high level of probability.[2] When Josephus, for example, writes of the Aqueduct Riot, that evidence is falsifiable.

2. Corroboration. Multiple pieces of corroborating evidence, of any sort, are better than a single primary source. When we can cross-examine multiple sources, our interpretations are likely to attain higher levels of probability. Strong corroborations are agreements between different types of evidence, such as numismatics and literary evidence, or two independent strands of literary evidence, while weaker corroborations exist among sources that have some sort of connection. John agreeing with Mark or Josephus agreeing with Tacitus is strong corroboration. Weak corroboration is when Matthew agrees with Mark. Since Matthew likely used Mark as a source, his agreement with Mark may be merely a matter of copying from a text (in which case, it is hard to speak of corroboration at all), but it may also be that Matthew's agreement with Mark signals his acknowledgment that his own received tradition agrees with Mark. Bear in mind that Matthew's editing of Mark includes the intentional omission of some material. When he excludes this material, he does so for a reason, and usually the application of some basic redaction criticism (the analysis of how authors edit their sources) reveals his theological or

---

fabrication of events. Cf. N.T. Wright, *The New Testament and the People of God* (Minneapolis: Fortress, 1992), 426.

1. For detailed discussion, see Bauckham. At least a few such witnesses likely continued to be meaningful sources up to about sixty years after the time of the event. It is important to distinguish fabrication from bias, agenda, perspective, theological reflection, and redaction, all of which are common in first-generation sources. Eyewitness evidence, of course, presents challenges of its own, for it is a legal commonplace that multiple eyewitnesses tell different stories that can sometimes be difficult to reconcile.
2. Falsifiable evidence is, by its nature, also verifiable by the original readers.

literary motives. On the other hand, Matthew's omission of some element of Mark's material could represent disagreement between Matthew's received tradition and what he reads in Mark. I will employ the term 'weak corroboration' to acknowledge these difficulties. Corroboration of any sort is most welcome to classical historians, for it increases the probability of our interpretations and it provides the opportunity for comparative analysis from multiple perspectives.

3. Consistency. Classical historians always ask: 'Is this piece of evidence consistent with all other relevant pieces of this particular puzzle, in this particular linguistic, historical and cultural context?' If so, the probability of the analysis rises; if not, we begin to ask other questions about the reasons for any inconsistency. Perhaps the problem lies with the bias of the source? Or with the assumptions of the historian? Perhaps we should look at the whole puzzle from a different angle? The principle of consistency, and grappling with inconsistencies among sources, keep the discipline of classical history honest and fresh.

4. Cui bono? Historians always ask of their sources, *cui bono?* or 'who benefits?' Historians have long given up the Enlightenment idea of scientific objectivity as impossible and misleading. Every source has its biases and agendas, and no modern historian is wholly objective, try as we might to keep our cherished notions and preconceived ideas at arm's length. Postmodern thought, despite occasionally going to self-referential extremes, has done historians a great service by bringing these concerns into focus. One of the ways historians grapple with the biases in every source is to raise the *cui bono* question.

One example should suffice: Josephus engages in a great deal of self-justification. This is understandable given the awkward fact that he is Jewish but writing under the patronage of the Roman imperial family, just after a major war between Romans and Jews. He benefits when he is able to demonstrate that reasonable Jews and Romans can get along. For this reason, his description of an episode like the Affair of the Standards, where non-violent Jewish resistance against Pilate results in a peaceful and beneficial conclusion, fits his bias perfectly. This bias does not mean that Josephus invented the event, but there can be little doubt that he has portrayed it in a manner that justifies his own position.

The *cui bono* principle is helpful in many respects, enabling historians to detect and counter biases among sources. The proximity of first-generation sources helps limit the effect of the *cui bono* principle. For sources farther removed from the events they record, in the second generation and beyond, the *cui bono* principle can also be helpful in raising questions concerning possible legendary embellishment or fabrication.

5. *Authorial Intent*. This principle is an essential tool, if a tricky one for the historian to employ effectively. To the extent that this can be discerned (and that is not easy and sometimes impracticable), the intent of an author can have a great deal of impact on how we weigh a source as historical evidence. For example, the intent of inscriptions, by their nature, is for someone in a position of power to announce something in public in a particular place. The intent of coinage, especially in the Roman Empire, grows out of the reality that coins are the only form of mass media in antiquity. Emperors thus used coins to send messages to their subjects. They could even subdivide their audiences by sending different messages on gold coins than on bronze or different messages via different regional mints. The intent of literary authors determines to a large degree their choice of literary genre. As we have seen, Josephus intended not only to grapple with the Jewish War, but to justify his own position. I think the evidence is fairly clear that Matthew had little interest in chronology or geography. Rather, his intent was to portray parallels between Jesus and Moses as well as how Jesus fulfilled Hebrew prophecy, among other things. Luke, on the other hand, cared a great deal about chronological and geographical accuracy, along with other distinctive themes like Jesus's concern for the poor and marginalised. Even these few examples demonstrate the importance of grappling with authorial intent before employing a source as historical evidence. Coins can tell us a good deal about how an emperor wanted to portray his accomplishments, but they tell us little about his subjects. Josephus can tell us much of historical value about the context and events of the Jewish War, but his account is consistently self-serving. Matthew can tell us a good deal about the life and teachings of Jesus as well as early Christian interpretations of the Hebrew Bible, but we would be unwise, as is too often the case, to take a literal reading of his infancy narrative in preference to that of Luke.[1]

---

1. See Appendix I for more detail. In my judgment, Matthew is making few historical claims in his infancy narrative, but rather composing a haggadic Midrash, a form of creative storytelling that would immediately be recognised by his contemporary Jewish readers, though it is often lost on modern interpreters. The purpose of this Midrash is to draw parallels between Moses and Jesus. The creative nature of this kind of Midrash pays little heed to historical events, something an informed audience would appreciate and enjoy. To interpret a midrashic text as if it were making historical claims is to disregard the intent of the author. For further discussion, see R.H. Gundry, *Matthew: A Commentary on His Literary and Theological Art* (Grand Rapids: Eerdmans, 1982), 32-7; 54; 78ff; cf. Allison, *Moses*.

These basic principles should provide sufficient abstractions in terms of how classical historians approach evidence and practice their craft. The astute reader will notice, however, that there are several assumptions and methods regularly employed by some historical Jesus scholars that do not appear here, including a firm distinction between theological writing and historical writing, the use of Form Criticism, and the employment of the Criterion of Dissimilarity.[1]

Classical historians do not grant a firm distinction between history writing and theological writing. For example, it is common for some historical Jesus scholars to make the argument that if a particular statement in a Gospel can be shown to be theologically motivated, or at least consistent with the theological perspective and agenda of the author, then the statement in question is not historical or is at least improbable. That is, historical claims and theological agendas are incompatible. Classical historians certainly recognise the importance of grappling with the biases, political, philosophical, or theological agendas of authors under examination, but they do not grant this firm distinction. Take, for example, our discussion above of Josephus's account of the Affair of the Standards. One of Josephus's primary theological motifs is that God blesses his people when they engage in non-violent resistance, but they suffer terrible consequences when they turn to violence, as was the case with the disastrous Jewish revolt of 66-73. Since Josephus is making a theological point in recording this event, if we were to wield the firm wedge commonly employed by some scholars, we would need to conclude that the Affair of the Standards was probably not a historical event. Classical historians would not be inclined to jettison

---

1. Discussions of historical methodology, assumptions, and 'criteria of authenticity' abound among historical Jesus scholars. A few of the more important include: J.P. Meier, *A Marginal Jew: Rethinking the Historical Jesus* (New York: Doubleday, 1991), vol. 1; B. Ehrman, *Jesus: Apocalyptic Prophet of the New Millennium* (New York: Oxford University Press, 1999); L.T. Johnson, *The Real Jesus: The Misguided Quest for the Historical Jesus and the Truth of the Traditional Gospels* (San Francisco: Harper, 1997); B. Witherington, *The Jesus Quest: The Third Search for the Jew of Nazareth* (Downers Grove: Intervarsity, 2010); N.T. Wright, *The New Testament and the People of God* (Philadelphia: Fortress, 1992); C. Blomberg, *The Historical Reliability of the Gospels* (Downers Grove: Intervarsity, 2007), and C.A. Evans, *Fabricating Jesus: How Modern Scholars Distort the Gospels* (Downers Grove: Intervarsity, 2006); R. Bauckham, *Jesus and the Eyewitnesses* (Grand Rapids: Eerdmans, 2006); D. Allison, *Constructing Jesus: Memory, Imagination, and History* (Grand Rapids: Baker, 2010); C. Keith and A. Le Donne, *Jesus, Criteria, and the Demise of Authenticity* (London: T&T Clark, 2012).

such important first-generation evidence for such reasons, though we certainly recognise the function of Josephus's theological biases, not to mention those of the Gospels of the New Testament.

Classical historians seldom if ever employ the tools of Form Criticism and the Criterion of Dissimilarity, which are more properly applicable to literary criticism than historical method. Further, the use of these particular tools in the discipline of classical history would have the unwelcome effect of eliminating most, if not all, evidence from consideration.[1]

The discussion above should be sufficient in terms of abstractions. We could multiply such generic principles or argue the virtues of various methods or criteria for many pages, but the central methodological considerations must do justice to the fact that classical historians have to deal with evidence of all types across the entirety of the ancient world. Methodology is constrained by the nature of the evidence. Let us take a couple of examples, with a view toward elucidating the realities classical historians commonly encounter. In addition, please bear in mind our discussions of Philo and Josephus above, for the same issues apply to them. We will engage in a brief examination of two case-studies which demonstrate the kinds of issues concerning evidence and probability that classical historians encounter regularly: Alexander the Great and Apollonius of Tyana.

Alexander the Great. Any student of the historical Alexander the Great has encountered some of the typical problems faced by the classical historian. The nature of the evidence regarding the life of the great conqueror of Macedon is complex. Non-literary evidence consists of a number of coins and a few inscriptions. Literary sources are extremely problematic. There were several first-generation sources, but none of them survived the intervening centuries except in fragments or quotations by later authors.[2] Even these fragments are precious as evidence, but fragments are always fragmentary – removed from their original context and often freely edited by the authors quoting them.

---

1. Form criticism identifies individual units of text according to genre and literary form and then attempts to trace the literary and oral stages of transmission of that unit. The criterion of dissimilarity, employed by some New Testament scholars, assumes that sayings and actions attributed to Jesus may be accepted as authentic only if they can be shown to be dissimilar to characteristic emphases of both ancient Judaism and early Christianity. The application of the latter assumes that only the completely independent Jesus, who has no connection with Judaism or Christianity, is the authentic Jesus.

2. E.g. the *Ephemerides*, Chares of Mytiline, Marsyas of Pella, Aristobulus, Nearchus, Callisthenes, and Cleitarchus.

Because the first-generation sources have not survived, all analyses of the historical Alexander depend on ancient sources from later generations. Among these, the most important are Diodorus Siculus, who wrote in Sicily in the first century BC; Strabo, the Greek geographer and contemporary of Augustus; Quintus Curtius Rufus, who composed his *History of Alexander the Great* in Latin in Rome in the first century AD; Plutarch of Chaeronea, who composed his Greek *Parallel Lives of the Noble Greeks and Romans* in the early second century AD; Lucius Flavius Arrianus, better known as Arrian, who, a generation after Plutarch, wrote his *Anabasis of Alexander;* and Marcus Junianus Justinus (Justin), who wrote his *Epitome* sometime between the second and fourth centuries AD.

Anyone who wishes to analyse the life of the historical Alexander must depend primarily on sources dated to anywhere from three to six hundred years after Alexander's death. Because the later sources depended in part on earlier sources, there are complex historical and literary interrelationships among them, not unlike the synoptic problem increased by an order of magnitude.[1] The serious student must come to terms with these issues as part of any attempt to understand the historical Alexander. After our best efforts, it remains quite difficult to ferret out the first-generation evidence embedded in these later sources, much less to reconstruct Alexander's life.

This complex web of relatively late extant sources which in turn depend upon earlier sources is fairly typical of the types of puzzles classical historians regularly encounter. Moreover, each of these later sources is biased and shaped according to the rhetorical, philosophical, political, and religious agendas of the individual authors. The same can be said of the earlier sources upon which these later sources depended. We must therefore be honest about the difficulties and the reality that any reconstruction based on such evidence will not rise to a very high level of

---

1. Diodorus primarily used Cleitarchus, as did Curtius, who also borrowed from Ptolemy. Plutarch based his *Life of Alexander* on Ptolemy, Aristobulus, and Cleitarchus. Arrian's use of sources concentrated upon Ptolemy, Aristobulus, and Nearchus. Justin wrote an *Epitome* (abbreviation) of the first century BC work of Pompeius Trogus. Cleitarchus is particularly problematic as a source, engaging in pretentious, melodramatic language, fanciful settings and superficial psychologising, although even he did not present a mythological Alexander. For the fragments of Cleitarchus, see Jacoby, *Die Fragmente der griechischen Historiker* (Leiden: Brill, 1950), IIB/1, 741-52; IID/1, 484-98. For analysis, see W.W. Tarn, *Alexander the Great: Sources and Studies* (Cambridge: Cambridge University Press, 1950); cf. N.G.L. Hammond, *Sources for Alexander the Great* (Cambridge: Cambridge University Press, 1993).

probability. Because of the nature of the evidence, virtually anything we can say about the historical Alexander represents much lower probability than just about anything we can say about the historical Jesus. Classical historians do not throw up their hands in the face of such evidence; rather, such evidence calls upon the best of historical sleuthing, creativity, and problem-solving.

Apollonius of Tyana. I begin my course on Jesus in History and Archaeology by studying the historical Apollonius, for an analysis of the evidence for his life provides a bit of perspective that is most helpful when later studying the life of Jesus. In part, I do this exercise for the common reasons – that there are interesting parallels (real or imagined) between two men from roughly the same era who were renowned for their holiness. More importantly, I start this way in order to give students a chance to experience the evidentiary challenges that characterise the discipline of classical history.

Apollonius hailed from Tyana, southern Asia Minor, during the second half of the first century AD, but the nature of the evidence for understanding the historical Apollonius is problematic. Modern study of Apollonius depends almost entirely on a single, highly rhetorical, highly biased source: the *Life of Apollonius of Tyana* by Philostratus, who flourished in the first half of the third century, some hundred and fifty years after the time of his subject. There are also some letters purported to have been written by Apollonius, but scholars consider most of them spurious creations of at least a century after his death, and thus of limited historical value. Philostratus claims that he had access to some writings of Apollonius, some local traditions, and the written works of Maximus of Aegae, Damis of Nineveh, and Moeragenes, but none of these are still extant.

In a way, analysing the historical Apollonius creates challenges not unlike the historical Alexander. Philostratus is a very late source relative to the lifetime of Apollonius, but not as late as many of the sources for Alexander. On the other hand, at least for Alexander, we have multiple late sources which provide some opportunity for cross-examination. The fact that we are so dependent on a single source for Apollonius largely denies us such opportunities.[1]

Beyond modest corroborations of the existence of Apollonius, one must analyse Philostratus with care to gain any historical traction, all the while acknowledging that we can almost never check him

---

1. We do, however, have a few testimonia, also from late sources, that attest to the life and writings of Apollonius: Dio 67.18.1, 4; *Life of Severus Alexander* 29.2.

against other sources. Because of these limitations, any reconstruction of the life of the historical Apollonius will always be haunted by relatively low probability. In this case, we have barely twenty pieces of our one thousand piece puzzle, most of which are tarnished by time. Nevertheless, this kind of challenge is commonplace for ancient historians. We must adapt our methods to deal with the nature of the evidence and recognise that modest probability is the best we can hope for.[1]

This brief survey of the nature of the evidence for two historical figures from the ancient world gives a good sense of the types of challenges regularly encountered by classical historians and how our methods must adapt to the nature of the evidence.

We could multiply examples, but these should suffice to clarify why many of the rigid and restrictive assumptions, methodologies and criteria employed by some historical Jesus scholars will not work if we hope to approach the study of the historical Jesus like any other historical issue. It turns out that some of what is today called historical Jesus scholarship bears only modest similarity to what classical historians actually do when they study other ancient persons.

The discipline of history is a complex interaction between historians and evidence in which we bring our own experiences with life, culture, literature and the broader scope of history to the task of interrogating ancient evidence. The types of questions we ask grow out of those experiences, and every new question we ask has the potential to cause us to view complex puzzles from alternative vantage points. For these reasons, the discipline of history is never rigid in its handling of evidence. The methods we employ must necessarily adapt to the types of questions we ask and the nature of the evidence available to respond to our inquiries. In the end, classical history is a challenging, analytical, energising, creative, and humble discipline in

---

1. For a helpful survey of the evidence for Apollonius see the online article by Jona Lendering at www.livius.org/ap-ark/apollonius/apollonius01. html. See also the excellent recent text, introduction, and translation by C.P. Jones, *Philostratus: Apollonius of Tyana* (Cambridge: Harvard University Press, 2005), *Loeb Classical Library* 458, in 3 Volumes; the third includes the letters attributed to Apollonius as well as Eusebius's *Against Hierocles.* The standard edition and analysis of the letters is R.J. Penella, *The Letters of Apollonius of Tyana: A Critical Text with Translation and Commentary, Mnemosyne Supplement* 56 (Leiden, 1979). Sherwin-White provided similar evidence from Plutarch, Herodotus, and Thucydides (186-93).

which we must inevitably be happy with modest probability wrapped in meaning, insight, and stimulating dialogue with fellow historians and colleagues in related disciplines.[1]

Given the nature of the evidence for the last days of Jesus and the historical methods commonly employed among classical historians, I will seek to examine first those areas where we encounter significant corroboration among our earliest sources, for these represent the points of highest probability. Second, where corroboration is weaker or lacking, we will keep our focus on the earliest sources available to us. When we examine the career of Pilate, for example, Josephus and Philo will be most important to us, but when it comes to the details of Jesus's arrest and trial, our attention will largely be drawn to the Gospel of Mark. Matthew and Luke, because they are mostly dependent on Mark in this portion of their respective texts, provide primarily weak corroboration except where they differ from Mark in a manner that suggests the use of other early sources. Since the Gospel of John seems to preserve a separate strand of tradition about these events, we will utilise it in a complex manner, at times to complement our analysis, at times to challenge our understanding based on the earlier evidence, and at times to illuminate our analysis from a unique angle. Moreover, because of John's inclusion of a number of vivid, incidental details, it is conceivable that his evidence was to some degree based upon an eyewitness, with all the strengths and weaknesses of such testimony. By following these basic methods of classical history, we will be in a position to understand and interpret the fascinating puzzle of the final days of Jesus to the highest degree of probability feasible given the nature of the evidence.

Now, with a firm grasp on the texts and historical methodology, let us pack up our evidence and travel back to the Roman province of Judaea, to the palatial Jerusalem home of the prefect of Judaea.

---

1. For a helpful introduction to the relationship between classical historians and their sources as well as the range of questions historians pursue, see M. Beard and J. Henderson, *Classics: A Very Short Introduction* (Oxford: University Press, 1995). For a more detailed discussion of historical methodology and the nature of the evidence that classical historians regularly encounter, see C.W. Hedrick, *Ancient History: Monuments and Documents* (Oxford: Blackwell, 2006). The discussion of methodology by N.T. Wright, while philosophical in focus, more closely approximates that of the classical historian than any other I've encountered by a Biblical scholar, perhaps hearkening back to his initial degree in Classics from Oxford: *The New Testament and the People of God* (Philadelphia: Fortress, 1992), 81-120.

III
Praefectus Iudaeae:[1]
Pontius Pilatus and his World

Pontius Pilatus, prefect of the Roman province of Judaea, awoke with the rising sun as was his custom.[2] He surveyed with appreciation his luxurious bedroom in the Jerusalem palace that had once been the pride of that extraordinary builder, King Herod. But the opulence of his surroundings did not diminish the challenges he would face with the dawning day. It was the third day of the Roman month of *Aprilis,* the nineteenth year of the Emperor Tiberius, and the year 786 *ab urbe condita* (from the founding of the city of Rome). We call it April 3, AD 33. It was *dies veneris,* the day of Venus, which English speakers would later call Friday, after another god from the frigid north. Pilate would have begun this day with some anxiety, for he was governor of the Jewish 'promised land', and his first seven years as prefect had not gone very well. This Friday fell on 14 Nissan of the Hebrew Calendar.[3] With the setting of the sun the night before, Passover, the greatest of all Hebrew festivals, had begun. For Pilate, this festival would be anything but festive, for every year at Passover the city of Jerusalem was packed with Jewish pilgrims from the four corners of the Roman Empire. He well knew that those crowded conditions, combined with the strong sense of Jewish passion and identity that always accompanied this festival, spelled trouble for any foreign ruler. Passover was a celebration of liberation, of deliverance from oppression, and Pilate was all too aware that he could be cast in the role of Pharaoh, for he was heir to a long and troubled history of Passover violence. He needed to be ready on this day.

---

1. *Praefectus Iudaeae,* 'prefect of Judaea', was the official title of Pontius Pilate and other early governors of the province of Judaea. The title appears on the Pilate Inscription discussed below.
2. The image of the rising sun is a common motif in classical literature, stemming in large part from Homer's many references to the breaking of dawn, extending her rose-red fingers over extraordinary people engaged in epic conflict. Such an image seems appropriate to our topic.
3. For a detailed discussion of the chronology of Pilate and Jesus, see Appendix I.

Little did he know that his anxieties were misplaced; that the message from the high priest he was soon to receive that morning would make this Passover unlike any other. Little did he know that on that day, he would become one of the most famous men who ever lived.

Pontius Pilatus and the trial he presided over that day have become the stuff not only of legend but of historical reconstructions and speculations ranging from the ingenious to the absurd. For the most part, however, they have been narrowly construed. Was Pilate an angry thug, agent of an oppressive and violent empire, just waiting for the opportunity to crucify anyone who might dare to challenge Rome's authority? Or was he a victim of circumstances, haplessly manipulated by the Jewish people who demanded the blood of a blasphemer? Both of these unfortunately common interpretations are demonstrably false, but the reality is complicated and few serious students of the Bible, even too few scholars, have taken the time to place Pilate in the context of his world. Pontius Pilatus was a Roman of equestrian class who as prefect of Judaea served as a small cog in the complex machinery of Roman governance. We will never understand Pilate, or his infamous trial, until we examine the evidence with care, with the aim of placing the life of this one individual within the larger context of Roman provincial government. This examination will in turn provide us with the most important pieces of the puzzle that is the historical Pontius Pilate.

Evidence for the Life of Pilate

The first question in the mind of the historian is always this: what is the nature of the evidence? As discussed in Chapter II, the evidence for the life of Pilate is both relatively early and relatively abundant, resting primarily on the first-generation sources written by Philo, Josephus, and the Gospel authors of the New Testament.[1] Tacitus, in the second century, corroborates the claims that Pilate was governor of Judaea under the Emperor Tiberius and that he condemned Jesus to execution.

The written evidence for the life of Pontius Pilatus is supplemented by evidence from coins and an inscription. The coins of Pilate, like those of his predecessors, were made of bronze, struck in Judaea and,

---

1. First-generation sources were written within the lifetime of at least some people who experienced the event the source discusses. Any sources written within about sixty years of the events they discuss would be considered first-generation. See Chapter II for further discussion on life-expectancy and the common ages of adult death.

in deference to Jewish sensibilities, did not include anthropomorphic images, such as the bust of the emperor or the inscription DIVIF ('son of the divine'), both of which were common in imperial coinage. Pilate did, however, strike some coins that included the vague pagan symbols of the *simpulum* (a sacrificial vessel or wine bowl) and the *lituus* (an augur's crooked staff), which has led some interpreters to view these coins as deliberately provocative to Jews. That interpretation, however, does not take into account the long history of the use of such relatively ambiguous pagan symbols on the coins minted by the Herodian kings and Roman prefects before him. There is no evidence that Jews considered Pilate's coinage offensive.[1] Of particular interest is the first issue to come from Pilate's mint (from AD 29/30) that includes on the obverse (heads) the symbol of three ears of barley, the central one upright, and the other two wilted, inscribed with the Greek words, *Iulia Kaisaros.* Julia (also called Livia) was the wife of the Emperor Augustus and mother of Tiberius. The reverse (tails) features the image of the *simpulum*, with the inscription naming Tiberius Caesar. In the same year, Philip, son of Herod the Great, in his realm to the north and east of the Sea of Galilee, also minted coins in honour of Julia, though he did what Pilate did not: he depicted her head on the obverse with the inscription 'Julia Augusta'. In addition, he honoured the city of Bethsaida with a new name, Julias. There he built a temple, most probably in Julia's honour, which has recently been unearthed. All these tributes to the Julian family were to commemorate the death of Julia, who had long been a benefactor of the Herodian family and the province of Judaea.[2] These tributes also provide evidence of the personal nature of Roman governance. Both Pilate and Herod Philip owed their positions to personal appointments by emperors from the Julio-Claudian family. They therefore felt a strong sense of personal obligation to honour the matriarch of the family. Personal relationships like these are at the heart of how the Roman Empire operated.

---

1. As we will see below, the coin that the high priests required Jews to use to pay the Temple tax (Tyrian sheqels) featured not only a graven image of a human and a bird, but a pagan god. By comparison, the ambiguous symbols on Pilate's coins were innocuous.
2. For further discussion of the coins of Pilate and Herod Philip, and the connection between Julia Augusta and Bethsaida, see F. Strickert, *Philip's City: From Bethsaida to Julias* (Collegeville, MN: Liturgical Press, 2011). On the temple, see R. Arav and R. Freund, *Bethsaida: A City by the North Shore of the Sea of Galilee* (Kirksville: Truman State University Press, 1999), Vol. II, 18ff.

Bethsaida: a Roman temple probably honouring Livia-Julia Augusta.[1]

All this discussion of coins minted by local governors concerns bronze denominations only, small change in Roman terms. Gold and silver coins circulated widely in Judaea, but these mints were controlled by the emperor. It was customary for these coins, such as the silver denarius Jesus used to make his point about 'rendering unto Caesar the things that are Caesar's', to include the name and portrait bust of the reigning emperor.[2]

Coins of Pilate.[3]

---

1. Photo by permission of the Bethsaida Excavations Project.
2. Matthew 22.19-21.
3. Photo by permission of J.P. Fontanille. For more detail, see http://www. numismalink.com/fontanille1.html.

The second piece of evidence that comes from the lifetime of Pilate is an inscription discovered during an archaeological excavation at Caesarea Maritima in 1961. The partially damaged dedicatory inscription was unearthed in the area of the great theatre that is still in use today. This inscription mentions a building or courtyard erected in honour of the Emperor Tiberius, appropriately called *Tiberiéum.* The second line mentions the patron of the project, *Pontius Pilatus.* The third line includes his title, *praefectus iudaeae,* 'prefect of Judaea'. This inscription corroborates written sources that name Pilate as governor of Judaea, and suggests that Caesarea was his place of residence (though on occasion he resided in the former palace of Herod in Jerusalem, probably during the great Jewish festivals and other times as he saw fit). Moreover, this inscription corrects an anachronistic error that appears in Tacitus.[1] In later years, the governor of Judaea would hold the title 'Procurator', but Tacitus used this term for Pilate. This inscription clarifies that Pilate, and other early governors of the province of Judaea, held the title of 'prefect'.

The Pilate inscription from Caesarea.[2]

We have no specific evidence for the early life of Pilate before he came to Judaea. What little we can reconstruct is based on evidence for the reign of Tiberius and the career of the praetorian prefect Sejanus

---

1. Anachronism is an important consideration throughout this discussion. For the historian, anachronism is an unpardonable sin. It literally refers to something 'out of time'. Usually, anachronisms consist in placing later ideas or words into an earlier chronological context where they do not fit. When Tacitus refers to Pilate as procurator (a later term) as opposed to his authentic title, prefect, he is committing an anachronism. We also encounter anachronism in rabbinic sources, which at times import into their discussions of the first century ideas or language developed by rabbis centuries later.

2. Photo by Brian LePort, by permission.

from the pages of Tacitus, Suetonius, and Dio, with some supplementary material provided by Philo and Josephus.[1] For the decade of Pilate's administration of Judaea, most of our evidence comes from Josephus, Philo, and the Gospels of the New Testament. While the Gospels deal primarily with Pilate's role in the trial of Jesus, which we will discuss in detail in Chapter V, our understanding of the remainder of Pilate's administration depends on evidence provided by Josephus and Philo.

Josephus provides us with glimpses of three formative events in Pilate's prefecture. The first, shortly after his accession in 26, was the infamous Affair of the Standards which appears in slightly different renditions in both the *Jewish War* and *Antiquities*.[2] The second, shortly thereafter, concerns a riot that grew out of Pilate's use of Temple funds to build an aqueduct for Jerusalem.[3] The third, included only in *Antiquities*, recounts Pilate's heavy-handed repression of a Samaritan uprising – an event that culminated in Pilate's being sent to Rome to answer for his actions, effectively ending his career in Judaea.[4] In addition to these three events, we also encounter Josephus's only reference to Jesus, the *Testimonium Flavianum*, which most scholars think suffered at least some interpolation by Christian scribes.[5] This passage appears to corroborate other pieces of evidence that Jesus was crucified under Pilate. Philo provides us with our only evidence of the Affair of the Shields. We will discuss all these events and passages in some detail below.

What's in a Name?

Now that we have a basic understanding of the nature of the evidence for the life of Pilate, we are in a position to put the pieces together. We can infer that Pilate was from the equestrian class, because it was standard procedure for emperors to appoint equestrians to governing posts in minor imperial provinces. *Equites*, as they were called in Latin, represented the second highest rung on the Roman social ladder, exceeded

---

1. The 'praetorian prefect' refers to the chief military officer and captain of the Praetorian Guard, the personal bodyguard and army of the emperor in Rome. In the first century, it was common for praetorian prefects to wield a great deal of power over the governance of the empire.
2. *Jewish War* 2.169-174; *Antiquities* 18.55-59. These events will be discussed in detail below.
3. *Jewish War* 2.175-77; *Antiquities* 18.60-62.
4. *Antiquities* 18.85-89.
5. *Antiquities* 18.63-64.

only by the senatorial elite. Equestrians were citizens of high standing and considerable wealth. Their high standing was often manifest in their military and administrative leadership positions.

The name Pontius Pilatus is intriguing. 'Pontius' indicates that his family could plausibly trace their roots to the important clan of the Pontii whose early renown came from Gaius Pontius, whose Samnite forces defeated the Romans at the Battle of Caudine Forks in 321 BC. 'Pilatus' seems to be a sort of nickname, for *pilus* is the Latin word for the spear or javelin regularly carried by Roman legionaries. Thus, 'Pilatus' means 'one who bears the *pilus*' or, more colloquially, 'spear-chucker', possibly with reference to a familial prowess in spear-throwing. A more likely explanation, however, is that one of his ancestors served as *primus pilus* (literally: 'First Spear') in the Roman military, the highest ranking among all centurions in a legion. Such men, upon retirement, received enough money to qualify as equestrians.

According to Josephus, Pilate was appointed to the post of prefect of Judaea in 26, a position he held for a decade, departing for Rome at the end of 36 or the beginning of 37. Because Judaea was an imperial province, the appointment of its governor fell to the emperor, Tiberius. It is probable that Pilate owed his nomination for this governmental post to the praetorian prefect, Sejanus, as military advancement was the surest way for an equestrian to come to the attention of the emperor. If this is true, it may well be that Pilate had served for a time in the Praetorian Guard, the personal bodyguard of the emperor in Rome. At the time of Pilate's appointment, Tiberius was in his twelfth year as Roman emperor, having inherited his power from his stepfather, Augustus.

Pontius Pilatus and Roman Imperial Government

Augustus, after his victory at Actium in 31 BC, put an end to the political factionalism and civil wars that had ravaged the empire for much of the previous century of the Roman Republic. Although consolidating his power through the might of legions, Augustus proceeded to take extraordinary steps to reduce the number of legions and his dependence on them. As a result, he launched one of the greatest accomplishments in human political history, the *Pax Augusta*, an official policy of peace, which would last, with few diversions, nearly two hundred years (after the reign of Augustus, it is often termed *Pax Romana*). Augustus also delivered the coup de grâce to the Roman Republic in 27 BC, replacing it with a form of government modern historians have dubbed the Principate: concentrating, with Senatorial legitimacy, the power of a proconsul and the power of a tribune in the hands of a single person, the *Princeps Senatus* Augustus. The *princeps* was better known as the Roman emperor. In some sources, because of his family lineage, he was called Caesar, a name that became a title in some sources. The new Augustan political and military establishment was characterised by remarkable stability and durability. Even emperors as unstable as Caligula and Nero did not succeed in destroying what Augustus had created.

The creation of the Principate had profound implications for Rome's governance of her provinces. Vergil's *Aeneid*, written under the patronage of Augustus, serves in part as the mouthpiece for the Augustan vision of Roman identity. One of Vergil's most famous passages provides a sort of mission statement for Roman governance:

> Others (so I believe) may fashion more smoothly images of bronze, coax living faces from marble, plead causes more eloquently, trace with the rod the wanderings of the heavens and foretell the rising of stars. But you, Roman, remember. These will be your arts: to rule the peoples with power, to cultivate the habit of peace, to spare the vanquished, and to pull down the haughty.[1]

Vergil served, to some degree, as a propagandist for Augustus. Without doubt, Augustus wanted to ensure that he would be celebrated as a virtuous and peaceful leader. He also wanted to erase the memory that he came to power as victor in a civil war. Toward that end, he promulgated his autobiographical *Res Gestae* (Accomplishments), inscribing it on monuments and imperial temples around the empire, emphasising the peace he brought to the provinces.[2] Augustus's coins, as the primary mass medium of the age, reinforced this message, often including either the name or the image of the goddess *PAX* (peace), accompanied by symbols of health and prosperity. With all propaganda, there is an inevitable degree of hypocrisy, but the most powerful propaganda has a firm foundation in reality. Augustus may have gained his position as emperor by the sword, but the evidence also indicates that he took Vergil's vision seriously, both in Rome itself and in the provinces. Yet while historians point to evidence of considerable economic expansion growing out of the cessation of the civil wars, provincials experienced the benefits of the Augustan peace only patchily, depending on their location and their social status.

---

1. *Aeneid* 6.847-853.
2. 26. The fullest extant version of this text was inscribed on the temple of Roma and Augustus in Ankara, though shorter fragments have been found elsewhere; cf. Velleius Paterculus 2.90; cf. Tacitus, *Annals* 1.2.

Shortly after his victory in the last civil war of the Republic and his emergence as emperor, Augustus fundamentally changed how Rome governed her empire. Before his time, to oversimplify a complex and organic structure, provinces had been governed under the auspices of the Senate, which conferred authority upon client kings or Roman governors. The Senate often preferred to rule indirectly by appointing a local client king (*rex socius*) who would rule with Rome's permission, in Rome's name, and in accordance with Roman policies – all with a significant degree of regional autonomy. The most important client kings who enter into our story are Herod the Great and his descendants, who variously and confusingly ruled over all or part of the province of Judaea for more than a century. Under Augustus, and increasingly toward the end of the first century BC, Rome chose to rule her provinces directly. For the most part, at the dawn of the Principate, proconsuls governed provinces under accountability to the Senate in Rome.

Augustus retained and rationalised this system to some degree, but he also modified it considerably. At the heart of Augustus's provincial reorganisation was a change in accountability and a change of objectives. Augustus converted those provinces he considered most valuable or most dangerous into imperial provinces, removing them from senatorial oversight and taking personal control over them. The empire was thus largely divided into Senatorial provinces, governed by proconsuls, and imperial provinces, accountable to the emperor alone.

The emperor could not, practically, govern all the imperial provinces, so he appointed trusted individuals to govern them in his name. The most common title of these governors, usually drawn from the elite of the senatorial class, was 'legate', at least for the larger and more important imperial provinces. Minor imperial provinces were often governed by prefects or procurators, who were usually drawn from the equestrian class.[1] It was not uncommon for legates to play a supervisory role over a local client king, prefect, or procurator. We encounter the intervention of the legate of Syria in several episodes in the province of Judaea, including the encounter that culminated in Pilate's permanent departure.

It is important to note the personal nature of much of Roman governance. The emperor personally appointed legates, prefects, and procurators. Moreover, it was not unusual for the emperor to intervene personally in the affairs of client kings, as he did when arbitrating the will of Herod the Great in 4 BC. Herod and his family were often found

---

1. Dio 53.12-15; For detailed description of provinces and their governance, see Strabo, *Geography* 17.3.24-25.

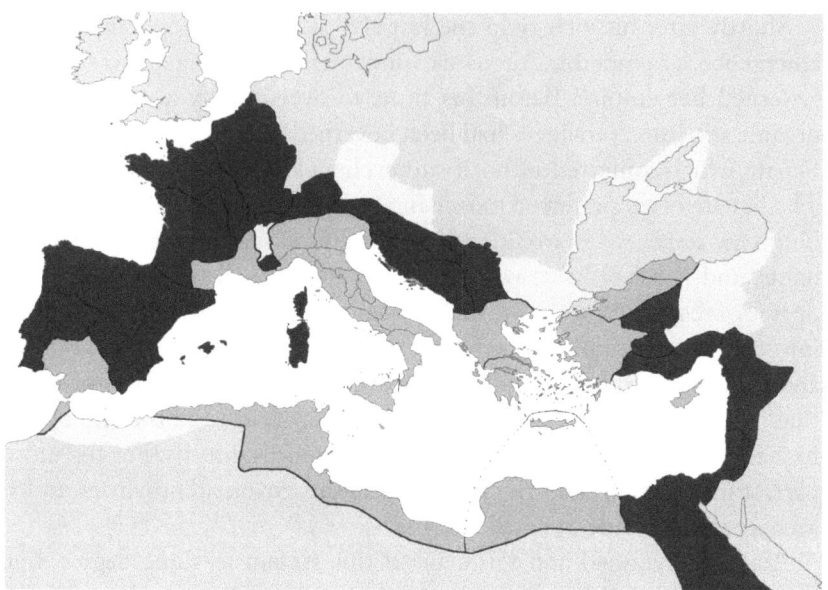

Map of the Roman Empire, distinguishing senatorial (lighter shading) and imperial (dark shading) provinces at the beginning of the reign of Tiberius.[1]

in the company of the imperial family. Personal benefactions cut both ways, such as the gifts Augustus conferred on Judaea, and the honorific naming of cities (Caesarea, Sebaste, Julias) and structures (such as the Tiberiéum or the Temples to Augustus or Julia) by governors or client kings. One particularly striking piece of evidence for the personal nature of Roman governance is that, according to Roman law, Roman citizens had a right of appeal to the emperor himself. It is difficult to imagine the reality created by such a policy, but we have abundant evidence that many took advantage of this extraordinary level of open, personal access. Emperors were regularly pestered by individuals wanting to be heard, while imperial administrators created lengthy waiting lists. In the New Testament book of Acts, Paul of Tarsus took advantage of the right of appeal and at the end of the book he was still awaiting his hearing before the emperor, more than two years after his initial appeal. The personal nature of imperial administration meant in practice that relationships, appeals, favours, benefactions, patronage, and the conferring of honours among elites were of immense importance throughout the empire.

---

1. Map source: Coldeel, 2009.
   https://commons.wikimedia.org/wiki/File%3ASenatorial_and_Imperial_provinces_in_14_AD.png

While Augustus shaped this reorganisation, it was not entirely consistent or stable.[1] Despite the organic and developing nature of this structure, however, Augustus brought a singular clarity of vision to the provinces to which all governors, of whatever title, were held accountable. Above all, after the debilitating turmoil and civil war that had dominated the late Republic, Augustus sought to impose a policy of peace and he believed the best way to create and maintain that peace was by providing the provinces with the benefits of Roman law, protection, infrastructure, and prosperity, along with a high degree of regional autonomy. To the extent that governors operated according to these principles, Augustus seems to have believed that the empire would prosper, tax revenues would multiply, and his political stock would soar. Events proved him more than prescient.

Roman rule was often benevolent, but it was not benign. All depended on upholding the *Pax Romana*. Provincial governors were empowered to pursue peace by force if necessary, for the Roman peace was a hegemonic peace. Rome did not rule with an iron fist but with an open hand; nonetheless, that open hand could draw a Spanish sword as quickly as Jupiter could unleash a lightning bolt. Imperial power was not to be trifled with.

So it was that Roman governors received their orders: maintain the strength of Roman rule with integrity, administer Roman justice with dignity, direct Roman troops and resources with restraint and efficiency, bring in Roman tax revenues with alacrity, respect local customs with benevolence, and above all, keep the peace with diligence.[2]

---

1. For example, Cyprus was annexed as a senatorial province, then converted to imperial status and subsequently reverted to Senatorial status, all at the hand of Augustus. Judaea may have been the most unstable of all, lurching from a single client king, to multiple client kings, to a prefect in the midst of client kings, to the restoration of client kings, to the establishment of procurators, to full-scale revolt and imperial military intervention, all over the course of about seventy years.

2. The evidence for this set of attitudes and policies is widespread, but some sense of its range is in order. Both Vergil and Horace, partisans of Augustus, ring the changes on the benefits that have come with Augustus's policy of peace, and Pliny the Elder concurs (e.g. *Aeneid* 1.288-95; *Carmen Saeculare*; *Natural History* 2.45.117; 3.5.39; 27.1.3). Even some provincials, like the second century Greek orator, Aelius Aristides, extol the virtues of the *Pax Romana* (*Rome*); cf. Epictetus 3.13.9; cf. Pomponius Mela, *On Places*. Others were more measured, like the historian Florus (*Epitome* 2.21, 29), or the moralist Plutarch (*Precepts of Statecraft* 32), not to mention Josephus or Philo, who acknowledge the benefits of Roman peace while also grappling

These principles of Roman governance rested on three of the oldest and most potent of Roman cultural values: *libertas, dignitas,* and *pietas. Libertas* refers to the 'liberty' Rome offered her citizens and subjects. *Libertas,* however, had always to be exercised within the bounds of *dignitas,* the proper respect owed to one's superiors. *Pietas,* the focal point of all Roman virtues, means much more than our rather anaemic word 'piety'. It refers to a robust sense of 'duty' – duty toward the gods, duty toward family, and duty to Rome itself. While we moderns would see these three as separate obligations, they were inseparable in the Roman mind, with *pietas* serving as an ethical lodestar, a central point of reference for most any question of proper behaviour.

This Roman triumvirate of values had profound import for the governance of the provinces. The Roman governor was charged to respect the *libertas* of the local provincials, but that *libertas* must always be balanced by the expectation that Rome's appointed governor would be honoured with proper *dignitas,* all resting on the mutual obligations of *pietas.* So long as both governor and governed played by these rules, all would be well from the Roman perspective. The problem is that too often the provincials failed to grasp the subtleties of these ethical and linguistic tensions, while Romans failed to understand the cultural sensitivities of their provincials. When provincials sought to exercise their *libertas* without *dignitas* and *pietas,* the ire of provincial governance could be provoked, with severe consequences. Such a system required a pressure-relief valve, and that invaluable role was filled by local elites, whom Roman governors recruited and utilised with varying degrees of effectiveness.[1]

---

with the provincial experience of subjugation (*Jewish War* 2.220; *Embassy* 300). We can get some sense of the dynamics of enforcing the policy of peace in the provinces through the eyes of the correspondence between Pliny the Younger, governor of Bithynia and Pontus in the early second century, and the Emperor Trajan. Ulpian, *Digest* 1.18.3.pr: 'A governor . . . should ensure that the province he rules remains peaceful and quiet.'

1. E.g. Aelius Aristides, *Rome* 26.64. It is important not to whitewash Roman governance and to note that tensions between *libertas* vs. *dignitas,* and instances of Roman corruption or abuse of power, resulted in several pockets of resistance and violence during the early *Pax Romana.* Among the more celebrated were the military conflict in Germania that culminated in the defeat of Roman legions at the Battle of Teutoburg Forest in AD 9 (Dio 56.18-22). Britannia, which Claudius added to the empire in AD 43, suffered severe, if short-lived, conflict with the rebellion of Boudicca in 61 (Tacitus, *Annals* 14.30ff; *Agricola* 30.6). The violent persecution of Jews in Alexandria under the Roman prefect Flaccus left lasting scars on Philo and

Rome and Judaea

The Roman province of Judaea provides a helpful case study on how Roman theory worked in practice. It has become fashionable in recent years for historical Jesus scholars to portray Rome as the consummate Evil Empire, imposing its blood- and gold-thirsty will on its unwilling subjects, thus generating widespread resentment. As a result, any resistance against Rome can be viewed as an expression of human dignity and resilience in the face of oppressive hegemony. While this paradigm, informed by the modern post-colonial experience, serves as a helpful corrective to earlier studies that tended to whitewash Rome, it is equally misleading. When one views the evidence as a whole, it becomes clear that the relationship between Rome and its provincial subjects was complex and diverse: chronologically, regionally, and socially. In historical context, most sources agree that the development of the *Pax Augusta* fundamentally altered the provincial experience relative to the chaos and civil wars that immediately preceded it, what classical historians call the Roman Revolution (usually dated to 133-27 BC). A thoughtful analysis of the evidence must bear in mind the broad effects of the Roman Revolution and the ensuing *Pax Augusta,* while also doing justice to the diversity of local provincial experience.

Relations between Rome and Judaea began with an early treaty of friendship with the independent Jewish monarchy, the Hasmonaeans, in the second century BC.[1] The Roman general, Pompey, annexed

Jewish-Roman relations, despite Philo's generally positive attitude toward Roman rule (Philo, *On Flaccus*). We know about such events precisely because they were not the norm for Roman governance of the provinces but rather newsworthy breaches of the *Pax Romana*. The Romans were an imperial power, imposing their will on their provincial subjects. They may have been committed to peace with an unusual level of benevolence and regional autonomy, but the modern experience of post-colonial resentment has taught us a healthy scepticism. Even the most well-intentioned imperialism has problematic consequences.

1. I Maccabees 8; Josephus, *Antiquities* 12.414-19. The Hasmonaeans were a Jewish dynasty that ruled over an independent Israel from the time of the Maccabean revolt to the annexation of Judaea by Pompey the Great: 167-63 BC. The Judaean experience of the *Pax Romana* must be understood in its own context. In the hundred and fifty years before Augustus, the Jews of the region faced the brutality and oppression of Greek Seleucid rule, leading to the Maccabean revolt. The Jewish Hasmonaean rulers were notorious for their instability, infighting, corruption, occasional brutality, and disruptions of significant populations. It was because of Hasmonaean internal conflict

Syria and Judaea in 63 BC, putting an end to Hasmonaean rule after years of internal turmoil. Thereafter, the Romans established a client kingship, settling eventually on the Herodian family as Rome's regional representatives. In the process, Rome permitted a good deal of autonomy and recognition of the ancient venerability of Jewish religion, even if many Romans considered Jewish belief in a single, invisible god peculiar. Julius Caesar had, in exchange for their support, conferred several benefits upon Jews, including exemption from military service and some tax reduction.[1] Augustus reaffirmed Roman recognition and protection of the Jews.[2] When Herod the Great died in 4 BC, Augustus intervened and ultimately determined that Herod's kingdom would be divided among his three sons. Augustus confirmed Herod Archelaus as ethnarch (though he was popularly called 'king') of Judaea in the south, Herod Antipas as Tetrarch of Galilee in the northwest and Perea, east of the Jordan, and Philip as tetrarch over Gaulanitis (modern Golan Heights) and the regions to the northeast.[3] These three clients of Augustus were closely watched by his personally appointed legates of Syria.[4]

---

that the Roman general Pompey was invited to intervene, which happened to be in the midst of the Roman Revolution. The last few decades of the Roman Revolution degenerated into conflict among generals and legions, eventually culminating in multiple civil wars. These conflicts made their presence felt in Judaea in the interventions of Crassus, Caesar, Antony, and Cleopatra – not to mention the military incursions of the Parthians and Nabateans. In the midst of all this turmoil, the Romans appointed the Herodian family to keep a lid on things. From the perspective of Jews living in Judaea, those hundred and fifty years represented anything but ideal living conditions. There can be little doubt that the peace, stability, and relative prosperity established under Augustus, not to mention his favourable policies toward Jews, came as a relief to most inhabitants of Judaea, even though such conditions came at the cost of subjugation to the unstable rule of the Herodians. This context goes a long way toward explaining the ambivalence evident in some first-century Jewish sources. It also makes more challenging the task of explaining why Jewish attitudes toward Rome degenerated in the first century AD.

1. Josephus, *Antiquities* 14.185-216.
2. Philo, *Embassy* 145-58, 309-18.
3. Josephus, *Jewish War* 2.93ff. The sons of the great Herod usually appear in the sources as 'Herod'. Thus it requires some care to determine which Herod is in view in any particular context.
4. Indeed, in the midst of the chaos that ensued when Herod the Great died, Varus, legate of Syria, intervened in force to restore the peace.

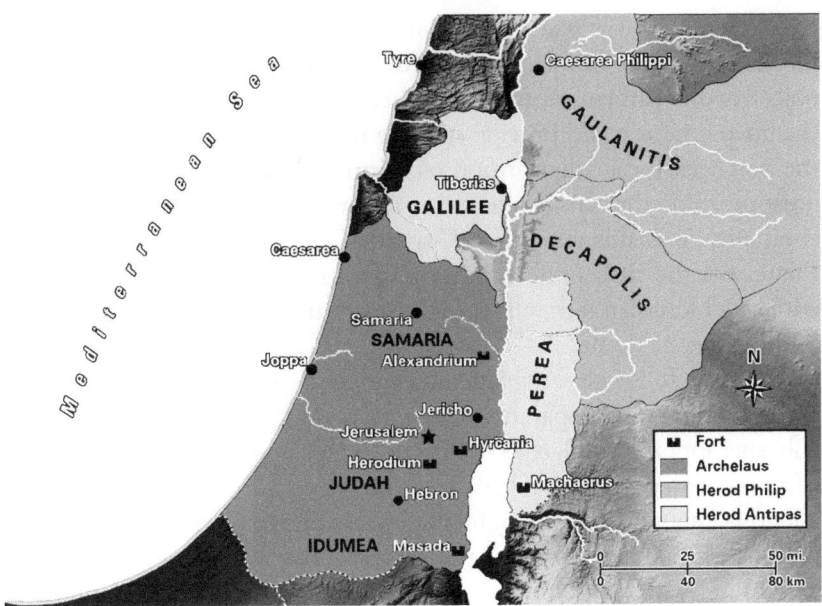

Map of Roman Judaea indicating the division of the realm among the three sons of Herod the Great after 4 BC. From AD 26-36, Pilate ruled the southern region, including Jerusalem and his seat of government, Caesarea Maritima. Herod Antipas continued to rule in Galilee and Perea, while Herod Philip continued to rule in the region of Gaulanitis to the north and east of the Sea of Galilee.[1]

This arrangement among the three Herodian brothers lasted nearly a decade until AD 6 when Augustus summoned Archelaus to Rome to answer to charges of excessive brutality, and breaches of the *Pax Augusta*.[2] While Rome had little sympathy with any provincials who would disturb the *Pax Augusta*, neither would it tolerate a client king or regional governor who acted with excessive violence. Augustus exiled Archelaus to Gaul, and then made a fateful decision: he would not expand the realm of the other Herodians but would instead leave them in place while appointing a Roman prefect to rule directly over Judaea and Samaria, the realm formerly ruled by Archelaus. In the interim, between the departure of Archelaus and the arrival of the first prefect, the legate of Syria, Publius Sulpicius Quirinius, stepped in to oversee the transition. Through Quirinius, Augustus did what he had done

---

1. Map by A.D. Riddle. Online: https://www.bibleodyssey.org/tools/map-gallery/h/map-Herod.
2. Archelaus inaugurated his reign with violence at his first Passover, killing some three thousand Jews. While Josephus does not provide specifics, it appears that his leadership did not improve (*Jewish War* 2.13, 111).

elsewhere when reorganising provinces. He commissioned a census of Judaea, limited to the realm that Rome would now rule directly. The objective of a Roman census was to ascertain the resources of a region so the government could provide suitable infrastructure, and to determine the potential for auxiliary troop recruitment and tax revenue. This was most probably the census referred to in the Gospel of Luke.[1] The census complete, Augustus appointed Coponius as the first prefect of Judaea. Pilate was the fifth prefect, inheriting all the awkwardness of sharing with two Herodian tetrarchs the administration of the Jewish homeland in the name of Rome.

Tiberius followed Augustus as emperor, inheriting the political and administrative apparatus of the Principate in AD 14. By the time Tiberius appointed Pilate as prefect of Judaea in 26, the imperial system of provincial governance had been maturing for some four decades. Tiberius maintained and tightened what he received from Augustus, with emphasis on rationality and responsibility, taking an accountant's delight in fiscal affairs. For all his personal woes and the scurrilous gossip that surrounded his personal character, Tiberius was widely regarded, at least in his early years, as an exemplary leader and administrator. Although he spent much time ensconced in his spectacular palace, the ruins of which are still visible on the island of Capri, Tiberius was able to run the empire effectively, largely through the agency of his praetorian prefect, Sejanus, until the year 31. Sejanus, commander of the personal bodyguard of the emperor and second only in power to Tiberius, was important for the life of Pilate in two respects. First, according to Philo, Sejanus harboured anti-Jewish sentiments. Second, it is likely that Pilate received his appointment as prefect at least in part through the influence of Sejanus. There is no specific evidence, however, that Pilate shared Sejanus's prejudices. Nevertheless, Pilate's relationship with Sejanus may have put him on tricky footing when in 31 Tiberius executed Sejanus and some of his followers on charges of *maiestas* (high treason).

For most of the imperial period, Roman rule was not, as it is often depicted, heavy-handed and violent, and many provincials, even including some Jews, responded favourably to their inclusion in the empire. Therefore, one might well ask, if the Romans were really so committed to peace and local autonomy, why did a certain percentage of Jews, a percentage that seems to have grown over time, chafe under Roman rule, considering it distasteful if not intolerable? There were at

---

1. On the census under Quirinius, see Josephus, *Antiquities* 17.355; 18.1, 26; 20.102; Luke 2.2. For a detailed discussion, see Appendix I.

least four reasons: 1) a history of periodic Roman violence perpetrated against Jews; 2) Roman taxation; 3) the elitist nature of Roman rule; and 4) the rise of Zealot political theology.

Roman Violence against Jews

The earlier discussion of the Roman governance of Judaea intentionally sidestepped a number of formative and troubling episodes. Now we must face squarely the fact that Roman violence against Jews had a long, if sporadic, history. While it is well to remember that a hundred years of Roman indirect or direct rule over Jews had been largely stable, respectful, and even beneficial, it began with violence; and that violence was periodically reinforced in such a manner that it was not easily forgotten. Those painful memories endured, even amidst extended periods of peace. The Roman proconsul Pompey entered Judaea initially by invitation of the Hasmonaean family to resolve a dispute. When his relationship with the Jewish ruling family broke down, however, he annexed the province in 63 BC by marching his legions into Judaea. He besieged Jerusalem, killed a significant number of Jews, and then did the unthinkable in Jewish eyes, defiling the Temple by entering the Holy of Holies.[1] A few years later, the Roman general Crassus violated the Temple precinct again and confiscated Temple funds to pay for his war effort against the Parthians, violently suppressing all resistance (he was subsequently defeated).[2] Herod, after the Roman Senate appointed him as client king, took control by force, in the process killing some of the elites of Jerusalem.[3] In the aftermath of Herod's death in 4 BC, Varus, the legate of Syria, cracked down on Jewish insurgents by sacking the city of Sepphoris and crucifying two thousand dissidents around Jerusalem.[4] Archelaus, Rome's client king, slaughtered three thousand Jews during an uprising at Passover.[5]

Such a record has misled many students of this era. These incidents of violence were serious, but isolated. Over the course of nearly a hundred years, there were only a few instances of such Roman violence perpetrated upon Jews, and most of these were in contravention of

---

1. Josephus, *Jewish War* 1.148-53; *Antiquities* 14.64ff; Tacitus, *Histories* 5.9.
2. Josephus, *Jewish War* 1.179-80; *Antiquities* 14.105.
3. *Jewish War* 1.358; *Antiquities* 14.175, 15.6.
4. Josephus, *Jewish War* 2.66-75.
5. Josephus, *Jewish War* 2.8ff. It is difficult to know how seriously to take these large, round numbers. Nevertheless, Josephus does suggest that these acts of violence were significant and well known.

Roman policy. The remainder of the time, peace and relative prosperity prevailed, especially after Augustus established the Principate in 27 BC. Between AD 6 and 33 (indeed, into the 40s), we have evidence of only one act of Roman violence against Jews in Judaea and that on a small scale, during the Aqueduct Riot which we will discuss below. Indeed, Tacitus claimed that during the long reign of Tiberius, all was quiet in Judaea.[1] Nevertheless, it is certainly understandable that the memories of earlier violence endured, and that Jews in Judaea had good reason to be anxious about the next time they might suffer the wrath of Rome.[2]

Reinforcing this concern was a degree of inconsistency in Roman policy toward their Jewish subjects. Julius Caesar had rewarded Jews for their support by treating them with respect and even favour, including exemption from military service.[3] Augustus continued to treat them well, even making contributions to the Temple in Jerusalem and requesting that a regular sacrifice be made on his behalf, but Tiberius ousted some Jews from Rome in AD 19, only to reverse that policy toward the end of his reign.[4] Caligula was particularly ill-disposed toward Jews because they refused to acknowledge his divinity – an

1. *Histories* 5.9. Here Tacitus refers to the absence of substantive uprisings; at the same time, he acknowledges the continued use of capital punishment against individuals the Roman governors considered real or potential threats to the *Pax Romana* or common criminals from the lower classes. In addition, individual Roman soldiers developed a reputation for rapacity which manifested itself in the form of confiscations of goods or services, not to mention questionable financial transactions (e.g. the confiscation of an ass in Apuleius's *Transformations*; the requisition of labour referenced in Matthew 5.41, and the tampering with loan paperwork: *P. Yadin* no. 11; cf. M. Goodman, *Rome and Jerusalem: The Clash of Ancient Civilizations* (New York: Vintage, 2007), 72; see also p. 379 for discussion of the lack of conflict in Jerusalem in the era of Tiberius. For further discussion of Roman capital punishment, see Chapter VII.
2. Josephus also records the later violent suppression of Jewish uprisings by Cumanus (*Jewish War* 2.223-46) and Florus (*Jewish War* 2.284ff.). As in the cases of Pilate and Archelaus, both appear to have been removed from office for their heavy-handed use of force against Jews. For similar reasons, Flaccus was removed from his prefecture in Egypt. All of these suggest that emperors took a dim view of excessive use of force at the hands of provincial governors.
3. *Antiquities* 13.251-2; 14.204.
4. Philo, *Embassy* 154-58; 309-18. On Tiberius's expulsion of Jews from Rome: Josephus, *Antiquities* 18.81-84; Tacitus, *Annals* 2.85.4; Suetonius, *Tiberius* 36. The curious detail of four thousand Jews conscripted into military service suggests that the expulsion may have been limited.

issue that came to a head with his determination to install his statue in the Temple in Jerusalem.[1] Claudius rescinded this order and restored Jewish privileges in Alexandria, but he also restricted Jewish assembly in Rome and eventually expelled Jews from Rome in 49 over riots concerning someone named 'Chrestus'. Priscilla and Aquila, two refugees from this expulsion, landed in Corinth, where they soon joined the ministry of Paul.[2] Some of these events may have been local and modest in scope and at times the better part of a generation passed without any conflict. Nevertheless, this history of sporadic violence and unanticipated political disadvantages created an understandable long-term tension among Jews. These tensions and anxieties were only exacerbated by financial concerns.

Roman and Jewish Taxation

One of the most commonly cited reasons for Jewish resistance to Roman rule is the burden of Roman taxes. There is no question that taxation was a contributing cause, but it is important to consider why some Jews considered Roman taxes particularly objectionable. Most commentators assume that the problem was that Roman tax rates were too high. This assumption is mere conjecture, for there is little evidence that would permit us, for example, to compare Roman tax rates with Herodian tax rates. Jews had certainly paid taxes under Hasmonaean and Herodian rule. Herod the Great engaged in massive and luxurious building projects, including Caesarea, Sebaste, Herodion, Machaerus, Masada, and his palaces at Jericho and Jerusalem (among many others), not to mention his greatest building project, which continued long after his death: the lavish remodelling of the Temple Mount complex in Jerusalem. Herod also built at least three large temples in honour of the imperial cult at Caesarea Maritima, Sebaste, and Panias. These projects were staggeringly expensive and there can be little doubt that Herod's subjects had to pay much of the bill. We do not know a great deal about taxation under the Herodians but the burden was significant, so much so that, immediately upon Herod's death, a Jewish crowd petitioned Archelaus for tax relief.[3] Herodians appear primarily

---

1. Philo, *Embassy.*
2. *Antiquities* 19.279ff.; Dio 40.6; Acts 18.2; Suetonius, *Claudius* 25.4. 'Chrestus' may well be a misspelling of 'Christus', or Christ.
3. *Jewish War* 2.4; *Antiquities* 17.200-5. Some scholars have suggested that the overall tax burden may have been reduced under direct Roman rule relative to the era of the Herodians.

to have levied taxes on crops and on goods bought and sold. There can be little doubt that Rome received its cut of tax revenue from the Herodians, but evidence of how and how much is elusive.

Under the Herodians, Jews also paid religious taxes: tithes and the Temple tax. The tithe referred to one-tenth of the produce of the land which went to support the priests in Jerusalem.[1] In addition, there was the annual Temple tax, calculated at ½ sheqel (roughly the pay for two days for a labourer) per adult male for all Jews no matter where they lived. The Temple tax, which supported the expenses associated with Temple cult, could not be paid using Roman coins. Rather, the priests required all coinage to be changed to the Tyrian sheqel (which, intriguingly, bore the images of the pagan gods Herakles/Melqart, with an eagle featured on the reverse).[2] This combination of significant Herodian taxes on top of a set of religious taxes was a significant burden to bear. Moreover, there is some evidence that the Temple tax had been increased dramatically not many years earlier, as high priests demanded an annual tax rather than the long-standing tradition of a once-in-a-lifetime tax.[3]

---

1. A number of Jewish sources speak of a 'second tithe' or a cycle of tithes, up to 14 over the course of seven years (Numbers 18.21-32; Deuteronomy 14.27-9; Nehemiah 10.37-9; Tobit 1.7ff.; Josephus, *Antiquities* 4.69, 205, 24), though the 'second tithe' would likely have been consumed by the family that offered it during the major pilgrim festivals. For detailed discussion, see E.P. Sanders, *Judaism Practice and Belief 63 BCE-66 CE* (London: SCM, 1992), 146-69.

2. One might well wonder why the Jewish high priests would require payment in the form of a foreign coin that features pagan graven images. Numismatists offer a partial answer. First, Tyrian sheqels were consistently pure (over ninety percent silver) and of a consistent weight. They were thus the most valuable and stable silver coins in the region. Second, Tyrian sheqels were minted at Tyre only from 125/6 to 18 BC (for discussion, see Y. Meshorer, *Ancient Jewish Coinage* [New York: Amphora, 1982], II, 9. Thereafter, the mint may have been transferred to Jerusalem and placed under the control of the high priests, thus providing Jewish religious leaders with a way to ensure the continued purity of the coinage they would receive (against the practice of debasing other silver coinage in the region). Moreover, control of the mint would have provided a lucrative source of income for the high priestly family. The continuation of the pagan iconography may be a way of retaining local confidence in the coins as they changed the location of the mint. Only at the beginning of the Jewish War in AD 66 did the high priestly mint stop striking pagan imagery on the coins. For detailed discussion of scholarly controversies over dates and minting, see D. Hendin, *Guide to Biblical Coins* (New York: Amphora, 2010), 476-85.

3. According to Philo, at least some Jews paid their religious taxes 'gladly and cheerfully', but as an elite member of the Jewish diaspora, his comments

*Tyrian sheqel, with the head of Hercules/Melqart on the obverse
and an eagle on the reverse.*[1]

When Augustus exiled Archelaus in AD 6 and decided upon direct
Roman rule of Judaea, one of his first steps was to impose a census. It is
no coincidence that a Jew named Yehuda of Gamla (sometimes called
Judas of Galilee) raised a rebellion in the wake of this census, for he
understood that a census was a prelude to direct Roman taxation. It is
important to note, however, that there is no evidence that Yehuda was
concerned about the *amount* of taxation. His concerns lay elsewhere.[2]
Under the prefects of Judaea, the religious taxes remained unchanged.
They did, however, change the Herodian system concerning what was
taxed, how taxes were collected, and what the tax revenues funded. A
Roman census required people to register where they lived and owned
property, providing a record of head count as well as land titles. Based
on census results, the Romans proceeded to impose a head tax (*tributum*

---

are not entirely representative (*On Special Laws* 1.141-4; Sanders, *Judaism*,
52). Sectarian documents from Qumran, as well as a significant hoard of
Tyrian sheqels unearthed in the excavations of the settlement, suggest that
this group of sectarian Jews rejected the annual assessment while collecting
the once-only tax (see J. Magness, *Stone and Dung, Oil and Spit: Jewish
Daily Life in the Time of Jesus* [Grand Rapids: Eerdmans, 2011], 101-2). The
combination of a significant increase in tax assessment with control over the
mint that produced the required coin, the exchange rate, and the commission
on currency exchanges can go a long way toward explaining both the wealth
of the high priestly family of Annas and its relative disrepute in the sources.

1. Photo: https://www.forumancientcoins.com/numiswiki/view.asp?key
=tyrian%20shekels.
2. *Jewish War* 2.118.

capitis) and a tax on the land and what it produced (*tributum soli* or *tributum agri*), though these were often confused. In addition, there were taxes on such things as ports, transportation of goods, and inheritance.[1] It is not at all clear that tax rates were higher under direct Roman rule than they were under the Herodians, but they were different. Jews did bear a relatively heavy tax burden, for their religious taxes alone were substantial, and any taxes imposed by any government increased the weight of that burden. That burden was heavy enough that the provinces of Judaea and Syria applied to Tiberius for the reduction of their head tax in AD 17.[2] Yet our sources do not point to the amount of tax as the primary Jewish concern, but rather to two other aspects of Roman taxation: what the taxes funded and how they were collected.

While the tax burden under Herod may have been heavy, the proceeds went largely to local projects which hired local builders and produced visible local results, not to mention increasing employment and stimulating local economies. Roman taxes also built local infrastructure such as aqueducts, baths, theatres and hippodromes, but much of the proceeds of the *tributum* went to fund Roman government, including Roman soldiers. Moreover, a substantial portion of the head tax flowed into the imperial coffers in Rome. The latter, along with the idea that their hard-earned money helped pay for the soldiers who would sooner impose their will by force than relinquish Roman hegemony, surely did not sit well with the local population.

Another concern was how taxes were collected. Roman prefects were in charge of collecting taxes but, given their minimal staff, they customarily farmed out collection duties to local tax collectors (*telonai* in Greek) whose reputation for rapacity haunts the pages of the New Testament. Since tax collectors commonly contracted with the Roman government to supply a predetermined amount of tax revenue, they could always create a higher profit margin by collecting more taxes than required. They were notorious for distorting tax rates and pressing subjects to pay more than was required. Jesus's encounter with Zacchaeus, a diminutive tax collector from Jericho, is instructive. In a fit of repentance, Zacchaeus promises, '[I]f I have defrauded anyone of anything, I will pay back four times as much.'[3] Such a promise may suggest that he felt some measure of guilt for defrauding Jewish taxpayers. On the other hand, he may be

---

1. Dio 55.27; for detailed discussion, see B.D. Shaw, 'Roman Taxation', in *Civilization of the Ancient Mediterranean: Greece and Rome*, edited by M. Grant and R. Kitzinger (New York: Scribner, 1988), Vol. 2, 809-27.
2. Tacitus, *Annals* 2.42.5.
3. Luke 19.8.

suggesting that he had been relatively honest compared to his fellow tax collectors. Jesus was known as one who ate with 'tax collectors and sinners', among whom was Matthew, one of the twelve Apostles.[1] This association earned Jesus a measure of ill-repute. The Pharisees and Herodians did not come to Jesus asking, 'Is the tax burden too high?' but rather, 'Is it lawful to pay taxes to Caesar?'[2] For some provincials, the regular payment of Roman taxes, using coins featuring the bust of the emperor, served as a constant reminder of their subservience. The combination of the distasteful destination of taxes, and their collection by avaricious agents of empire formed a potent brew for Jews. Some of them drank of it deeply and used it to fuel rage and resistance movements.

Roman and Jewish Elitism

A third reason for Jewish resistance to Roman rule undergirded the second, for many of those tax dollars funded the luxurious lifestyles of elites. One glance at the remains of the Promontory Palace in Caesarea, or Herodion, or the sumptuous homes of the high priests, or even the Temple itself provides eloquent testimony of taxes at work, and for many of the poor or destitute of Judaea, the sight must have been infuriating. To a large degree, those hard-earned sheqels, paid from the purses of Jews living in poverty or teetering on its brink, brought them little benefit.

We Americans like to quote Lincoln's Gettysburg Address, that ours is a 'government of the people, by the people and for the people'. It is a lofty ideal, but we all know that that ideal masks a high degree of elitism in our government as well as our rapidly growing wealth disparity. Romans, along with other ancient cultures, did not cherish any such ideals. Rather, theirs was a government of the people, by the elite and for the elite. Moreover, far from hiding the reality, they flaunted it. Elites wore distinctive clothing, including varying configurations of purple depending on one's rank, not to mention the elaborate *toga virilis,* the symbol of Roman citizenship. They travelled by horse or litter, accompanied by a great entourage of slaves and retainers. A trip to the forum by an elite Roman matron, bedecked in sparkling jewels, often became a parade of retainers – the larger the parade, the higher the standing of the person in the litter.[3] Senatorial, equestrian, and provincial elites competed for honorific titles, beneficial marriage alliances, patronage, and public recognition for their

---

1. Matthew 9.10; 10.3.
2. Mark 12.14; cf. E.M. Smallwood, *The Jews under Roman Rule: From Pompey to Diocletian, A Study in Political Relations* (Leiden: Brill, 1976), 153.
3. E.g. Suetonius, *Julius* 43.1; *Domitian* 8.3; Dio 57.15.4.

generosity. Their spacious villas dominated domestic landscapes while their largesse was celebrated on public inscriptions and elaborate tombs. Elites were characterised in some Roman sources as venal and arrogant, contemptuous of the poor who deserved their lot, and jealous of the honours shared only by their peers. It would be quite impossible for a Jewish peasant to visit Rome or Ephesus or Jerusalem and not encounter evidence of elitism on every hand.[1]

In the modern world, we often think of elitism in economic terms: elites are rich. That was true to a large degree in the ancient world as well, but not entirely. Ancient elitism was focused on the family much more than its income; that is, one was born elite, or not. It was difficult for a person who was not born into an elite family to join those lofty ranks (though some social mobility was possible through military advancement or other connections with elite families). Elites were usually wealthy, but there were also stories of elite families who squandered much of their wealth.

Elitism was not a Roman monopoly. Indeed, most all ancient governments were dominated by some sort of ruling class. Even the Athenian democracy was, for most of its existence, largely dominated by a few elite families. Jewish society in this era was also fundamentally elitist. The independent Hasmonaeans had been elitist in their own way, and the Herodians had made quite a show of it.[2] Under direct Roman rule, the conspicuous wealth represented by the luxurious Jewish homes in the Upper City of Jerusalem, some of which were the homes of priestly families, testifies to the continuation of Jewish elitism, and

1. For detailed discussion, see R. MacMullen, *Roman Social Relation: 50 B.C. to A.D. 284* (New Haven: Yale UP, 1974), who suggests that the Roman social pyramid was unusually steep, with the senatorial elite (at the time of Tacitus) accounting for about 0.002% of the population of the empire, and equestrians accounting for about 0.1%. Both elite classes together amounted to less than one percent. The bulk of the population probably lived relatively close to the subsistence level. Such stratification was matched in language, as elite Greek and Latin authors developed a detailed 'lexicon of Snobbery' (138-41).Cf. J. Stambaugh and D. Balch, *The Social World of the First Christians* (London: SPCK, 1986), 63ff.
2. Herodian elitism is evident in all of his spectacular building projects. Hasmonaean elitism is not as ubiquitous, but the lavish palaces of these independent Jewish kings in Jericho and the monumental tombs of Jason and Bene Hazir in Jerusalem bear witness to a conspicuous elitism that long pre-dated direct Roman rule. For further discussion of Jewish elitism, see M. Goodman, *The Ruling Class of Judaea: The Origins of the Jewish Revolt against Rome A.D. 66-70* (Cambridge: Cambridge University Press, 1987).

literary sources make it clear that the 'ruling class of Judaea' centred on the high priestly family. The Temple itself, in all its glory, represents an immense accumulation of wealth, largely collected from Jews who struggled to feed their families.

Because Roman government was fundamentally elitist and personal, the emperor appointed elites to rule imperial provinces, and those elite governors, in turn, ruled in collaboration with elite provincials they considered worthy. In Jerusalem, the most important local elite was the high priest who, in our period, was personally appointed by the Roman prefect. As we will see in the next chapter, the family of the high priest represented the highest form of elitism in the Jewish world. It was precisely this combination of Roman elitism and Jewish elitism that gave rise to a Roman-Temple alliance.[1] That alliance may have been more or less functional at different times, depending on the relationship between governor and high priest, but there can be no doubt that the combined interests of these elite individuals had a great deal to do with how the province actually functioned.

Many scholars have studied the social and economic stratification of first-century Judaea in an attempt to uncover the causes of the great Jewish War. While they disagree on details, most agree that the disparity of wealth and status combined with the significant tax burden, especially as experienced by Jewish peasants, created a strong sense that the Roman-Temple alliance was an agent of oppression. That oppression kindled a smouldering resentment which can help explain the many resistance movements that arose around the time of the death of Herod, as well as the years immediately before the outbreak of full-scale revolt in AD 66.

It is important to note, however, that such resistance movements arose before direct Roman rule. They were in abeyance (at least to judge from the silence of our evidence) during the early decades of direct Roman rule, only to resurge after the middle of the century. In addition, the Romans did not introduce elitism to Judaea. Rather, they brought their own elitism to bear on the home-grown variety that had long antedated their arrival. The self-interested elitism that caused so much resentment was thus exacerbated but not created by Rome and the objects of this resentment were not only the Roman governor and his entourage, but the aptly termed Roman-Temple alliance. It is precisely this power dynamic that set the tables that were soon to be overturned.

---

1. M. Borg and J.D. Crossan, *The Last Week: What the Gospels Really Teach about Jesus's Final Days in Jerusalem* (New York: HarperOne, 2006), 15ff. They refer to this alliance as a 'domination system', with emphasis more on its systemic than its personal dimensions.

Josephus and Philo, both Jewish elites who felt most directly the benefits of Roman rule, represent the perspective of privileged status, and it is important to remember this fact when interpreting the evidence they provide. The Gospels of the New Testament, however, provide something of a corrective.

All this discussion of elitism and Roman-Temple alliance may be abstract, but it becomes palpable when viewed from the perspective of the disenfranchised. Although peace and stability, after the chaos of the civil wars, benefitted all inhabitants of the Roman empire, the chief beneficiaries were the elites. Grinding poverty and frustration combined with a lack of social mobility continued to dominate the experience of many if not most peasants – which brings us to one of the more important resistance movements of the era.

'Zealot' Political Theology

A fourth reason for Jewish resistance to Roman rule was the development of a relatively new political theology associated with the rise of the Zealots.[1] Josephus connects the dots between the exile of Archelaus, the

---

1. I employ the term 'Zealot' reluctantly, in deference to popular usage. It may be anachronistic to use this term, at least with reference to any coherent group or ideology, in the early first century AD. Zealots as an organised and recognisable group seem to emerge later, in the 50s or even 60s. Yehuda of Gamla might not have referred to himself as a Zealot but, at least from Josephus's perspective, some later Zealots traced their heritage back to him. There is also a significant problem with the terms Josephus employs. The Greek word most commonly translated 'Zealot' is *lēstēs*. The basic meaning of the term is 'bandit' or 'brigand'. The term is problematic, however, for it admits of at least four applications with quite disparate implications. The first two would be considered criminals in most any society: 1) violent thugs intent on destruction and self-aggrandisement; 2) robbers who seek to enrich themselves by taking other peoples' property. The second two, however, would be considered criminals by some in positions of power but not by others, especially those in subjugated social positions: 3) economic brigands: those who steal (and sometimes may resort to violence in the process) because they have no other means of subsistence, such as those who have lost their land, jobs, or homes and engage in banditry to survive; 4) 'social brigands': those who engage in acts of brigandage as a form of social protest against what they view as oppressive political/social/economic circumstances (think Robin Hood, at least as portrayed in modern media). The fourth group may be motivated by a range of ideological or practical motives. Technically, the Zealot political theology Josephus describes is a variation on #4, with a focus on theological motivation, though Josephus's narrative often seems to

appointment of the first prefect of Judaea, the census under Quirinius, the new imposition of Roman taxes, and the rise of a resistance movement led by Yehuda of Gamla (Judas of Galilee). Josephus's earliest reference to Yehuda is brief but instructive, for the resistance movement he founded was rooted in a potent political theology: 'He declared that Jews were cowardly if they submitted to paying taxes to the Romans, tolerating mortal lords, after they had served God alone.'[1] At the heart of Yehuda's resistance was a vision which Josephus articulated in more detail in his

consider #4 and #1 roughly equivalent. The linguistic and historical challenge is that these four distinctions are abstract and often blur in reality, especially as Josephus describes them. Yehuda of Gamla may well have been purely a social brigand based on a particular political theology, but those who joined him in his rebellion against Rome may well have included individuals or groups representing all four definitions. Most often, it is impossible to distinguish them, but the best method is to analyse the supporters of any particular group. If a group of brigands is supported by local peasants, we may have a case of social brigandage, especially if the targets of their brigandage are exclusively elites. Without such indications of broad peasant support, the term *lēstēs* may refer to any of the possible definitions. This whole problem is exacerbated by the reality that there was no distinction in Roman law between civil and criminal law. It is ill-conceived to assume that 'brigands' always refers to people who modern historians would class as violent criminals and it is equally ill-conceived to consider all 'brigands' to be 'freedom fighters' or victims of oppression. For his part, Josephus seems to oppose Zealot political theology and uses *lēstēs* in all senses. *Lēstēs* appears fifteen times in the New Testament. In most cases, it is clearly employed in the criminal sense (in the parable of the Good Samaritan [Luke 10], in the Good Shepherd Discourse [John 10], and in the 'Cleansing of the Temple' [Mark 11.17; Matthew 21.13; Luke 19.46]). In a couple of cases, the usage is ambiguous enough that economic or social brigands could be in view, though they could point to criminal definitions just as well (Mark 15.27; Matthew 27.38; John 18.40). For detailed discussion, see M. Hengel, *Zealots* (London: Bloomsbury T&T Clark, 2000). The fascinating study by B.D. Shaw, 'Bandits in the Roman Empire', *Past and Present*, 105 (November, 1984), 3-52, helps contextualise the evidence from first century Judaea, geographically, textually, and chronologically. Even shepherds (who were often accused of rustling), veteran soldiers (from disbanded units or on the losing side of a civil conflict), military deserters, or pirates could be termed 'bandits' under Roman law. They were 'outlaws' in the literal sense of the term. Pompey was renowned for clearing the Mediterranean of pirates, while Augustus seems to have been nearly as successful at clearing Italy of bandits, but precise definitions continue to be complex and elusive, so it is best to avoid overgeneralisation, beyond the following: evidence of brigandage appears largely to be inversely proportional to the local presence of strong state authority.

1. *Jewish War* 2.118.

later *Antiquities* as the 'Fourth Philosophy' of the Jews: if God alone
is to be their only ruler and Lord, then Jews should do everything in
their power to assert their liberty including both passive resistance (not
paying Roman taxes) and, potentially, active resistance (which in some
cases led to violence and insurrection).

From the perspective of Josephus, this movement spawned many
others, variously called 'brigands', '*sicarii*' (so called because of their use
of the small curved dagger, the *sica* in Latin, which they employed to
great effect by stabbing Jewish Roman sympathisers in the midst of large
crowds), or 'Zealots'. For Josephus, Yehuda of Gamla laid the egg that
Shimon bar Giora hatched, for Shimon led his fellow Zealots in the later
stages of the great revolt against Rome later in the century. For Josephus,
the Zealot political theology was one of the primary causes of the great
misfortunes that would later befall the Jewish people.[1] On the other hand,
Josephus does indicate throughout his larger narratives of the next sixty
years that Yehuda of Gamla and the disparate groups that followed his
example were significant players only because they tapped into a larger
sense of resentment among a significant number of Jews.[2] On a deeper
level, that resentment grew out of a long-standing hope that permeated
Jewish culture and tied together the variegated strands of Jewish belief
and praxis – a hope for the vindication and restoration of Israel in its
fullness, a complete return from exile, and a return of the Temple to its
highest degree of integrity and sanctity.[3] Jewish attitudes toward Rome,
even Zealot political theology, grew out of this pervasive sense of hope.

Josephus was probably right that the vast majority of Jews were not
willing to engage in violence against their Roman overlords, for they
understood some of the benefits of the *Pax Romana*, not to mention that
wrangling with Rome was risky business. They had enough accumulated

---

1. *Antiquities* 18.1-10. In Luke 6.15, one of Jesus's disciples is named 'Simon
   the zealot'. Some scholars point to the name of another of his disciples, Judas
   Iscariot, suggesting that it derives from an association with 'sicarii'. The
   interpretations of both of these names are problematic, as is any attempt to
   associate them with the later Zealot theology and rebellion that culminated
   in the Jewish War.
2. Studies of ancient Jewish names suggest that Joshua (Yehoshua or Yeshua)
   and Judas (Yehuda) were two of the most popular. To the extent that these
   names reflect a degree of veneration for Joshua, son of Nun, and Judas
   Maccabeus, two of the greatest warriors in Jewish history, this habit of
   naming children may be a measure of the tension in the atmosphere of first-
   century Judaea.
3. For detailed discussion of the 'hope of Israel', see N.T. Wright, *The New
   Testament and the People of God* (Minneapolis: Fortress, 1992), 280ff.

memory of occasional misrule or violence or persecution at the hands of Romans, and enough experience with paying their taxes to Rome only to see their hard-earned money shipped off across the Mediterranean, that the development of significant resentment was a reasonable response. They never knew when the next prefect might resort to unwarranted violence or might violate their religious sensitivities, intentionally or not. Some Jewish elites found a way to collaborate with Roman rule for their own advantage; others lived with a perennial sense of frustration with the Roman-Temple alliance, while still others were willing to engage in resistance, whether passive or active, with some advocating violence as a justifiable means to restore the rightful rule of God over his chosen people. A growing number of Jews, however, seem to have been united in one sentiment: better that the Romans should sail back to Italy and better still that God should intervene on behalf of his chosen people.

When Pilate received word in late 25 that Tiberius had appointed him as the fifth prefect of Judaea, he knew it was a mixed blessing. On the one hand, this was a senior administrative post, and a significant step forward in his career. On the other hand, prefect of Judaea was surely the worst governmental position in the entire Roman empire. He knew that his patron, the praetorian prefect Sejanus, the second most powerful man in the Empire, harboured a certain contempt for Jews, and that Tiberius had recently banished them, yet he was being asked to govern the Jewish homeland. Moreover, he was to travel to the far reaches of the empire, to a land flowing not with milk and honey, or even with rivers and verdant landscapes like Italy, but rather, from his perspective, a land flowing with heat, scorpions and touchy subjects. He probably understood little about Jews, except that they rejected the gods of Rome and had what appeared to him strange preoccupations with diet and the mutilation of their private parts. He knew that he was in for a challenge, standing as the embodiment of Rome between a potentially hostile praetorian prefect and a potentially hostile provincial populace. Governing well under these circumstances would take an exceedingly deft hand, something that, as it turned out, Pilate did not possess.

Pontius Pilatus, Prefect of Judaea

The nature of the evidence for the life of Pilate is, as we have seen, quite strong with multiple first-generation sources. When, however, we examine the evidence for the major events of Pilate's prefecture, excluding the trial of Jesus, most of it consists of single attestations by early if significantly biased sources: Josephus or Philo.[1] For the most part, corroborating evidence does not exist, but the fact that these are early sources lends a reasonable degree of probability to the following reconstruction. The evidence for the early years of Pilate's prefecture centres on three events: the Affair of the Standards, the Aqueduct Riot, and the Affair of the Shields.

The Affair of the Standards

No sooner had Pilate arrived at his new home, the spectacular Herodian Promontory Palace in Caesarea Maritima, than he made his first substantial blunder as prefect – a blunder that would set the tone for much of his administration. The Affair of the Standards appears only in Josephus.[2] It was the responsibility of the Roman prefect to direct the soldiers (auxiliary cohorts) under his control with restraint, efficiency, and military authority, with the peace and stability of the province as his primary aim. Pilate probably had under his command five auxiliary cohorts and one infantry regiment drawn from the regional population of pagan non-Roman citizens.[3] It makes perfect sense that Pilate would periodically rotate where he stationed particular cohorts to bring fresh perspective and attentiveness to all areas of the province. According to Josephus, the precipitating event happened when Pilate moved the cohort that had been stationed in relatively pagan Caesarea, the seat of

---

1. When I employ the term, 'bias', I am using it in the general sense. In some respects, every written source is biased: written with a particular point of view and written with a particular agenda, whether personal, political, ideological, or political. One of the essential tasks of the historian is to detect and analyse biases so that they may be carefully considered and, in many instances, counterbalanced, in the process of putting the evidence to the question and reconstructing the past. We do not dismiss sources from consideration for reasons of bias. If we did so, we would have little or nothing left to analyse. Rather, we integrate our understanding of bias into our interpretations.
2. *Jewish War* 2.169ff.; *Antiquities* 18.55-9.
3. Auxiliary cohorts were groups of soldiers under Roman command which consisted primarily of non-Roman subjects from the provinces. Service in these units often created a path to citizenship. Jews had been exempt from military service since the time of Julius Caesar. I use the term, 'pagan', with some misgivings, for in some circles it has pejorative overtones. Classical historians, while rejecting the pejorative connotations, continue to use 'pagan' as a convenient umbrella term for all the myriad and disparate religious groups in the empire who were neither Christian nor Jewish. In this context, one might substitute the equally useful but problematic term 'Gentile'.

his government, to Jerusalem. This would not have been a problem under ordinary circumstances. It became a problem because every cohort had its own military standards that carried words or symbols, as commonly depicted on reliefs or coins such as the illustration below. Roman standards provided rallying points and facilitated communication in time of conflict, but even in time of peace they provided a strong sense of identity and allegiance among soldiers. Standards were even occasionally venerated with religious rites.

Legionary standards on the reverse of a Roman coin of Marcus Antonius.[1]

All of this Pilate well understood, but he had trouble understanding the Jewish sensitivity concerning 'graven images' of all sorts.[2] Conflict arose because the standards of the particular cohort Pilate transferred to Jerusalem included 'images of Caesar', likely referring to Tiberius. It appears that all other cohorts in Judaea had standards that were inoffensive because they did not contain 'graven images' of humans or gods, and only they had been posted in Jerusalem under Pilate's predecessors. When Pilate made the decision to move the Caesarean cohort to Jerusalem, he unwittingly created a dilemma for himself: he could not ask a cohort to change its standards without offending his soldiers, and he would not allow what he undoubtedly considered trifling sensibilities among his subjects to dictate to him where he would station his troops. He therefore determined upon an expedient that demonstrates his underdeveloped perspective as governor. He transferred the cohort as planned, but he

1. Photo: http://www.downies.com/aca/auction307/Catalogue_078.html.
2. One of the ancient Hebrew commandments prohibits the making of 'graven images'. Jews around the turn of the millennium interpreted this commandment with some margin for error, prohibiting not only idols (representations of God), but any artistic portrayals of humans or animals.

had it move 'at night, under cover', presumably thinking that, once the standards were firmly ensconced in the Fortress Antonia just north of the Temple precinct, his Jewish subjects would be none the wiser and even if they found out they would acquiesce to this *fait accompli*. If this is at all representative of his thinking, he gravely miscalculated. Dawn brought with it the discovery of the iconic standards and the beginning of a public outcry that precipitated an impromptu march to Caesarea to accost Pilate. After the gathered mob 'begged him to remove the standards from Jerusalem out of respect for their ancestral customs', Pilate refused, for he realised that his blunder had placed him in an untenable situation.[1] If he were to grant their request and move the cohort, his leadership would thenceforward be in question among subjects and soldiers alike. If, however, he were to refuse the request, he would offend only a mob of hostile Jews. He decided upon the latter course, whereupon the gathered crowd 'fell prone all around his house and remained motionless for five days and nights' – forming a sort of 'occupy Caesarea' protest.

Pilate decided to wait them out, but on the sixth day his patience ran short. He decided to put an end to this protest, by force if need be. He set up his tribunal in the 'great stadium', which seems to refer to the recently discovered hippodrome Herod had built just north of the Promontory Palace. When the crowd gathered, Pilate gave a signal for his troops to surround them, hoping by intimidation to cow the mob into submission. Again, he miscalculated, making his position even more untenable. As the tension rose to a climax, Pilate gave the order for the soldiers to draw their swords in a final attempt to warn off the mob. Once again, he miscalculated. He was ready for a violent melee, but he was not prepared for what happened next. One after another, Jews lay down on the ground and bared their necks to the Roman swords, 'ready to be killed rather than transgress their law'. Pilate could never have anticipated that he would encounter anything like this. His bluff had been called. He knew that he could not give the order to attack defenceless subjects. In the end, Pilate put his commitment to law, peace, and stability over his own personal pride, but self-interest also played an important part in his decision: Rome would look with extreme displeasure on a new prefect who inaugurated his office by shedding innocent blood. He relented, recalling the offending cohort back to Caesarea and replacing it with another, much to his own chagrin and his soldiers' irritation. So ends the Affair of the Standards, an incident which sheds helpful light on our understanding of Pontius Pilate.

---

1. Josephus, *Jewish War* 2.171.

In the foreground is the Promontory Palace in Caesarea Maritima, which served as Pilate's primary home, with the Hippodrome to the left where he sat in judgment over Jewish protestors at the conclusion of the Affair of the Standards.[1]

From the perspective of Josephus, this whole episode is close to the heart of his political and theological agenda, for it serves as a model for Jewish resistance done right. For Josephus, if Jews respond to disagreement with Roman leadership with humility and non-violence, putting their faith in God, God will deliver, and Rome will respond reasonably.[2] From the perspective of Pilate, however, this whole episode was a stupid and unnecessary blunder that could have ended his administrative career before it began. Doubtless, in public, he blamed Jewish hypersensitivity and inflexibility for this debacle, but he also had to realise, at least in private, that he had created the whole problem; he had no one to blame but himself.

Regardless of blame, the event served as a lesson in cross-cultural understanding. Pilate now knew that he needed to become better informed about Jewish religious sensibilities, even as he learned by

1. Photo by Ferrell Jenkins: bibleplaces.com, by permission.
2. In the later *Antiquities,* Josephus attributes a much more negative motive to Pilate; that he actively sought to violate Jewish law. While Josephus was in no position to know the motives of Pilate, this editorial revision from his earlier account in *The Jewish War* is consistent with the increasingly negative portrayal of all prefects and procurators in the later work, thus shifting the blame for the escalating conflict, to some degree, in the Roman direction.

experience why Judaea had been so difficult to govern for so long. He would not make that mistake again, but he also knew that there would be consequences resulting from his actions. He had failed to flex the strong arm of Roman power, and even though he could console himself that he had made the best decision in a bad situation, his actions sent a troubling message to his Jewish subjects: their new prefect had weaknesses and was susceptible to popular pressure. Henceforth, Pilate's ability to do his job, to maintain the *Pax Romana* and rule his province with discipline and stability, was compromised, though how much he could not know. He needed to be very careful in the future. He does seem to have tried, but he was not careful enough.

The Aqueduct Riot

Within the next year or two (the chronology of Josephus is not precise), Pilate faced his second encounter with a group of defiant Jews, this time over the funding of an aqueduct. The project itself was sensible, meaningful, and close to the hearts of Roman and Jew alike. The water supplied by the Gihon spring and other sources was, while dependable, insufficient for the needs of Jerusalem, especially when great throngs of pilgrims arrived to celebrate and sacrifice during the most important holidays in the Jewish calendar. Pilate, perhaps in an attempt to set things right and enhance his political capital among his Jewish subjects, sought to make an enduring contribution that would be remembered with gratitude. He therefore commissioned an aqueduct to bring water from the region of Bethlehem and the so-called pools of Solomon (yet another building project completed by the great Herod), to fill the great subterranean cisterns of Jerusalem. Yet even such a beneficent project could backfire if not handled properly, and backfire it did.

The problem was funding, for aqueducts were expensive. Without doubt, Pilate had been apprised that taxes were a touchy subject. There was no way he could raise them without incurring Jewish wrath, and he certainly could not fund the project out of his own resources. There was, however, a local source of funding that, from Pilate's perspective, perfectly solved this problem: the Temple treasury, which contained the proceeds of the annual Temple tax as well as the many offerings brought to the Temple. Its primary function was to defray the expenses of Temple maintenance. Since the water provided by the aqueduct would surely contribute to the support of the Temple's substantial needs for ritual and actual cleansing, Pilate reasoned that he should be able to tap into these funds to support a project of great benefit to all.

The Arrub Aqueduct, which may represent a portion of Pilate's aqueduct project.[1]

There must be a back story here that Josephus does not tell. Rather, he blandly explains that Pilate stirred up trouble 'by expending the sacred treasure known as the Corbonas upon the construction of an aqueduct'.[2] The missing piece of the puzzle is this: either Pilate requisitioned those funds by force, or he did not. There is no evidence that Pilate took the Temple funds by force, and that silence speaks volumes. The treasury was stored in the Temple, and any attempt by a Gentile ruler to enter the court of Israel, much less the treasury, by force, would have been cause for full-scale revolt, something Josephus could hardly have ignored.[3] If it is unlikely that Pilate took the funds out of the Temple treasury by force, then he probably did so by permission, in collaboration with someone

1. American Colony Photo Department, *Section of Wadi Arrub aqueduct cut in the rock. 1934-39,* black and white photographic print. G. Eric and Edith Matson Photograph Collection. Available at: https://www.loc.gov/ item/mpc2010004136/PP/. For detailed discussion of the archaeology of aqueducts around Jerusalem, see A. Mazar, 'The Aqueducts of Jerusalem', in *Jerusalem Revealed: Archaeology in the Holy City 1968-1974,* edited by Y. Yadin (Jerusalem: Israel Exploration Society, 1975), 79-84.
2. *Jewish War* 2.175.
3. According to Josephus, revolt is precisely what happened when the Roman Procurator, Florus, confiscated funds from the Temple treasury in 66 (*Jewish War* 2.289ff).

in Jewish leadership. Only the chief priests who controlled the Temple precinct could provide such permission. Of course, Pilate might have brought any number of threats or promises to bear on Jewish leaders to manipulate their support, but, short of violence, he required their assistance, or at least their compliance. That Josephus mentions nothing about priestly cooperation, grudging or otherwise, is intriguing.[1]

Instead, Josephus narrates the scene which ensued when Pilate came to town to dedicate the new aqueduct, and word got out that Pilate, a Gentile overlord, had used their sacred Temple funds to pay for this project. The outcry was even more virulent than it had been in the Affair of the Standards. This time, Pilate was ready for it. When he set up his tribunal, he had his soldiers prepared, dispersed throughout the crowd, dressed in civilian clothes, with their weapons at the ready beneath their tunics. They had their orders: no swords unless absolutely necessary, but be ready to use clubs. As the angry protestors grew restive, and hurled ever more violent insults and threats toward Pilate, he issued the signal for his soldiers to act. As they pummelled the rioters, tempers flared, violence escalated, and Pilate lost control of the situation. The result was a bloody melee with an unspecified number of Jews beaten to death or trampled in the attempt to evacuate the premises. It may be that this event formed the context for the reference in Luke to some Galilean Jews in Jerusalem 'whose blood Pilate mixed with the blood of their sacrifices'.[2]

For the agenda of Josephus, the contrast between this event and the Affair of the Standards is stark. Passive resistance works, but violent Jewish resistance to Rome only results in Jewish blood being spilled.[3]

In other ways, the Aqueduct Riot was akin to the Affair of the Standards. In both cases, Pilate revealed that he did not have a clear sense of how Jews would respond to his actions. Perhaps he talked himself into believing that the benefits of the aqueduct would so far outweigh any concerns about the funding that Jews would see their way to appreciating his benevolence. Perhaps this was simply an attempt to reassert his authority. Whatever his motives, that he had his soldiers at the ready suggests that the protest did not take him by surprise. The reference to his order to use clubs rather than swords seems to represent the prefect as one who did not wish to use excessive force, but who wanted to keep violence to a minimum while reasserting his authority.

---

1. For further discussion, see Chapter IV.
2. 13.1.
3. *Jewish War* 2.175-77; *Antiquities* 18.60-62.

Both of these conflicts resulted from the ham-fisted acts of a neophyte governor who was out of touch with the scruples of his subjects and did not have a clear sense of the consequences of his decisions. Neither event seems to have been a deliberate act of provocation, for Pilate had much to lose and nothing to gain from such conflicts. If he wanted to provoke, he had surer means ready to hand. Pilate appears in the pages of Josephus more as an oaf than an ogre.

Despite these similarities, however, there is a fundamental difference between these two events. In the first case, Pilate kept the peace by bowing to popular non-violent resistance, thus appearing weak and ceding the high moral ground to those who opposed him. In the second, he imposed the peace by meeting violence with Roman might, thus appearing stronger, if less humane. In both cases, he appears largely incompetent. Neither confrontation was necessary, both were precipitated by Pilate's own actions, and neither resulted in a satisfactory conclusion for anyone.

The Affair of the Shields

The third recorded event of Pilate's governorship appears only in Philo's *Embassy*: the Affair of the Shields. Philo's chronology, like that of Josephus, is not clear, but many think this event took place after the Aqueduct Riot but before the trial of Jesus, perhaps in 31 or 32. The conflict arose from simple beginnings. Pilate commissioned a group of splendid, polished, gilded shields to honour his patron, Tiberius. They did not contain any graven images, for Pilate had learned that lesson, but they did feature a prominent inscription in honour of the emperor, including the names of both Tiberius and Pilate. We are not told the exact words that were inscribed, but they must have contained something that offended Jewish religious sensibilities, or this whole account would serve only to make Jews look unreasonable.

What was it about the words inscribed on the shields that rendered this event a *cause célèbre*? Philo does not tell us, but it is a reasonable conjecture that Pilate's name appeared as it did on the inscription at Caesarea, as the dedicator: PONTIVS PILATVS. The most common form of the name of Tiberius on the coins he produced in Rome is: TIBERIVS CAESAR DIVI AVGVSTI FILIVS AVGVSTVS, 'Tiberius Caesar, Augustus, son of the divine Augustus'. If this conjecture is correct, or something like it, then the offence lay in the written reference to the claims to divinity within the imperial family and to the imperial cult that had already made its presence felt in the

Jewish homeland. It is one thing to have a temple dedicated to Augustus in Caesarea, or to Julia Augusta in Bethsaida, but it is quite another to bring this explicit reference to the imperial cult into Jerusalem.

Pilate displayed these shields *inside* the *praetorium*, the Roman administrative headquarters of his palace, not outside for all to view. Moreover, he seems deliberately *not* to have included the portrait of the emperor that was common to such dedications. Pilate seems to have learned from his earlier experience with the standards, and might have thought that his new decorations were inoffensive precisely because they lacked graven images. If so, his motive was honorific, not antagonistic. He undoubtedly wished to honour Tiberius but once again he misjudged the scruples of his Jewish subjects. When the presence of these shields became widely known, an outcry arose in Jerusalem, but there was no riot this time to be put down by Roman soldiers. Rather, those who were offended complained to the Herodian princes who were present in Jerusalem, and these unnamed Herodians brought a complaint to Pilate with the request that the shields be removed. Pilate refused their request and one might well ask why.

In this case, he faced no restive mob. One would think that he could easily have granted the request, defused the situation, and set up the shields elsewhere. Was it merely a matter of Pilate yet again exhibiting his penchant for stubbornness? Was it a matter of pride, demonstrating his superiority over the Herodian intercessors? Was he simply fed up with Jewish sensitivities? Perhaps all of these came into play, but there is another possible reason based on turbulent developments that had recently rocked Rome.

As Tiberius spent more of his time in Capri and away from Rome, leaving much of the government of the empire in the hands of his praetorian prefect, Sejanus, he seems increasingly to have developed paranoid thoughts and conspiracy theories, fearing that various people in positions of power were out to usurp his authority. In response, Tiberius had Sejanus arrest and execute purported enemies on charges of *maiestas*; high treason. These treason trials came to a head in 31 when Tiberius had Sejanus himself and many of his followers executed for treason. If, as many scholars think, the Affair of the Shields took place in the early 30s, after the execution of Sejanus who had probably been Pilate's patron in his earlier career, Pilate likely experienced some trepidation that his name might come up as a treasonous associate of Sejanus. If Pilate entertained any such thoughts, then that fear would have provided a potent motive for his dedication of the shields in the first place, as a demonstration of his loyalty to Tiberius when it was most necessary. If Pilate dedicated his shields to deflect any suspicions that might implicate him in the treason of Sejanus, then we have a very good reason why Pilate *had* to refuse the petition to remove the shields from Jerusalem. To remove them would be tantamount to dishonouring Tiberius at the very moment when it was most risky to do so. In such a case it was, from Pilate's perspective, much preferable to stand by his dedication and let Tiberius decide the matter, even if Pilate had to endure yet another blot on his administrative record.

Whatever his precise reasoning, Pilate refused the petition of the Herodians, and they, in turn, sent a letter of complaint to Tiberius. According to Philo, with due recognition of his tendency toward amplified rhetoric, Tiberius responded with a strong denunciation of Pilate's judgment and ordered him to remove the shields from Jerusalem and install them instead in the Temple of Augustus in Caesarea.

From the perspective of Philo, the negative portrayal of Pilate provides opportunity to present Tiberius as the noble emperor who supports the Jews against his own governor. Philo contrasts the nobility of Tiberius with Caligula's disregard of Jewish sensibilities. From the perspective of Pilate's career, we see in the Affair of the Shields a continuation of the pattern we have already discovered. Pilate can be credited with learning not to bring graven images into Jerusalem, and never again did he tamper with the Temple treasury. On the other hand, his insensitivity to Jewish religious concerns is once again on display, though this time it is more subtle. Once again, this conflict was wholly generated by Pilate's action – a cultural blunder that was entirely unnecessary. The Jewish outcry as described by Philo appears to have been substantial. So also is the virulence of the written reply of Tiberius, at least as Philo tells it. Pilate was stubborn, arrogant, and a bit thick, but he was hardly malevolent. We here get a glimpse of his vulnerability after squandering his political capital in the first two debacles. His position, relative both to his subjects and to his emperor, was shaken, and the response from both sides represented a growing sense of disrespect for the *dignitas* of the prefect.

For the sake of completeness, there is one more event in Pilate's career included in the pages only of Josephus's *Antiquities*: the conflict that culminated in Pilate's departure from Judaea in late 36 or early 37. A tumult arose among some Samaritans on Mt. Gerizim. Fearing an insurrection, Pilate's troops first blocked and then fell upon the Samaritans, executed the ringleaders, and put the others to flight. Thereafter, some Samaritans complained to Vitellius, legate of Syria, who took control of Judaea and sent Pilate to Rome to answer for his heavy-handed use of force to subdue his subjects.[1] When he arrived at Rome, Tiberius had passed away and Caligula had taken his place. Whether Pilate was ever tried on these charges and what became of him is unknown. After 37, he disappears from history.

As Pilate began his day the morning of April 3, AD 33, he looked back over the last seven years and could not have been happy with what he saw. He had somehow retained office, despite the debacles of the Standards, the Aqueduct, and the Shields, but it had not been easy. He was in a vulnerable position and he knew it. Only recently had he realised the common theme. In every one of these conflicts, the family of the Jewish high priest had been conspicuously absent. They were neither among the crowd of bared throats in Caesarea nor the angry mob in Jerusalem. Nor did they participate in the Affair of the Shields. Pilate may have tried to work with them once, when he requested funds from the Temple treasury, but, if so, for some reason it had not gone well.[2] Yet that curiously absent high priestly family was a potent force, perhaps the most potent force, in his realm. By means of such observations, Pilate seems to have begun to realise the error of his ways as governor. He had tried to govern for many years without engaging the most ancient principle of Roman governance: *non quid, sed quis.* 'It's not what you know, but who you know.'[3]

Pilate had tried to rule on his own authority, but he had little to show for it. He finally had to come to terms with the fact that he needed help. He needed a depth of local cultural knowledge, he needed connections in high places, and if he hoped to accomplish anything that would redeem his tenure in office, he needed support and guidance. Although the high priest of Jerusalem owed his appointment to the prefect of Judaea, he was neither a puppet nor a lackey. Pilate might have despised the priests' obsession with ritual bathing, their strange diet, their sensitivity about art, and their superior attitude, but the simple fact was that he had no other alternatives.

---

1. 18.85ff.
2. The next chapter will discuss this matter in more detail.
3. An inversion of a Latin proverb. Much of Roman governance, in Rome and abroad, was built on personal relationships among aristocrats, the granting and receiving of favours, and the conferring of honour. References to these things are pervasive in Roman literature, especially that of Cicero, Pliny, and (with some self-effacing critique) Seneca (e.g. Cicero, On *Duties*; Pliny the Younger, *Epistle* 2.13; Seneca, *On Benefits* 1.2.2-3; 4.30.2-3; Apuleius, *Florida* 9).

His realisation was tardy, but he finally came to understand that a strategic alliance with the high priest and his family was the key to his future. Priestly guidance could have saved him from some of his early blunders, if only he had sought it, and their intervention could have mollified angry crowds, though we have no evidence that he ever requested it. He had begun the slow and awkward process of cultivating common interests with the high priestly family. It was a new and promising alliance, but it was fragile and fraught with mutual suspicion. Pilate knew it would not be easy, but he also understood that it was the only way forward. What he could not know was that it was precisely this fragile alliance that would shape those momentous events of April 3, AD 33, when the high priest and his family would bring to his *praetorium* an obscure itinerate teacher from Galilee.

IV
Pontifices Maximi:[1]
Annas, Caiaphas, and the
High Priesthood of Jerusalem

As the sun rose over the hills of Moab on 14 Nissan, April 3, AD 33, as the Roman prefect rose from his troubled sleep, Chanin ben Seth did not, for he had been up all night dealing with a family crisis. While the prefect, Pontius Pilatus, admired the luxurious palace he had inherited from Herod, Chanin (Ananus in Josephus or Annas in the New Testament), the patriarch of the chief priests, might have looked with pride at his own sumptuous home, which he had built for his family not far from the Herodian palace in the Upper City of Jerusalem. While the prefect was anxious about the challenges he would face with the dawning day, Chanin was not, for he knew what to expect and he knew what had to be done. He had just one problem to deal with, and then he would be free to celebrate with his family the *Pesach*, the Passover, the great feast of deliverance for his people. Chanin was not destined, as was the Roman prefect, to become one of the most famous men in history by the end of the day, but his relative lack of renown does not do him justice. Chanin, as much as anyone, set the agenda on that day which would, to an astonishing degree, change the world.

While we do not hear the name of Chanin, Ananus, or Annas frequently in the primary sources, and he gets short shrift among modern scholars, we do find two provocative hints in the New Testament, which can serve as a starting point for our query. The first comes from a list of synchronisms at the beginning of the third chapter of the Gospel of Luke:

---

1. *Pontifices Maximi*, 'high priests', is the plural of *Pontifex Maximus*, the chief priest at the Temple of Jupiter Optimus Maximus on Capitoline Hill, overlooking the Forum in Rome. This was the most prestigious priesthood in the Roman Empire. In later years, Augustus took the title, and still later, the Pope inherited it. This is also an appropriate Latin translation of the Hebrew, *kohen ha-gadol*, the title of the high priest of Israel.

> In the fifteenth year of the reign of Emperor Tiberius, when
> Pontius Pilate was governor of Judaea, and Herod was ruler of
> Galilee, and his brother Philip ruler of the region of Ituraea
> and Trachonitis, and Lysanias ruler of Abilene, during the
> high priesthood of Annas and Caiaphas, the word of God
> came to John son of Zechariah in the wilderness.[1]

All these synchronisms make sense except one. How is it possible to talk
about the era of the 'high priesthood of Annas and Caiaphas'? There
was only one high priest at a time. From other sources, we know that
Caiaphas was the high priest during the adult years of John and Jesus.
Why, then, the superfluous reference to Annas?

The second hint comes from the Gospel of John which says that,
immediately after Jesus was arrested, he was taken to the home of
Annas – the high priest. Annas sent him to Caiaphas – the 'high priest
that year'.[2] Both of these strange references to Annas beg for explanation,
while at the same time giving us a hint that there is something more to
this man than initially meets the eye.

Before we attempt to reconstruct the role of Annas and his family
in the trial of the millennium, we would do well to place them in the
historical, functional, and social context surrounding the highest position
in Jerusalem.

The High Priesthood of Israel

The high priesthood of Israel was long considered hereditary, tracing
its lineage back to Aaron, the brother of Moses. Priestly descendants of
Aaron were divided into twenty-four divisions or family branches, some
of which, over time, carried more prestige than others. From the time of
King David, the high priestly office was in the hands of the descendants
of Zadok. The Zadokite line may have continued (though the evidence
is scant) down to the second century BC when its hold on the office
was broken in the aftermath of the Maccabean revolt, that great Jewish
rebellion led by Yehuda ha Makkabi (or Judas Maccabeus) against the

---

1. 3.1-2.
2. 18.13; 19-24. The reference to 'that year' is also strange, for as we shall see,
   high priests were not one-year appointments. The phrase has the connotation
   of 'that momentous year'. The connection in this passage between Annas
   and the title of high priest is loose. In context, Caiaphas could be the high
   priest questioning Jesus. Josephus, on several occasions, applies the title
   'high priest' to a former high priest no longer in office, perhaps as American
   presidents still retain the title after the expiration of their term.

oppressive rule of the Seleucid Greeks – an event commemorated in the festival of Chanukah. The newly-formed independent Jewish hereditary monarchy, the Hasmonaeans, eventually established themselves as both kings and high priests.[1]

When the Romans annexed Judaea in 63 BC, and the Herodian family began its long rule, Herod himself appointed or deposed high priests and took control of the high-priestly vestments, storing them in the Fortress Antonia at the northwest of the Temple Mount.[2] The high priest could request them only seven days before any major festival. Moreover, Herod chose high priests who were from relatively obscure families of the line of Aaron, some from the regions outside Judaea, likely so that they would never be in a position to usurp any of Herod's authority. In all, Herod appointed seven different high priests and Archelaus, his son, appointed two more after him. This relatively rapid turnover created the important phenomenon of the 'chief priests' – a term used by Josephus and the New Testament to refer to former high priests and their families. These prestigious and highly-influential individuals, not unlike former presidents, wielded a considerable amount of clout, and in some cases, continued to be addressed as 'high priest' years after they left office.[3]

When Augustus decided to place Judaea under direct Roman rule in AD 6, the legates and prefects continued in the Herodian tradition, appointing high priests, with the difference that now the high priest served at the pleasure and discretion of the Roman governor. Romans also inherited from the Herodians control over the high-priestly vestments. In the Roman Empire, as in all other ancient states, there was no distinction between the state and religion: all religions were political and all politics were religious. These distinctions are modern inventions. The high priesthood of Jerusalem thus combined what moderns might call sacred and secular roles.

---

1. For the history of the high priesthood, see J.C. VanderKam, *From Joshua to Caiaphas: High Priests after the Exile* (Minneapolis: Fortress, 2004).
2. Perhaps referring to the triple-tiered gold crown, the Ephod, and the breastplate worn during the great festivals. After the death of Herod, control over the priestly vestments remained in Roman hands until the time of Vitellius, legate of Syria (*Antiquities* 15.403-5).
3. This seems to be the case for Annas in the New Testament, as well as Annas, Jonathan, and Ananias in Josephus (*Jewish War* 2.243, 441; *Antiquities* 18.34, 95; 20.205; *Life* 193). For further discussion, see Sanders, *Judaism*, 319-27; H. Bond, *Caiaphas: Friend of Rome and Judge of Jesus?* (Louisville: Westminster John Knox, 2004).

The high priests found themselves in a delicate position under Roman rule. On the one hand, theirs was the most prestigious position among the Jewish people. They controlled the very heart of Jewish identity: the Temple. As priests, they were the official mediators between the Jewish people and their holy God. At the same time, they were, beginning in AD 6, placed in a different kind of mediatorial position, between the Jewish people and their Roman overlords. Tension between these obligations must regularly have vexed these men. In a sense, the high priests were in a position to do real good for their Temple, for their people, for their families, and for their own reputation. In another sense, they were in a no-win situation. The Romans could call upon them to implement policies they considered distasteful, for example. Or, even if they favoured a Roman policy, it might prove unpopular with the Jewish people, and thus place the high priests in a compromising position. High priests were not elected representatives of their people, yet at any time they could find themselves as the only Jewish voices in the Roman process of decision-making. They were Roman appointees and could be denigrated as Roman lackeys. They were also Jewish and could thus be dismissed as mere subjects to be manipulated by their Roman superiors. As priests, they were called to be neither, but rather to serve as leaders of the Jewish people.

The position of the high priests relative to the Jewish people was also delicate. On one hand, they were servant-leaders, called to mediate on behalf of their people, to serve their needs for corporate worship and to offer atonement for their sins through sacrifice. On the other hand, high priests were wealthy, aristocratic leaders, comfortable in their positions of power and their beautifully appointed homes, and thus to a large degree out of touch and out of step with the hurts, needs, and desires of the greater Jewish population. Moreover, at times they were viewed as Roman sympathisers. To the extent that Jews of Judaea felt oppressed under Roman rule, members of the high priestly family were viewed as Roman collaborators, contributing by their attitudes and actions to the oppression of the Jewish people. For reasons such as these, high priests are seldom praised and often vilified in Jewish sources, even among those as sympathetic to their position as Josephus. In particular, Josephus refers to several high priests who acted in a manner that was detrimental to the larger Jewish population, thus incurring popular wrath.[1]

---

1. E.g. Josephus, *Antiquities* 20.204-10; *Jewish War* 2.426-7; 7.260. Cf. *The Testament of Moses* 6-7. Close to the heart of the identity of the sectarian community at Qumran was condemnation of the corrupt high priests of Jerusalem who plundered the people and polluted the temple through their accumulation of wealth (e.g. 1QpHab 8-9). For further discussion, see Goodman, 40.

Along similar lines, a text from the *Babylonian Talmud* based on the earlier *Tosefta* reflects back on the careers of former high priestly families of the first century with a note of disdain:

> Abba Shaul ben Batnit said in the name of Abba Yosef ben
>   Chanin. . . .
> Woe to me because of the house of Chanin [Annas];
> Woe to me for their whisperings!
> Woe to me because of the house of Katros;
> Woe to me for their pens![1]

In context, *b. Pesachim* describes the many ways in which high priestly families of the first century ruled by force and exploited their position of power for their own gain. The tone is distinctly negative. What were the 'whisperings' for which the house of Chanin was derided? Is this a reference to a penchant for gossip-mongering? Or to functioning as informants? Or to secretive business or political machinations? Might the whisperings refer to the remarkable capacity of the house of Chanin to curry favour with Roman governors? We cannot be certain from this brief, late reference, except that, from the perspective of the rabbis who composed this text, the house of Chanin was disreputable and this opinion was widely shared. The house of Chanin was certainly the most powerful family in Jerusalem in the first half of the first century, and they may have received the deference of the people by virtue of their position, but that does not mean that their behaviour had earned the allegiance of the bulk of the Jewish population.

---

1. *b. Pesachim* 57a; *t. Menchot* 13.18-21. The *beth Chanin* almost certainly refers to the family dynasty of Annas. The *beth Katros* refers to the high priestly family that probably lived in the famous Burnt House, now a poignant archaeological site, open to visitors in the Jewish Quarter. We can connect this house with the Talmudic text above because inscribed on a loom weight there was the Aramaic name of its owner, 'bar Katros'. The *Babylonian Talmud* and *Tosefta* are late sources, so their primary role in this analysis is to corroborate the negative assessment of our earlier sources. For other evidence of the avarice of high priestly families, see Josephus, *Antiquities* 20.181-207; *Life* 195; *t. Menchot* 13.22; II Maccabees 4.7-10, 24, 32; *b. Yebamoth* 61a; *Testament of Levi* 14.5; *Covenant of Damascus* 6.15-6; *Psalms of Solomon* 8. There may well have been high priests in our period who were men of integrity and piety, so we should not overgeneralise, but there were also enough Jewish criticisms of their own priests to demonstrate an abiding tension between many Jews and the high priest. For further discussion, see J. Jeremias, *Jerusalem in the Time of Jesus* (Philadelphia: Fortress, 1969), 49, 96-99, 195-8; cf. Sanders, *Judaism*, 182ff.

Note that many of these derogatory references to high priests as corrupt or oppressive or out of touch with the Jewish people come either from late sources or from contexts in the later part of the first century. Given the bias of Josephus, however, it is a reasonable assumption that, if anything, he undervalues the perspective of the lower classes and underestimates the tension between the bulk of the Jewish population of Judaea and the aristocratic family of the high priest. Not only was the high priest unrepresentative of popular Jewish sentiment, but he may often have stood in ignorance of it or in opposition to it.[1]

From AD 6-33, the high priest in Jerusalem occupied an awkward space between two worlds. He knew the governor could remove him from office at any moment, so he had to be careful or he was out of a job. He also knew that some Jews, perhaps many, chafed under Roman rule and detested how he filled the position. Yet he had one great thing in his favour: his family. The high priests were not just Jews of the priestly line, they were aristocrats, and Romans held social elites in high regard. Pilate would never understand Annas's concern for ritual bathing any more than Annas could understand Pilate's love of pork; yet they had much in common. Both were wealthy and had a taste for high culture. Both held their own honour and that of their families in high regard. Both disdained the noisome rabble. Both were successful players in the game of political influence. Both had much to gain from collaboration and much to lose from conflict. Above all, both had strong motivation to maintain the status quo insofar as that was possible, for it had profited both of them immensely. Both shared a common goal: to keep the peace – Pilate because the *Pax Romana* was at the heart of his job description, and Annas because any revolt among the Jewish people would likely dislodge his family from its lofty perch. Naturally, they saw these things differently, but they had much common ground on which to build an alliance.

---

1. Josephus does acknowledge class tensions, e.g. *Jewish War* 7.260-1. It will therefore come as no surprise that one of the earliest persons assassinated by the *sicarii*, the urban Jewish terrorists, was Jonathan, son of Annas, who succeeded Caiaphas as high priest (*Jewish War* 2.254-57). According to the most significant study of the Jewish elite of the period (Goodman), the high priestly families, especially the house of Annas, were so entrenched in pursuing family interests, and so disconnected from the perspective of the vast majority of Jews that their myopia, infighting, and incompetence were primary causes of the tensions in Judaea and ultimately the Jewish War of 66-73. For detailed discussion of the evidence for the abuses by and criticism of high priestly families in the first century, see C. Evans, 'Jesus' Action in the Temple: Cleansing or Portent of Destruction?' *Catholic Biblical Quarterly* 51 (1989), 256ff.

When Pilate arrived in Caesarea in 26, as a neophyte prefect of modest ability, Annas had already succeeded in placing his family in power for eighteen years. Caiaphas had already served as high priest for eight. Annas had already exercised his considerable influence under four prefects. He knew what he was about, and he knew how to get things done, even if the new governor had much yet to learn.

The House of Annas

Josephus, our lone source, tells us nothing about the family roots of Ananus son of Sethi, as he calls Chanin or Annas. In AD 6, when Archelaus had been deposed and sailed off to Rome to face eventual exile, the legate of Syria, Quirinius, stepped in to supervise the transition to direct Roman rule and to administer his famed census.[1] In the midst of those tumultuous changes, Quirinius appointed Annas as high priest, a position he held for nine years, outlasting the first two prefects of Judaea. Thereafter, until 41, high priests were appointed, deposed, and served at the discretion of the governors of Judaea. Annas was deposed in 15, for reasons that Josephus does not disclose, by the third prefect, Gratus, who seemed to change high priests like togas.[2] Whatever his reasons, Gratus's subsequent actions suggest that he continued to hold Annas and his family in high regard.

After Annas, he deposed and appointed four different high priests in as many years. Annas was succeeded by Ishmael ben Phiabi, who lasted for one year, only to be replaced by the son of Annas, Eleazar, in 16. He lasted no longer, with Gratus appointing Shimon ben Camith in 17. He, in turn, lasted a year, culminating with the appointment of Joseph Caiaphas, son-in-law of Annas, in 18. Gratus apparently considered Caiaphas more satisfactory than his predecessors, or maybe he just tired of Temple turnover. Whatever the reasons, Caiaphas became the longest-serving high priest of the Judaean prefecture, lasting through the remainder of Gratus's tenure, and through the whole prefecture of Pilate, finally being deposed by the legate Vitellius in 37. It is important to note, however, that Caiaphas was replaced by Jonathan, another son of Annas (37), who was, in turn, replaced by Theophilus, yet another son of Annas (38-41), and succeeded by yet another, Matthias (c. 41-44).

---

1. Josephus, *Antiquities* 18.26; Luke 2.2. See Appendix I for discussion.
2. Since this was the first year of Gratus's rule, it is reasonable to suggest that he changed high priests as a way of asserting his authority in the realm rather than because of any problems created by Annas. Later prefects did the same in their first year. See VanderKam, 420ff. for further discussion.

Later, in 62, Annas, the fifth son and father's namesake, was appointed. He held the high priesthood for only three months, but during his short tenure he earned a measure of infamy by stoning James, the brother of Jesus.[1] Thereafter, on the eve of the great revolt (65-67), one of the grandsons of Annas also served as high priest. In all, over the course of sixty years, eight of the high priests were from the house of Annas. Between the time of the appointment of Annas in AD 6 and the trial of Jesus in 33, the family of Annas controlled the office of high priest for twenty-five of twenty-seven years. Caiaphas had, by 33, served as high priest for fifteen years. In sum, Annas held the high priesthood of Jerusalem as a family fiefdom during the lifetime of Jesus and beyond. There was something about this particular priest that made the Roman authorities take notice and treat his family with extraordinary deference. Prefects and legates would come and go, but the house of Annas seemed as if it would endure forever, dominating the Jerusalem scene for more than half a century. It is little wonder, then, that the New Testament would continue to use the term 'high priest' to refer to Annas long after he vacated the official appointment. He was *the* high priest *par excellence*, and the power behind the Ephod when family members were subsequently appointed to the role.

Annas was not only a dominating force over the high priesthood; he was also extraordinarily wealthy. It is possible that his family owned significant land-holdings, but if they did, we have no evidence of it. What we do know is that the high priestly family controlled the Temple precinct, and as such, they were in a perfect position to make an immense profit by providing for the needs of worshippers, especially when multitudes thronged Jerusalem during the great festivals. Pilgrims undertaking the *Aliyah*, the 'going up' to Jerusalem, sang their Psalms of Ascent en route to the Temple where they joined in the corporate worship of the Jewish community. In particular, they had two practical objectives as they approached the Temple: to pay their Temple tax and to offer sacrifice. Jews traveling to Jerusalem from around the empire were unlikely to carry with them Tyrian sheqels. Before they could pay their Temple tax, they had to change their Roman (or other local) coinage into the only denomination the Temple would accept. This service appears to have been provided for them in the outer Temple courts, which were under the control of Annas and his family. Whether the house of Annas directly ran the operation or

---

1. Josephus, *Antiquities* 20.197-203. Some archaeologists believe that the ossuary of James has been discovered, though the Israel Antiquities Authority has judged a portion of the inscription a forgery. Debate still continues on this matter.

contracted it out to other priests or Levites, with the changing of coinage, there are always two ways to make a profit: commissions and exchange rates. In addition, numismatic evidence may suggest that the high priestly family controlled the mint that struck the Tyrian sheqels. Considering that hundreds of thousands of Jews needed to make currency exchanges yearly, the profits from this enterprise were likely considerable.[1]

Alongside the changing of coinage was another necessary enterprise: the sale of sacrificial animals. It was cumbersome to travel to Jerusalem from Galilee, not to mention from Alexandria or Babylon, while dragging along lambs or doves for sacrifice in Jerusalem. In addition, sacrificial animals needed to be without blemish, passing priestly inspection. It was much more convenient to avoid the hassle and instead purchase pre-approved sacrificial animals around or, in the case of doves, within the Temple precinct.[2] Once again, the family of Annas doubtless controlled this operation, and they surely charged a premium for their services, whether the inspecting of animals, the licensing of sellers, or the management of the operations. Both the sale of sacrificial animals and the changing of coinage were monopolies, so inflated profits were to be expected.[3] The luxurious homes in the Upper City of Jerusalem, some of which belonged

---

1. Rabbinic sources suggest that the commission could be as high as 4.2%. Given the fact that some Roman coinage in the period shows initial signs of debasement, priestly control over purity of the Tyrian silver (which remained over 90%) ensured favourable exchange rates, all to the benefit of the high priestly family. It is important to note that there is nothing in Torah that requires the payment of the Temple tax in Tyrian sheqels. That requirement itself was imposed by the high priests. For a sense of the magnitude of the Temple Tax from the diaspora alone, Cicero notes, in the first century BC, that Roman officials once confiscated some of the Temple Tax revenues from three Roman cities (Apamea, Laodicea, and Adramyttium); the total confiscated was two hundred and twenty Roman pounds of gold, roughly a hundred and sixty-five English pounds (*Pro Flacco* 28.66-9); cf. Sanders, *Judaism*, 84.
2. The synoptics mention only doves; John mentions also cattle and sheep (2.14). Considering that the context of this discussion was just before Passover, thousands of lambs needed to be available for purchase. On the other hand, it seems impractical for herds of quadrupeds to be held in pens covering large portions of the court of Gentiles. More practically, the vendors likely displayed a few examples of their wares near their tables, while customers purchased chits that enabled them to pick up their purchases outside the Temple courts.
3. Sanders rightly points out that there was a limit on what could be charged for sacrificial animals, since all, even the destitute, were expected to be able to participate in the sacrificial cult (*Judaism*, 90).

to important priestly families, bear lavish witness to the profitability of the priesthood, at least for some of its leading families. From the perspective of Josephus, the family of Annas seems to have been appropriately providing important services in support of divine worship. Josephus does not report any widespread concern about corruption among the high priests. Since he himself was a Jewish aristocrat of priestly family, however, we would not expect him to be much of a critic.[1]

Not only was the house of Annas distinguished by prestigious family connections and significant wealth, they also seem to have been adherents of the Jewish sect of the Sadducees.[2] Because we do not have any evidence from the pen of a Sadducee, we can give only a brief glimpse of their distinctive beliefs as gleaned from sources that are largely hostile to their tradition. We would therefore do well to treat this evidence with due caution. Josephus claims that the Sadducees rejected the idea of fate in favour of free will, accepted only written law, and denied the resurrection of the dead. They were thus not very popular with the bulk of the Jewish population.[3] Moreover, Josephus urges that the Sadducees were harsher than other Jews when dispensing justice.[4] Rabbinic sources record several disputes between Pharisees and Sadducees, with the expected Pharisaical bias.[5] Nowhere are we specifically informed that Caiaphas was a Sadducee, but his marriage into the house of Annas makes such an inference persuasive. Some of the references to Sadducees mention them in the context of priestly families and aristocrats, which suggests some, though not complete, association among these groups. This association of Sadducees with priestly aristocrats of Jerusalem may in part explain the virtual disappearance of the sect following the destruction of the Temple in 70.

Caiaphas did not command the same level of family prestige as Annas but, because his marriage with the daughter of Annas was likely arranged by the two sets of parents, his lineage, piety, faithfulness, and intelligence must have commended him to Annas. Whatever the

---

1. Jesus, however, was not so sympathetic, and he was not alone in this sentiment; *b. Pesachim* seems, for different reasons, to suggest that priestly dynasties which used their power to exploit others were corrupt. Similar disdain for the corruption of the high priesthood was evident among the sectarians who wrote the Dead Sea Scrolls (e.g. 1QpHab 8-9; 1 QM; 1QS 4).

2. Acts 4.1-6; 5.17; Josephus, *Antiquities* 20.199.

3. *Jewish War* 2.164-66; *Antiquities* 18.15-17; 13.297; Luke 20.27; Acts 4.2; 23.6-10.

4. *Antiquities* 20.199.

5. E.g. *m. Yadaim* 4.6.7; *m. Parah* 3.7; *m. Niddah* 4.2. The rabbis of later years were largely the spiritual descendants of the earlier Pharisees.

reasons for the marriage, Caiaphas did not disappoint. Anyone who could carry on the duties of high priest for nearly two decades, and work effectively under three prefects, had much to commend him. Without doubt, Caiaphas was a powerful high priest, but even he would likely have recognised that much of his power was derivative, rooted in the house of Annas.

Because of his wealth, his connections, his lineage, his position of influence, and his capacity to shape his world, there can be little doubt that Chanin ben Seth was the most powerful Jew in the world. It is precisely this power, combined with that of Caiaphas and Pilate, that would determine the course of events on 14 Nissan, AD 33.

The family of Annas, for more than two decades, had been tried by four different prefects and found reliable. This reality amplifies the priestly silence during the early years of Pilate's prefecture. It appears that for his first five or six years Pilate attempted to rule Judaea on his own, without support from local leaders. The high priestly family could have saved him from many an indignity, but there is no evidence he consulted them. They may well not be mentioned in the context of the Affair of the Standards, the Aqueduct Riot, or the Affair of the Shields because they chose to keep their distance, to let the stubborn, inexperienced governor suffer the consequences of his own indiscretions. If this is true, it was a risky strategy from the perspective of Annas, and one that was not sustainable.

One gap in our evidence, however, begs for explanation: the participation or lack thereof of Annas and Caiaphas in the funding of the aqueduct project. Josephus tells us that the project was funded by the Temple treasury, but he does not tell us whether Pilate obtained that money by permission of the high priest or not. No matter which way we turn, this silence is deafening. If Pilate did not have permission, but took control of the Temple treasury by force, that would have been a gross violation of earlier Roman agreements with the Jews, a slap in the face of Annas and Caiaphas, and an act of profound provocation against Jewish cultural and religious sensibilities. The Roman triumvir, Crassus, had done something of the sort once before, and the consequences were horrific.[1] Had Pilate done such a thing, there can be little doubt that Josephus would have devoted plenty of papyrus to the outcry and the uprising that would surely have followed. For these reasons, it is not probable that Pilate took these funds by force.

---

1. One Sabinus also did something of the sort during the violence that threw Jerusalem into chaos after the death of Herod (Josephus, *Antiquities*, 17.221-264; cf. Goodman, *Rome and Jerusalem*, 380).

If Pilate used these funds with permission, then the only person who could grant that permission would be Caiaphas. If he did grant permission, one might well wonder whether he did so willingly or under constraint. If he did so willingly, agreeing that funding the aqueduct was a justified expenditure on behalf of the Temple, it is reasonable to expect that he and his family would have defended Pilate's decision when popular Jewish opposition arose. That they nowhere appear in Josephus's account of the public hearing and fracas that ensued is another noisy silence. It is possible that the silence of the high priestly family may indicate that they themselves were surprised by the vehemence of the public outrage, yet another indication that they were out of touch with popular Jewish sentiment. If this is the case, then their silence would represent mere face-saving. An alternative and perhaps more plausible explanation that accounts for both the evidence and the silence is that Pilate did get permission from Caiaphas, but it was under some sort of threat or constraint. The high priestly family was not happy about it. They therefore resolved to wait for the information to go public (or they leaked it), and to let Pilate squirm in his tribunal as he tried to extricate himself from the mess he had made. In this way, Annas and Caiaphas could let the angry mob punish Pilate for forcing their hand and taking their money. Either way, if Pilate received permission from the high priestly family to use those funds, their apparent unwillingness to intervene in the scandal must have seemed like a betrayal.

If this reconstruction is anywhere near on target, Pilate did try to work with the high priestly family early in his prefecture, but the attempt broke down, for Pilate had treated Annas and Caiaphas as obstacles to overcome rather than as partners in governance. When push quite literally came to shove among the crowd of Jewish protesters, and Roman soldiers pulled out their clubs, the house of Annas did not stand behind the Roman prefect, but looked on from a distance as Pilate (and many Jews in the crowd) paid the price for his insolence.

This incident could have been satisfactory neither to Pilate nor to the family of Annas. They both had to recognise that this kind of relationship, marred by constraint and contempt, did not further either of their agendas. They needed to find a better way of working together, something with which Annas and Caiaphas had experience, even if Pilate did not. It took some time, but it appears that the Affair of the Shields provided the impetus to push prefect and priest together. Force of circumstances provided the common ground on which they could build a meaningful alliance on the time-tested Roman model. A much-chastened and vulnerable Pontius Pilatus was able to bring a new level of respect to their relationship which the venerable patriarch of the high priesthood seemed willing to match, but it was important that they not repeat the mistakes of the past. If they were to have a meaningful alliance that worked well to achieve mutual ends, there could be no more high-handed impulsiveness, no more desertion of one another. They needed to work together, and they needed to be prepared to support one another when need arose. Annas may not have experienced the same vulnerability as Pilate, but he knew that his family would stand or fall based upon the favour of Rome; he may not have wanted to admit it, but he needed Pilate nearly as much as Pilate needed him. It would not be long before this fledgling alliance would be tested.

The Archaeology of Priestly Purity

The nature of the evidence for Annas and his family closely parallels that for Pilate, though it is not quite so abundant. Once again, we can be thankful that the evidence is unusually early and multiple, but we will also face some of the same issues we faced in the last chapter. Four lines of evidence are central: archaeology, the New Testament, Josephus, and other Jewish sources.

First, let us examine the archaeological evidence for both Annas and Caiaphas. South of the old city of Jerusalem, near the place where the Kidron and Hinnom valleys intersect, is a collection of tombs dating from the first century. This burial ground, which now includes the modern monastery of St Onuphius, has traditionally been referred to as Akeldama, 'the field of blood', based on a reference to the death of Judas, the disciple of Jesus.[1] Archaeology has revealed that, far from a field for indigent burials, this group of tombs includes some of the most luxurious and ornate in the entire region. One of these tombs has been tentatively identified as the tomb of Annas and his family. The evidence for this identification is minimal but intriguing. Josephus, in a detailed description, places Annas's tomb in precisely this area.[2] Given this specificity, the most opulent tomb that fits the geographical description is located on a terrace just below the monastery. The construction and decoration of this tomb bear remarkable similarity to the motifs that remain from the Herodian Temple Mount, including a triple gate,

1. Matthew 27.8; Acts 1.19.
2. *Jewish War* 5.505-6.

The proposed family tomb of Annas.[1]

engaged pillars that appear to emerge from the wall, and an ornate double-rosette motif on the ceiling bordered by acanthus leaves. In such a tomb, a high priest could rest quite comfortably in familiar surroundings. That is it for the evidence, however. The grave was robbed in antiquity, with the result that any grave goods or inscribed limestone bone boxes (ossuaries) that might have included individual or family names have not been preserved.[2]

We are much more fortunate, however, when it comes to archaeological evidence for Caiaphas. In November 1990, a tractor working in the Peace Forest, not far south of the proposed tomb of Annas, collapsed the roof of a first-century rock-cut tomb. There are many tombs in the area, so such accidental discoveries are not uncommon, but this one is of great significance for our inquiry. The tomb is relatively simple in design and plain in decoration, consisting of a single chamber with four burial niches (*kokhim* in Hebrew), like mini-caves cut into the walls. Most of the tomb had been robbed, but six limestone ossuaries remained, some of them inscribed with names. Some pottery shards also survive that help date the use of this tomb from the first century BC into the

1. Photo by permission of www.holylandphotos.org.
2. For further discussion, see K. and L. Ritmeyer, 'Akeldama: Potter's Field or High Priest's Tomb?' *Biblical Archaeology Review* (November/December, 1994), 22-35, 76, 78.

The Caiaphas Ossuary.[1]

Stone vessels from Jerusalem.[2]

---

1. Photo: Eric Huntsman. http://huntsmansintheholyland.blogspot.com/
   2012/07/a-day-at-museums.html. Used by permission.
2. Photo by permission of www.holylandphotos.org.

first century AD. Two of the ossuaries had not been disturbed by the robbers, including the largest and most ornate of the group (Ossuary 6), which was decorated with elaborate rosettes and other botanical motifs. Inside this ossuary were the remains of six people, a man of about sixty years of age, an adult woman, two infants, and two children. Ossuaries containing multiple individuals were not uncommon, and names were sometimes inscribed on them. The name inscribed twice in Aramaic on this particular ossuary is uncommon: *'Yehosef bar Qyp'.'* Most scholars agree that this inscribed name, 'Joseph son of Kaiapha' refers to the oldest skeleton in the ossuary. Given the rarity of the name, that skeleton probably belonged to the 'Joseph who is called Caiaphas' in Josephus,[1] the high priest Caiaphas of the New Testament. If this identification is correct, we have found the final resting place of one of the most important players in our story.[2]

Beyond these two tombs, the archaeology of ritual purity can teach us a good deal about the life of a priestly family. This evidence takes three forms: stone vessels, ritual bathing pools, and two surviving inscriptions from the Temple.[3]

An immense quantity of stone vessels has been discovered in Judaea, extending as far away as Sepphoris in Galilee and Bethsaida, on the north shore of the Sea of Galilee. Most, however, have been unearthed in the area around Jerusalem, along with some stone carving workshops in the vicinity. Elegant homes of the Upper City, where some of the more important priests resided, were well stocked with such vessels. Either turned on a lathe or hand-carved, usually from limestone, these vessels ranged from large jars for ritual washing purposes, holding upwards of thirty gallons (such as those discovered in the Burnt House and which, according to John, Jesus used at the wedding at Cana),[4] to cups resembling coffee mugs, to modest plates and bowls. Stone vessels were found only in Jewish homes, but not in all Jewish homes, for pottery vessels were much less expensive. Why, then, did some Jews favour them? Vessels moulded from clay, according to

---

1. *Antiquities* 18.35.95.
2. There are, however, some disputes over this identification. For details, see Z. Greenhut, 'The Caiaphas Tomb in North Talpiot', and R. Reich, 'Ossuary Inscriptions of the Caiaphas Family from Jerusalem' in H. Geva ed., *Ancient Jerusalem Revealed* (Jerusalem: Israel Exploration Society, 1994), 219-225; cf. J. Zias, 'Human Skeletal Remains from the 'Caiaphas' Tomb', *'Antiqot* (English Series) XXI (1992), 78-80; cf. Bond, *Caiaphas.*
3. For details, see Gibson, 54-5
4. John 2.6.

A Miqveh *near the southern entrance to the Temple Mount.*[1]

The excavations of the first-century Pool of Siloam suggest that it may have functioned as a large, public miqveh.[2]

---

1. Photo by permission of www.holylandphotos.org.
2. Photo by permission of www.holylandphotos.org.

Leviticus 11.33, become permanently unclean if they or their contents come into contact with anything ritually impure. Stone vessels, unlike pottery, were immune to such impurity; they could be cleansed and re-used, thus providing some assurance to their owners that they would not themselves become inadvertently defiled by using an impure container for food, drink, or holding water for ritual washing. Those willing to pay a dear price for stone vessels were highly motivated and able to afford such measures to ensure the security of their purity.

Ritual bathing pools (Hebrew = *miqveh* [sg.] or *miqva'ot* [pl.]), like stone vessels, were widespread around Jerusalem, and have also been unearthed as far away as Sepphoris in Galilee and Masada, near the Dead Sea. These excavated and plastered pools, which included steps to enable a person to climb down into them to the point of immersion, are ethnic markers of Jewish presence and concern for ritual purity. While it is not certain to what degree the later rules enshrined in the *Mishnah* were in force in the early first century, we do get some sense from that source of how and why they were important. According to the ancient rabbis, a *miqveh* must hold a minimum of forty *seahs* of pure, preferably running, water – about sixty to two hundred and fifty gallons, depending on how one calculates the modern equivalent. Some larger, public *miqva'ot* have been discovered at Qumran and around the Temple Mount in Jerusalem. Even the great public pools of Bethesda and Siloam, to the north and south of the Temple, may have served this function.[1] Many *miqva'ot* seem to have been designed for private use, for they were located beneath private homes. The upscale Upper City of Jerusalem housed a good number of these, including the famous Burnt House, which was burned by Roman legions in AD 70, shortly after the Temple was destroyed. *Miqva'ot* provided opportunity for ritual cleansing of impurities of many sorts, including contact with corpses or unclean animals, different types of diseases, or bodily emissions. Entrance into the courts of the Temple required significant levels of ritual purity, and priests needed to maintain a high level at all times. There can be little doubt that the home of Annas or Caiaphas would have included a *miqveh* in which the priests would have immersed themselves almost every day, if not multiple times per day.[2]

An inscription from the Temple courts in Jerusalem clarifies an additional element of ritual purity that would have been important to the life of any priest. The Temple was surrounded by three courts.

---

1. John 5.2ff.
2. For a detailed study of *miqva'ot*, see Gibson.

*The warning inscription forbidding Gentile entry
into the Temple's Court of Women.*[1]

outermost was the 'Court of Gentiles', because only there were Gentiles permitted. Inside that larger area was the 'Court of Women', into which only Jews could enter, both male and female. Inside that were the 'Court of Israel', reserved for male Jews, and, farther in, the areas restricted to priests alone. Two Greek inscriptions have been discovered, one complete and one partial, which were posted on the wall separating the Jewish courts from the Court of Gentiles, forbidding entry to Gentiles on pain of death.[2]

Herod the Great greatly expanded the Temple courts in a massive construction project that began about 20 BC and was not completed until shortly before it was destroyed in AD 70. Some portions of that great Herodian remodelling are visible, including the lower courses of stones in the western retaining wall, now commonly referred to as the Western Wall or Wailing Wall. To the south of the Western Wall, in a first-century paved street that skirts the western edge of the retaining wall, is a pile of large beautifully carved rectangular limestone blocks (ashlars), with the fringed facing typical of Herodian construction. These ashlars may have once formed part of the walls of the Temple. At the south end of the Temple Mount, one can still see the monumental staircase by which many, including Jesus, would have entered the Temple

---

1. Photo by permission of www.holylandphotos.org.
2. Gibson, 48.

Monumental stairs: south end of the Temple Mount.[1]

courts. The entrances at the top of those stairs are now blocked, but those who make proper arrangements ahead of time with the Muslim religious authority may be allowed to enter those extraordinary vaulted sub-structures, built by the great Herod, that still support the southern end of what once was the Temple Mount.[2] This complex subterranean structure, popularly called Solomon's Stables, now functions as a mosque.

The Temple Mount was the workplace of the priests, and the high priest was in charge of the whole precinct. Every day, the high priests of the family of Annas would undergo ritual cleansing in their private *miqveh* and don their priestly vestments. Once properly purified and attired, they would enter the Temple precinct, pass the partition where Gentiles were forbidden, and proceed to the area reserved for priests. There they would offer sacrifices on the great altar in front of the most holy place of all, which only the high priest could enter, and that only one day a year: Yom Kippur, the Day of Atonement. From their priestly headquarters, they would oversee all functions of the Temple, from offerings, to treasury, to the Temple guards, to the clean-up of what must have been an extraordinary amount of blood and

---

1. Photo by author.
2. By international agreement, the raised platform that once housed the Jewish Temple and that now contains the Dome of the Rock and the Al Aqsa Mosque is controlled by the *Waqf*, the Muslim religious authority of Jerusalem. Access to the whole area around the religious precinct is controlled by the Israeli military.

Model of Temple precinct at the Israel Museum.[1]

The 'Place of Trumpeting' inscription.[2]

animal detritus. They were also in charge of leading the whole Jewish community in worship, especially on Shabbat and during the great festivals – which brings us to the next piece of archaeological evidence.

In excavations near the Temple Mount, archaeologists unearthed a Hebrew inscription that reads, '[Belonging] to the house [or place] of trumpeting. . . .' This was probably set into the top of the southern wall of the Temple. Josephus helps us understand its meaning when he describes one of the priestly duties: they would 'blow a trumpet to announce the beginning and end of Shabbat' every week.[3] This

---

1. Photo by author.
2. Photo by permission of www.holylandphotos.org.
3. *Jewish War* 4.583.

inscription adds an aural note to our inquiry. It is not difficult to imagine a member of the family of Annas, or one of their colleagues, standing above this inscription, pursing his lips and blowing with all his might. We can almost hear the clarion call welcoming the Jewish people to the great celebration of the Holy One of Israel.

One more group of archaeological discoveries will illuminate our quest: the excavations of the Upper City. The Six Day War of 1967 ravaged the Jewish Quarter of Jerusalem, but in its aftermath, Jewish archaeologists made a virtue of necessity, descending on the newly exposed ancient sites with energy and professionalism. One structure in that area, now identified as the Burnt House, provides an excellent example of a sumptuous Upper City home owned by a priestly family, complete with stone vessels and a *miqveh*. We know it was almost certainly the home of a priest because of the discovery of a loom weight inscribed with the name, Bar Katros, a priestly name reviled in the *Babylonian Talmud*.[1] It is called the Burnt House because its walls still retain the charcoal hue from the Roman razing of the Upper City in 70.

Two traditional sites have been identified as the 'House of Caiaphas', one associated with the Assumptionist Church of St Peter of the Cockcrow, on the eastern slope of Mount Zion, and the other in the court of the Armenian monastery of St Saviour, just outside the Zion gate. There are problems with both identifications, but the Armenian site does boast one of the finest Upper City homes of the period, complete with frescoes that rival many in Pompeii. That these frescoes include a painting of a bird renders it improbable that this was the home of a high priest of this period, given the prohibition of 'graven images'. The Assumptionist church is situated on top of a tomb, thus making any house built there ritually impure. If they knew of the tomb, it is unlikely that the family of Annas would choose to live in such a location. As a result of these problems, no solid identification is possible at this point, but from these examples, we can get a fairly good sense of the type of home the high priestly family likely inhabited. Excavated homes and artefacts in the nearby Herodian Quarter (and in the Wohl Archaeological Museum) preserve some of the most visually evocative remains of the world of Annas and Caiaphas, with stunning frescoes, mosaics, pottery, and Corinthian columns. These excavations have revealed what some consider the best single candidate for the home of Annas and/or Caiaphas: the 'Palatial Mansion', a six and a half thousand

---

1. *b. Pesachim* 57a.

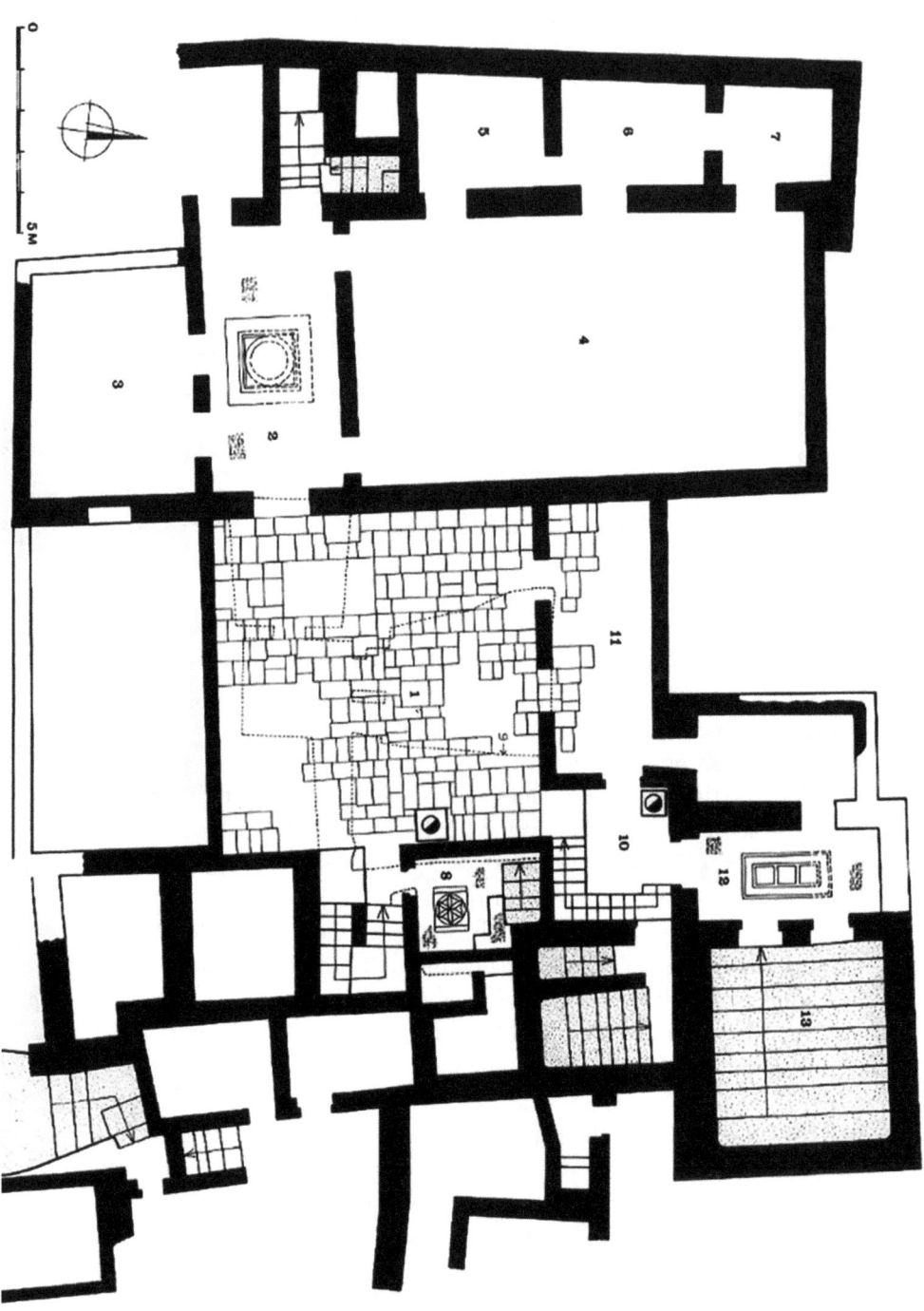

The plan of the Palatial Mansion in the Jewish Quarter (see note 1 opposite).

*The excavation of the Palatial Mansion
in the Jewish Quarter.*[1]

square foot courtyard home (not counting the second floor) which is one of the largest and finest homes thus far discovered in Upper City Jerusalem.[2] While many Jerusalem homes were of modest size, some of the large mansions of the Upper City seem to have been designed to allow extended relatives to live together in a family compound, sharing a single central courtyard. Households of extended families are known from many different times in ancient Israel. The Gospel accounts of the high priestly inquest of Jesus are consistent with this sort of living arrangement for the extended family of Annas, which may well have included Annas's daughter and her husband, Caiaphas.[3]

---

1. From Geva, *Jerusalem Revealed*, 11, Plate IV, by permission.
2. This is tentatively identified as the 'Palace of Annas' by Leen Ritmeyer, based on an earlier suggestion by archaeologist Nahman Avigad (http://www.ritmeyer.com/2012/08/28/the-palace-of-annas-the-high-priest/), cf. N. Avigad, 'How the Wealthy Lived in Herodian Jerusalem', *Biblical Archaeology Review* 2, no. 4 (1976): 1, 23-32, 34-35).
3. For further discussion, see Gibson, 85. Alternatively, it is possible that Caiaphas lived in a house near to Annas, or that a group of houses formed a sort of family compound. Any of these possibilities would be consistent with the available evidence.

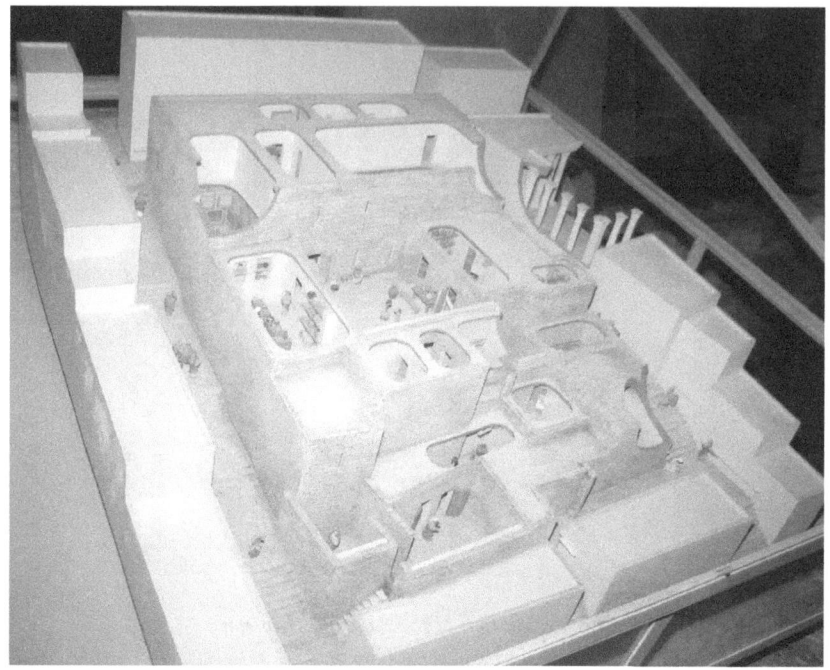

Model of the Palatial Mansion from Wohl Archaeological Museum.[1]

Concerning written evidence, Annas appears a mere four times in the New Testament. Three of these occasions have already been mentioned, from the Gospels of Luke and John.[2] The fourth appears in the Acts of the Apostles, in which Annas and Caiaphas participate in a judicial hearing of Peter and John.[3] Caiaphas is mentioned by name nine times, including twice in the Gospel of Matthew in the context of the arrest and inquest of Jesus.[4] In Mark 14 he is not named, but he is referred to as the 'high priest' several times. Luke appears to follow Mark's lead in this respect. We will discuss all of these in more detail in a later chapter.

Beyond the New Testament, the most important source is once again Josephus. Little needs to be added to our discussion from the last chapter, except two issues that may be of significance: Josephus was a Jewish aristocrat, and he was proud of the fact that he was from a priestly family. For these reasons, Josephus may offer a perspective that is not far removed from that of his elder contemporary aristocratic high priests: Annas and Caiaphas.

---

1. Photo by permission of http://www.theologische-links.de.
2. Luke 3.2; John 18.13, 24.
3. 4.6.
4. Matthew 26.3, 57; Luke 3.2; John 18.13, 14, 24, 28; Acts 4.6.

It is worthwhile to remember at this point one type of evidence that we do *not* have available to us: we have not a single piece of writing from a Sadducee. We will therefore inevitably find it challenging to see the world through the eyes of Sadducees like the house of Annas, as we must rely on the few and largely negative descriptions in the New Testament and Josephus. While acknowledging this limitation, ancient historians also recognise that it is not an unusual one. We have to deal with gaps in evidence and the ubiquitous reality that we do not have information that we would very much like to possess. We must work with the evidence available to us, taking into account its biases and perspectives, all the while acknowledging that most of the pieces of this, as most ancient puzzles, are missing.

Jesus and the House of Annas

Annas and Caiaphas would have been hearing reports and rumours of a couple of Jewish holy men in the region for some time. From their perspective, one of them, Yohannan (John), was cut from the camel's hair cloth of the prophets of old, a fiery apocalyptic preacher of repentance who baptised people in the River Jordan. His days were numbered after he challenged the moral standing of Herod Antipas. It was only a matter of time before Antipas executed him. The other was a teacher and healer from Galilee who had made his presence felt in the north. It seems unlikely that either of these men caused much of a stir in the house of Annas, for they were distant and appealed primarily to the lower classes, but there was some potential cause for concern in the teachings of this Yeshu ha-Notsri, Jesus of Nazareth. Word had it that he liked to talk about the 'Kingdom of Heaven' and that he had some tough words for Pharisees. This was not what would have troubled the high priestly family. It was when this would-be holy man critiqued the social hierarchy that his teachings touched a nerve. Some considered him a prophet. Some even used that potent word, *Meshiach*, in reference to him – the Messiah (*christos* in Greek), the anointed one, heir to the throne of David. This Yeshua was no threat to Annas, but he did bear watching. So far as the Gospel of Mark, our earliest source, is concerned, the high priestly family paid no attention at all to Yeshua until a few days before his execution.[1]

---

1. Mark 11.18 is the first appearance of the 'chief priests' in the Gospel, immediately after the 'cleansing of the Temple' incident. Jesus had already predicted this confrontation in Mark 10.33. Matthew and Luke follow Mark's lead. Before that time there is no evidence of any conflict or concern

The week before Passover in AD 33, this same Jesus entered Jerusalem amidst a fanfare created by some of his followers. Annas doubtless received reports that he entered the city, riding on a donkey in imitation of the words of the prophet Zechariah, with some laying their garments before him or waving palm branches. From Annas's perspective, such a spectacle may have had a potential air of blasphemy about it, depending on what this man intended to convey, but again, no cause for immediate worry. The next day everything changed.

Jesus and his followers, according to Mark, entered the Temple precinct and, in the Court of Gentiles, he approached the tables where one could exchange other types of coinage for Tyrian sheqels and purchase doves for sacrifice. Without warning, he proceeded to tip the tables over, making quite a mess, scattering doves and coins around the court, and disturbing the operation of the Temple complex. Then he shouted out: 'Is it not written, "My house shall be called a house of prayer for all the nations"? But you have made it a den of robbers.'[1] He was quoting the venerable words of Isaiah and Jeremiah. While some doubt that Jesus said or did any such thing, most scholars agree that Jesus did something provocative in the Temple courts, in some sense acting in imitation of the prophets of old, combining words and actions to challenge the status quo and its injustice.

---

relative to the high priestly family. John, however, does note some measure of conflict between Jesus and the chief priests surrounding the earlier feast of Tabernacles (7.32). If this chronology is correct, the high priestly family was already on alert before the 'triumphal entry' of Jesus. Because John places the 'cleansing of the Temple' incident early in the narrative, the textual distance between that event and the arrest of Jesus requires that the fourth Gospel find other factors to pique the wrath of the high priestly family, such as the raising of Lazarus and the relative popularity of Jesus that followed (11.47ff.). Because I think it most probable that John displaced this event in his Gospel, I have here followed the chronology of the Synoptic Gospels.

1. Mark 11.17, based on Isaiah 56.7 and Jeremiah 7.11. For those who argue that Jesus identified with Zealots (*lestai* in Greek) it is interesting here that Jesus refers to the chief priests as presiding over a band of *lestai* – here translated 'robbers', in the Temple court. In this context, *lestai* (following the *Septuagint*) seems to suggest rapacity, violence, corruption, and exploitation, not the 'social bandit' protests of the disenfranchised. In all probability, Jesus spoke Aramaic, in which case he may well have quoted Jeremiah in Hebrew. The Hebrew term in Jeremiah for 'robbers' is *paritsim,* a noun that generally connotes violence of any sort, including economic violence such as robbery, swindling, and oppression of the poor and needy (among other descriptors in Ezekiel 18.10-18). The emphatic 'you' conveys a similar force in Aramaic as in Greek.

In order to capture the force of these words, we will do well to remember the context of Jesus's quotation from Jeremiah. Here is the larger passage:

> Thus says the LORD of hosts, the God of Israel: Amend your ways and your doings, and let me dwell with you in this place. Do not trust in these deceptive words: 'This is the temple of the LORD, the temple of the LORD, the temple of the LORD.' For if you truly amend your ways and your doings, if you truly act justly one with another, if you do not oppress the alien, the orphan, and the widow, or shed innocent blood in this place, and if you do not go after other gods to your own hurt, then I will dwell with you in this place, in the land that I gave of old to your ancestors forever and ever.
>
> Here you are, trusting in deceptive words to no avail. Will you steal, murder, commit adultery, swear falsely, make offerings to Baal, and go after other gods that you have not known, and then come and stand before me in this house, which is called by my name, and say, 'We are safe!'– only to go on doing all these abominations? *Has this house, which is called by my name, become a den of robbers in your sight?*
>
> You know, I too am watching, says the LORD. Go now to my place that was in Shiloh, where I made my name dwell at first, and see what I did to it for the wickedness of my people Israel. And now, because you have done all these things, says the LORD, and when I spoke to you persistently, you did not listen, and when I called you, you did not answer, therefore I will do to the house that is called by my name, in which you trust, and to the place that I gave to you and to your ancestors, just what I did to Shiloh. And I will cast you out of my sight, just as I cast out all your kinsfolk, all the offspring of Ephraim (Italics added).[1]

---

1. Jeremiah 7.3-15. For detailed discussion, see Gundry, *Mark*, 644ff. The introduction of Jeremiah into this context points to a whole panoply of Hebrew prophetic texts that cited the corruption of the priests as a primary symptom of Judah's unfaithfulness and a primary cause for the destruction of the First Temple (e.g. Isaiah 28.7; Micah 3.9-12; Ezekiel 22.23-31; Lamentations 4.13; Zephaniah 3.4; Zechariah 14.20-1; cf. *Jubilees* 23.21; *Testament of Levi* 17; *I Enoch* 89; *Psalms of Solomon* 17-18). For further discussion, see C. Evans, 'Jesus' Action in the Temple: Cleansing or Portent of Destruction?' *Catholic Biblical Quarterly* 51 (1989), 237-70.

This context tells us a good deal about both the meaning and the motive of Jesus's symbolic, prophetic action. The movement of the context is from a note of possible hope (combined with warning) to a note of judgment, with an intervening sense of lament. If the Hebrews, and particularly their leaders, amend their ways, there is still the hope that God will 'dwell with you in this place [the Temple]'. But the leaders of the people have no interest in amending their ways. Therefore, God will bring about the destruction of his own house (in context, by means of the Gentile Babylonians) to purge his people of injustice. That is, for Jeremiah, God does not want to destroy the Temple, but the persistent injustice of its leaders, including the priests appointed to maintain the Temple's status as the central place of atonement, cannot be allowed to continue. Far from providing safety, the Temple leadership has caused the sanctuary of God to become the seat of injustice. As a result, Jeremiah, with a profound sense of loss, predicted that the Temple would be destroyed.

What is the nature of the injustice that has brought the Hebrews to this place of imminent judgment? Jeremiah gives us several hints. In general, the Hebrews have been guilty of numerous violations of Torah. Besides the general references to idolatry, adultery, and murder, there are several specific references to economic injustice: stealing, and the oppression of the alien, the orphan, and the widow; those most vulnerable and least able to fend for themselves. This combination of the shedding of innocent blood with stealing points to a context of violent rapacity. The reference to a 'den of robbers' is the culmination of these charges: even the Temple itself has become the home of oppression and violent rapacity at the hands of the very people God charged to administer justice and atoning sacrifices. If it has become a den of robbers, it has lost all meaning and purpose, and if the leaders continue on their current trajectory, if they fail to amend their ways, there will be nothing left worth preserving. God will have to render the only just judgment, and see to the destruction of his own Temple.

Jesus seems to be cast in a manner very similar to Jeremiah. According to a saying shared by Matthew and Luke, Jesus laments the sad state of Jerusalem in his time.[1] He does not wish to see disaster fall upon the holy city, but fall it will if Jerusalem's leaders continue on their present trajectory. As in Jeremiah's time, the priestly leadership of Jesus's time has converted the symbolic seat of God's presence among

---

1. Matthew 23.37-8; parallel: Luke 13.34-5.

his people, the place of prayer, forgiveness, worship, and atonement, into a new den of robbers, much like their predecessors had done some six centuries before. Thus Jesus, like Jeremiah, proclaims that a similar judgment is in the wings.

The 'chief priests' (Annas, his sons, and other former priests) knew their Isaiah and Jeremiah, and understood correctly that this was a personal affront.[1] From the perspective of the high priestly family, there was something pretentious about Jesus. It was one thing to teach love and forgiveness or to challenge the Pharisees for their legal interpretations and the elites for their greed in Galilee, but it was quite another to do such a thing in Jerusalem, in the Temple of God. For the high priest, the *chutzpah* of this young man of questionable lineage from the negligible village of Nazareth, to come to the sanctified centre of God's creation and disrupt, distort, and decry, was too much. Particularly infuriating for Annas and the chief priests was the reference to Jeremiah, who had dared in his day to challenge the permanence and venerability of the Temple. Above all was that 'you' (which is emphatic in Greek as in Aramaic) attached to the quotation from Jeremiah: 'You have made it a den of robbers.' That 'you', according to Mark's text, did not come from Isaiah or Jeremiah, but was Jesus's own contribution, and that single addition was effectively a declaration of war. In Mark's description, it is apparent that Jesus was pointing, verbally if not physically, an accusatory finger at the house

---

1. The passion narratives of Jesus in the Gospels contain many quotations of or allusions to the Hebrew Bible. Some scholars have suggested that these narratives are therefore examples of 'prophecy historicised', fictional fabrications that grew out of early Christian interest in searching the sacred Hebrew texts for ways in which Jesus fulfilled prophecy. That kind of phenomenon can happen in historical sources, but not during the lifetime of those who experienced the events in question. I suspect that, given the nature of the evidence, these references represent something more like 'history scripturalised'. That is, the memories of those who witnessed these events and the stories they told were shaped in an atmosphere that was steeped in the Hebrew Bible. I also think it probable that Jesus's speech often incorporated quotations or allusions to the sacred text. These words cohere very well with the circumstances and historical context. For discussion, see M. Goodacre, 'Scripturalization in Mark's Crucifixion Narrative' in Geert van Oyen and Tom Shepherd (eds.), *The Trial and Death of Jesus: Essays on the Passion Narrative in Mark* (Leuven: Peeters, 2006), 33-47; cf. N.T. Wright, *The New Testament and the People of God*, 427ff.

of Annas.[1] What Annas would have heard was something like: 'You' are the avaricious aristocrat robbing God's people – just take a look at the money on the ground; 'You,' in the name of shepherding the flock of God, are fleecing them. 'You' are at the heart of the Roman-Temple alliance that has long oppressed the Chosen People of God. If Jesus believed that his announcement of the Kingdom of God was fundamentally incompatible with current high-priestly practices, the house of Annas seems to have agreed.

It seems quite credible that Jesus engaged in confrontational actions and words in the Temple courts. One might well ask, 'Why?' He must have known that these kinds of words and actions were provocative. He must have known that the consequences of such provocation would be severe. If the chief priests were not inclined to challenge him beforehand, why did he decide to confront them? His public ministry might have lasted many years had he stayed in Galilee or just celebrated the Passover feast quietly like many another pilgrim, steering clear of the priestly elites. Whatever he was thinking, he chose confrontational tactics by employing these particular actions and words in the Temple courts.

I am sceptical of any attempts to discern the motives of Jesus, not least my own, but scholars have offered several ideas that may at least shed some light on the question. Some have suggested that Jesus sought symbolically to signify the eschatological destruction of the Temple or the end of the sacrificial function of the Temple. Others believe he meant to challenge the legitimacy of the Jewish priesthood, or to expose the impurity of those who at present held those offices. Still others argue that Jesus rejected the focus on externals characteristic of Temple worship, as a substitute for genuine, internal devotion to God. While different pieces of evidence can be marshalled in support of each of these theories, I do not find any of them compelling in context. If we are to understand the motive and meaning of Jesus's actions, we need to clarify several issues.[2]

First, the logistics of Temple worship required the availability of many sacrificial animals. Since Jesus and his family did, according to the Gospels, visit the Temple on occasion, a reasonable inference would

---

1. The immediate reference of the 'you' may have been those who managed the sales operations, but in context, it was focused on their supervisors: the sheqel stops with the house of Annas. In the context of Mark, it was the chief priests, not the money-changers, who heard Jesus's words and, in the very next verse, responded with fury: 'And when the chief priests and the scribes heard it, they kept looking for a way to kill him . . .' (11.18).
2. For a thoughtful review of several approaches to this evidence, see E.P. Sanders, *Jesus and Judaism* (Philadelphia: Fortress, 1985), 61ff.

be that they also engaged in normal Temple worship and sacrifice.[1] It is therefore something of a stretch to imagine that Jesus had any particular concerns about the reasonable provision, pre-inspection, and sale of sacrificial animals as a convenience for pilgrims.

Second, the primary purpose of the tithe, paid by every Jewish family, was to provide a living for priests and Levites. Jesus never denigrated the tithe, but rather commended the practice. Moreover, priests and Levites received income from sacrifices, first fruits, and heave offerings.[2]

Third, Jesus had many options when he entered the Temple courts if he wished to engage in prophetic action or public criticism. If he wanted to abolish the sacrificial system, he could have entered the priestly court and interfered with the sacrificial process. If he wanted to question the legitimacy of the Temple itself, he could have staged a protest outside of the Temple courts, even calling on his followers to help prevent entry, or he could have proclaimed his message in the Temple courts, perhaps something like Stephen did later, emphasising that 'The Most High does not dwell in houses made by human hands. . . .'[3] If he wanted to protest the separation between Jews and Gentiles, he could have broken down the wall that separated the Court of the Gentiles from the areas restricted to Jews, or defaced the Greek inscription mentioned above that warned Gentiles to keep out on pain of death. He had many options, but he chose instead to attack tables.

Fourth, Jesus could have chosen to say anything, to critique anything he wished. He could have denigrated the purity or legitimacy of the priests, as did some of the sectarians in Qumran; he could have condemned the priests for their character flaws or immorality as did the *Talmud;* he could have decried their injustice as did the *Testament of Moses.*[4] He chose to do none of these things.

Given the range of possible actions and words available to him in or around the Temple, we should pay careful attention to the things he did choose to do and say, according to our earliest sources. He did choose to attack the tables where money was exchanged and doves were sold for sacrifice. Why? I concur with most scholars

---

1. For further discussion, see A-J. Levine, *The Misunderstood Jew: The Church and the Scandal of the Jewish Jesus* (New York: HarperOne, 2006).
2. Numbers 18.21-26; Deuteronomy 14.27-9; Nehemiah 10.37-9; Matthew 23.23. For detailed discussion, see Sanders, *Judaism,* 146-57.
3. Acts 7.48.
4. 1QpHab 8-9; *b. Pesachim* 57a; *The Testament of Moses* 6-7.

who interpret Jesus's actions and words in light of ancient Hebrew prophets, like Jeremiah, who presaged the destruction of the Temple, (especially since, a couple of chapters later in Mark, Jesus made such a prediction).[1] But this idea does not explain the specific nature of his actions. What was it about these tables that became the focus of his symbolic action? If Jews regularly came to the Temple to pay their Temple tax, what is the problem with providing money changers as a convenience? If the selling of doves was a necessary and helpful service for those who wished to sacrifice, why would that enterprise concern Jesus?

To phrase the questions in this way blunts the issue. Jesus's concerns lay not with the money-changers but more likely with the idea that money needed to be exchanged into Tyrian sheqels.[2] The amount of the tax was set by biblical precedent, but the Hebrew Bible makes no demand as to what type of coin can be used to pay the tax. That demand was imposed by the high priests, and the result was that the high priestly family made a handsome profit on their mints, exchange rates, and commissions. Similarly, there is no evidence that Jesus was concerned about the idea of selling pre-approved doves for sacrifice. Rather, he was probably concerned about their elevated price resulting from the high-priestly monopoly on such sales, not to mention the fees charged for priestly inspection.[3] The relationship between limited supply

---

1. In the context of Jeremiah 7, the warning of the impending destruction of the Temple is based upon the Hebrew leaders' continued practice of oppression, exploitation, and stealing (along with other violations of Torah). Of course, Jesus's words and actions must also be viewed in the context of his persistent teaching about the coming Kingdom of God. The warning of impending destruction of the Temple is not isolated to this particular incident, but makes its presence felt in several passages in the Gospels (e.g. Luke 19.41-4; John 2.19; Matthew 21.18-19; Mark 13.1-2 [and parallels]; 14.58; 15.29; cf. Acts 6.14; *Gospel of Thomas* 71). For detailed discussion, see N.T. Wright, *Jesus and the Victory of God* (Minneapolis: Fortress, 1996), 413ff.

2. For a well-nuanced discussion of these issues, see J.H. Charlesworth, *Jesus and the Temple: Textual and Archaeological Explorations* (Minneapolis: Fortress, 2014), 145-81. He further suggests that Jesus may have rejected the violation of the second commandment evident in the imagery on the coins. Cf. Matthew 17.24-7.

3. It is important to bear in mind that doves were the common form of sacrifice for the poor. This bird-selling business was a monopoly not in the sense that one could only purchase birds in this one place (there were almost certainly alternatives), but it was a priestly monopoly in two senses: only

and high demand, especially during the major pilgrim festivals, surely pushed prices up, even though the general commitment to community worship may have limited inflationary tendencies. While one might argue that the providers of these services ought to be entitled to charge for their efforts, we should not forget that, since they operated in the Temple courts, these were very likely priests, perhaps even members of the extended house of Annas, and their income was already provided for through the tithes, offerings, and sacrifices. Any profit gained from these tables was over and above the normal and sufficient priestly sources of income.

These considerations point to very practical results. Whenever a pilgrim of meagre means (which was most pilgrims) came to the Temple to worship, that person would have visited those tables, paid the value of the Temple tax (half a sheqel, a significant financial burden), plus considerably more to cover the exchange and commission. That same pilgrim would then have moved to the next table, and there paid considerably more for a dove to sacrifice than one would have cost elsewhere, thus multiplying the financial hardship on a family that could ill-afford it. Where did all those profits, multiplied by the tens of thousands of pilgrims, go? One look at the luxurious priestly homes of the Upper City tells us a great deal. It was therefore neither the provision of sacrificial animals nor the provision of money changers that aroused Jesus's indignation, but the ruthless profiteering and exploitation perpetrated by the high-priestly establishment in the name of God.

With this understanding, we can return to Jesus's words: '"My house shall be called a house of prayer for all the nations", but you have made it a den of robbers.' Note in particular the term 'robbers'. Jesus did not refer to the chief priests as legalists, formalists, heretics, or hypocrites. 'Robbers' means not merely thieves but, in context, evokes the common ancient image of a cave full of violent criminals, plotting their next raid, intent on taking by force what does not belong to them, for their own benefit.[1] When we put these words together with Jesus's actions in the

---

priests manning the tables could guarantee that the birds they sold were officially approved for sacrifice at the time of sale and only priests were likely to have received permission from the high priest to sell such birds in the Temple court. Other bird-sellers outside the Temple courts were therefore at a distinct disadvantage. Concerning priestly inspection, see *m. Sheqalim* 5.1. Concerning excessive prices for doves, see *m. Keritot* 1.7.

1. '. . . robbing the helpless while themselves enjoying the safe refuge of privilege', N. Hillyer in *New International Dictionary of New Testament Theology* (Grand Rapids: Zondervan, 1979), III, 380-1. Though it was

larger context of the Roman-Temple alliance, their meaning comes into clearer focus.

While I have no doubt that Jesus's words and actions were symbolic and prophetic, his targets seemed to be largely social and economic: a protestation against exploitation.[1] Even this statement is oversimplified, for it misses something crucial.

I would submit that the Gospel of Mark, our earliest source, provides a convincing context and perspective. There, Jesus predicted that he would come into conflict with the chief priests and that the consequence would be his death.[2] While some have challenged that prediction, considering it a retrospective invention, I am not so sure, for there is nothing implausible about such predictions if Jesus planned provocative action against the Temple leadership. He never spoke against the sacrificial system, or the Jewish priesthood as an institution, so I think there is good reason to doubt that those were his targets. Jesus's words and actions were surely symbolic, but they were also deeply personal. While he did not target the priesthood as an institution, he did target the leadership of the house of Annas who controlled the Temple courts and whose management of the Temple precinct resulted in oppression and exploitation. I do not much like the traditional label for this event, 'The Cleansing of the Temple', for it seems to suggest that there was something ritually unclean about the whole Temple precinct. From Jesus's perspective, if there was anything that needed cleansing (or perhaps purging is a better word), it was the leadership of the house of Annas.

---

written in the second century, the Roman historian immediately calls to mind the extended narrative of violent exploits of robbers (*latrones* in Latin) based in their cave in Apuleius's novel, *Metamorphoses*. Fear of encountering robbers while travelling between cities is commonplace in Roman sources, including the New Testament (e.g. Luke 10.30; 2 Corinthians 11.26).

1. Note further that in Mark, just after Jesus overturned the tables, he also drove out buyers and sellers, as well as carriers of goods. That is, Jesus, at least for a moment, interrupted the regular commerce that seems to have been commonplace in the Court of Gentiles. This reinforces an economic focus of Jesus's protest. R. Bauckham, to a large degree, anticipated my analysis of 'Jesus' Demonstration in the Temple', though we arrived at this destination independently and by different paths: in *Law and Religion: Essays on the Place of the Law in Israel and Early Christianity*, ed. B. Lindars and R. Bauckham (Cambridge: James Clarke, 1988), 72-89; 171-6.

2. Mark 8.31; 10.33.

From the larger perspective of his teachings, Jesus seems to have considered the Kingdom of God to be in conflict with the Roman-Temple alliance. Many scholars have noticed this conflict, but most have failed to consider why he did not choose to confront the Roman authorities. There were many ways he could have engaged in symbolic, prophetic words and actions in the Fortress Antonia, or better yet, at the *praetorium* of Pilate. He could even have chosen to confront Pilate, mounted on a great warhorse and escorted by his personal guards, at his *adventus* (the typical form of proud and pompous Roman procession) from Caesarea to Jerusalem, which would have taken place about the same time as his own triumphal entry on the other side of the city.[1] That Jesus chose not to confront Pilate, but rather to confront the house of Annas in the Temple courts is significant.

It was the 'Temple' portion of the Roman-Temple alliance that seemed to hold pride of place among Jesus's concerns. It was not so much the abstract oppressive power of the great empire, as the personal, daily exploitation of the Jewish people in the name of God that Jesus chose to confront. To the extent that his 'good announcement' of the Kingdom of God urged that the last should be first, that the poor and meek are blessed, that the great banquet table of God was open to all, that personal and community transformation, forgiveness, and love of one's neighbours as well as one's enemies were central ethics of the Kingdom, and most of all, that the Kingdom would be ruled by God, not the Roman-Temple alliance – the house of Annas stood in direct opposition. Much of what Jesus stood for, Annas stood against.

As a result, Jesus seems to have believed that open confrontation with the house of Annas in the Temple courts was essential for demonstrating his message to the gathered Jewish pilgrims in Jerusalem. He also understood the consequences, that confrontation with the house of Annas was a challenge to the elitist and personal nature of the entrenched power structure. In provoking the Temple portion of the alliance, he knew he would also incur the wrath of Annas's Roman allies. Jesus seems to have understood what he was doing and the kind of trouble he would likely face – and he seems to have thought it was worth it.[2]

---

1. J.D. Crossan and M.J. Borg, *The Last Week: What the Gospels Really Teach About Jesus's Final Days in Jerusalem* (New York: HarperOne, 2006), 4. While Jesus surely challenged many aspects of Roman hegemony, these are not the focus of his prophetic words and actions.

2. He had access to a rich Jewish heritage whose sacred texts (and other textual traditions) provided several ways to understand how his suffering on behalf of his people could be instrumental in their redemption: e.g. 2 Maccabees;

From the perspective of Annas and his family, Yeshu ha-Notsri, over the course of perhaps a single minute, grew from a person worth watching into a deadly enemy bent on undermining their lofty stature. Moreover, to be a bit crass, Jesus threatened the high priestly family's accustomed standard of living. None of these things were acceptable to the house of Annas. This man had to be stopped.

Annas, however, faced a big problem. The progression in the text of Mark is instructive. Jesus acts, then speaks his prophetic words; the chief priests react with vehemence but also fear because of Jesus's popularity with the people. A significant number of people in Jerusalem seem to have been quite taken with this would-be holy man, and crowds often gathered round him. From Annas's perspective, therefore, caution was in order. This whole situation needed to be handled with great discretion; as privately as possible. It would not do to involve Pilate too soon, for he would not understand. Nor would it do to make enemies of many of their fellow Jews, as the house of Annas sought to eliminate its newest enemy.

Annas was likely not overly concerned with the teachings of Jesus, nor terribly offended that Jesus had called into question the social norms, nor worried that Jesus might start a revolution that could topple Rome or even his own position. John the Baptist was more of a threat in these respects, and he had never warranted the wrath of the high priestly family. The fact that Jesus did not show proper respect within the Temple precinct, that he insulted the leadership of the high priestly family, that he seemed to think his own agenda for the Temple more worthy than the tradition of generations of priests: *these* things kindled the wrath of Annas. To compound matters in his mind, if rumours were accurate, this Jesus had a rather lax attitude about matters of ritual purity and the observance of Shabbat. Furthermore, there was that hint of blasphemy, the troublesome rumblings that suggested Jesus might be the long-awaited *Meshiach*, and a threat to the lucrative family business. These considerations combined to convince Annas that there was no room in Jerusalem for Jesus.

A careful examination of the evidence in context indicates that Annas and Caiaphas were neither hapless formalists nor greedy tyrants, though they cared about the formalities of Temple worship and their

---

4 Maccabees; *Martyrdom of Isaiah*; Wisdom 2-6; 1QHab. 8, 11; Daniel 11, 12; Zechariah 9-14; Ezekiel 4; Isaiah 40-55. None of these texts precisely anticipates early Christian understanding of the suffering of Jesus, though they do provide its context and contribute to its formation. For detailed discussion, see N.T. Wright, *Jesus and the Victory of God*, 553ff.

family livelihood. Nor were they devoted to destroying any movement that disagreed with their theology. Rather, they were a family of Jewish aristocrats, high priests who had risen to a position of unparalleled prominence. Their motives grew out of their position. More than anything else, they viewed themselves as the protectors of the corporate worship of Israel, models and enforcers of the ritual purity appropriate to the worship of a holy God, defenders of Jewish dignity in their relations with Rome, champions of peace and the status quo. Above all, they believed in family values as only Jewish aristocrats could. Anything that threatened the established power structure, or the function of the Temple, or the wealth and prestige of the house of Annas had to be squelched. In this case, a singular threat challenged everything Annas held dear. Yeshu ha-Notsri had to be stopped.

Annas immediately sought to find a way to apprehend Jesus in a quiet place that would not draw crowds. His family finally succeeded in engaging the services of one Judas Iscariot, from whom they received word that Jesus and a few others would be alone on Thursday evening on the lower slopes of the Mount of Olives in a place called Gethsemane, where there were a few olive presses. They sent a contingent of hand-picked soldiers to arrest this man, with orders *not* to take him to the *praetorium* of the prefect, or to the Fortress Antonia, the normal holding places for criminals, but rather to take him directly to the Upper City, to the private home of Annas and Caiaphas.[1] Once the high priestly family had him under their control, without a crowd of followers, they would know what to do.

So it was that Annas, the high priest *par excellence*, the most powerful Jew in the world, did not rise with the sun on the morning of 14 Nissan, April 3, AD 33. He had spent all night doing what had to be done to protect his family. He did not know that his every action on that day would be scrutinised by millions of eyes over the course of multiple millennia. He did not know that the fate of his prisoner would change the world. What he did know was that he could not solve the problem of Yeshu ha-Notsri on his own. More than ever, he needed the support of the Roman prefect, Pontius Pilatus.

---

1. John's account amplifies the size and nature of the guards who arrested Jesus, referring to it as a *speiran*, the Greek term for a Roman cohort – a sizeable military contingent (18.3).

V

Quaestio:[1]
The High Priests' Inquest

Traditional interpretation of the 'trials' of Jesus suggests that Jewish leadership, vested in the representative council of the Jewish people, the Sanhedrin, arrested Jesus and then subjected him to two trials: a Jewish trial followed by a Roman trial. Jesus was convicted of blasphemy in the Jewish trial, but the Sanhedrin subsequently changed the charge to treason or something of the sort and bound him over to Pilate for the Roman trial. There, a great gathering of Jews demanded the crucifixion of Jesus, even calling down his blood on themselves and their children. Pilate, cowed by the crowd, ultimately gave the order to crucify him while washing his hands of the matter.

There are many problems with this interpretation, not least, that it has fuelled many centuries of Christian anti-Semitism and persecution of Jews. The belief that 'the Jews' killed Jesus has helped to justify the Crusades, the Inquisition, and pogroms. Some have even cited such logic, at least indirectly, as one of the roots of the Holocaust. In response, recent years have seen the rise of revisionist interpretations, some of which argue that Gospel accounts of any involvement of any Jews in the 'trials' of Jesus must be purely fictional, growing out of the anti-Jewish biases of the authors rather than history.

As with everything in this study, the most probable historical reconstruction is much more complex and nuanced than these interpretations suggest, and the only way we can begin to analyse this puzzle is to pay close attention to the puzzle pieces available to us.

---

1. *Quaestio* is the Roman term for a legal inquiry or investigation preliminary to a trial. It is therefore a rough equivalent of the English term 'inquest' which, in American law, describes the work of a grand jury as it examines evidence and determines what, if any, charges should be brought to trial.

The Nature of the Evidence for the High Priestly Inquest of Jesus

As we turn our attention fully to the evidence in the New Testament, I am conscious of the fact that, as a classical historian, I am a visitor stumbling into a crowded club, or perhaps Daniel descending voluntarily into a certain den. I wish to express my appreciation for the extraordinarily detailed work of historical Jesus scholars and exegetes in this arena. I benefit greatly from their efforts and have no intention of duplicating them. Rather, I hope to offer a fresh glimpse of the evidence through a different set of spectacles: in this case, spectacles manufactured in ancient Rome.

As the stories of Jesus, Annas, Caiaphas, and Pilate converge, the evidence gets stronger. Most of what we have been able to learn about the lives of these three central figures thus far was drawn from Josephus and Philo. Both are relatively early first-generation sources, both are biased, and both are extremely valuable, providing for a reasonably probable interpretation.[1] Nevertheless, in most cases, our knowledge of particular events depends on a single source (such as the Affair of the Standards or the Affair of the Shields). When we consider the evidence for this High Priestly Inquest of Jesus, all our evidence comes from the Gospels of the New Testament and, from the perspective of the ancient historian, that's a considerable improvement. These sources are for the most part earlier than Josephus, thus providing closer proximity of source to event, and they also provide multiple lines of evidence that allow for cross-examination. While the proximity and multiple nature of the evidence is an improvement, multiple sources create their own interpretive and analytical challenges that we will need to consider. Where there are multiple sources, there is always the potential for both corroboration and discrepancy.[2]

After understanding the nature of the evidence, the first question the ancient historian asks is about the range and degree of agreement among the sources, along with the nature of any corroboration or any discrepancies among the sources. For the sake of convenience and clarity of analysis, I have placed the evidence from the four Gospels in parallel columns at the end of this chapter.

---

1. As noted in Chapter II, first-generation sources were written within the lifetime of at least some people who experienced the event the source discusses. Any sources written within about sixty years of the events they discuss would be considered first-generation.
2. For a discussion of the dates and interrelationships among the Gospels, see Chapter II.

Analysis of these texts suggests that Matthew and Luke created their accounts of the high priestly inquest almost entirely out of material provided by Mark.[1] If they had a copy of Mark in hand, they provide only weak corroboration and, since there is no evidence that they had access to other sources for this episode, any changes introduced by Luke or Matthew should be considered editorial redactions of Mark rather than independent evidence. John provides some corroboration, but does not appear to have verbal dependence on the synoptic Gospels. When all four Gospels agree, we have a very high level of corroboration. Even if we consider only the most credible evidence, we have a firm outline of the high priestly inquest. Although the Gospel accounts do not agree on all details, all four agree on the following:

1. Jesus was arrested at night and brought to the home of the high priest.
2. Peter followed and ended up in the courtyard of the high priest.
3. People questioned Peter who denied being associated with Jesus.
4. The high priest questioned Jesus.[2]
5. Jesus was beaten.
6. Early the next morning, they bound Jesus over to Pilate on the charge that he claimed to be 'King of the Jews'.[3]

---

1. Luke, however, omits much of the material from Mark for reasons that are unclear. Perhaps he wished to portray the high priestly family as 'lawless men' (Acts 2.23) or perhaps he did not consider matters pertaining to the Temple or blasphemy to be of interest to his Gentile readers. Whatever his reasons, he abbreviates and conflates Mark's account of these events.
2. The sequence of events in John 18 is difficult to unpack. At first blush, in the NRSV translation, Jesus is arrested, then taken to Annas for an initial round of questioning, then 'sent' to Caiaphas. On closer inspection, however, this chronology is not so clear. The primary problem is that John refers expressly only to Caiaphas as 'high priest', and it is the 'high priest' who presides over the initial round of questioning of Jesus. It may well be that John's sequence is that Jesus is arrested, taken to Annas, then sent to Caiaphas who presides over all of the questioning. Whether Annas or Caiphas presided over the inquest in John, the questions asked by the high priest are not the same as in the synoptics. This is one of those cases where John seems to complement the synoptics; he does not specifically corroborate the questions asked by Caiaphas in the synoptics, but he does corroborate the outline and setting of the events. Luke compresses this whole episode and employs the plural to express the inter-rogation, thus making it unclear which individual was doing the questioning.
3. The charge, 'King of the Jews', appears in the sources in the context of the trial before Pilate which is the subject of the next chapter.

Since John and the synoptic Gospels represent different lines of evidence, these areas of agreement represent a single case of strong corroboration combined with two cases of weak corroboration, despite the different perspectives, biases, and agendas of the four sources. In addition, we have another point of corroboration provided by Josephus in his reference to Jesus: the *Testimonium Flavianum*. Much debate has swirled about the textual criticism of this passage and its probable interpolation (intentional change) by Christian scribes. Despite this controversy, one portion of the text, which does not appear to have been subject to Christian interpolation, is significant for our understanding of the high priestly inquest: 'Pilate, upon hearing Jesus accused by men of the highest standing among us, condemned him to be crucified. . . .'[1] While Josephus provides no details about the inquiry, his reference to the 'men of highest standing among us' seems to be a reference to the high priestly family. If so, this evidence provides important corroboration that the trial before Pilate found its impetus in charges brought by the house of Annas. Behind this claim must have been some mechanism by which the 'men of highest standing' determined the charges they would bring to the prefect. The high priests' inquest makes perfect sense in light of Josephus, even if he does not provide a narrative account.

With this very probable skeleton of events in place, we can now begin to wrap it in muscle, cartilage, and skin as we consider matters that, while still probable, do not rise to the same level. We will depend primarily on Mark, our earliest source. Matthew follows Mark closely, while adding some details that serve to heighten the drama and to cast the high priestly family in a more negative light. Luke omits most of the details, greatly abbreviating his narrative. There is an unusual level of agreement between the synoptics and John. John also provides some interesting incidental details that suggest an eyewitness source, particularly the kindling of the fire and the presence of the unnamed disciple who knows someone in the high priestly retinue and goes inside ahead of Peter to get permission for Peter to enter the courtyard.[2]

---

1. *Antiquities* 18.63-4. For further discussion, see Chapter II.
2. John 18.15-16. Given these vivid incidental details, it is probable that the eyewitness material was provided by Peter and/or the unnamed disciple (though anyone present could have provided reports). The identity of that unnamed disciple has been the source of considerable speculation. John and Judas seem to be the most likely candidates, though several others have been nominated. Both Peter and the unnamed disciple were in a position to report on the high priests' inquest, and it is a reasonable inference that they would have followed the group with the captive Jesus the following morning

Evidence that appears in John or Mark alone should be considered in much the same way that we considered material about Pilate that appears only in Josephus: single attestation by a first-generation source. It is good evidence, but it does not lend itself to the very high level of probability that comes with multiple levels of corroboration. There is nothing in John's account of the inquest that directly conflicts with the synoptics; we can therefore consider his material complementary in nature, as we did with Josephus and Philo.[1]

In sum, we have a solid core of high probability evidence, rooted in agreement among early sources, including significant levels of corroboration. Evidence this early with this much corroboration is rare for the ancient historian. These areas of agreement must therefore be considered more reliable than anything else discussed thus far.

The Participants

It is highly probable that Jesus was arrested at night, in the presence of a small group of his followers, on orders from the house of Annas. After his arrest, he was brought not to a local prison, or to the *praetorium* of the prefect, but to the home of the high priestly family. This little detail is of great significance, for it points to a unique and private set of circumstances. In the high priestly household, Annas held sway as patriarch and Caiaphas held the highest position in the land as the high priest of Israel. Because this gathering was at a private home at night, those who were present were there by invitation only. Who received invitations? The answer to this question is one of the keys that unlocks the whole story, for it will cause us to reconsider some common interpretations.

First, there is broad agreement among the sources that the high priest was there. Only John includes a specific reference to Annas, but if Annas and Caiaphas lived in the same high priestly palace, which is a

---

to the *praetorium* of Pilate, thus also providing those vivid incidental details of John's account of the trial. Other possible sources of information for the proceedings of the inquiry would be the slaves and guards mentioned in the courtyard, as well as Joseph of Arimathea, who may have been present (Mark 15.43; Luke 23.50-1). It is possible, of course, that these vivid, incidental details merely represent a literary device suggesting verisimilitude. On the other hand, John's language and composition are remarkable for their simplicity, not their literary sophistication.

1. There is one problematic difference in John, and that concerns the chronology of the inquest, trial, and execution of Jesus relative to Passover. Detailed discussion of this issue appears in Appendix I.

reasonable assumption, then the presence of both Annas and Caiaphas at these proceedings would follow. Since Luke refers to both Annas and Caiaphas as high priests, it is hard to imagine one without the presence of the other at these proceedings.

Second, the synoptics agree that the chief priests were there; that is, the former high priests. This title refers to Annas and his sons, along with any other living ex-high priests, thus providing additional confirmation of John's reference to the presence of Annas.[1]

Third, there were 'elders' – that is, elite Jewish aristocrats. No family was more aristocratic than the house of Annas, suggesting that this is a reference to the remainder of his extended family, especially those of his sons who had not yet donned the high-priestly Ephod (a sacred priestly vestment). 'Elders' would also include the extended family of Caiaphas. It is also possible that there were included in this group some other Jewish elites who were close to the house of Annas, and thus merited an invitation to this nocturnal gathering.

Fourth, there were the 'scribes'. The identity of this group is somewhat controversial, but they were widely considered experts in the Torah. It is common in the New Testament for scribes to be found in association with Pharisees, but this was not always the case. Priests, such as Ezra or Josephus, were literate experts in the Torah and thus worthy of the scribal designation.[2] Annas and his family were doubtless experts in the law and it is possible that some of his sons were designated scribes. This term could thus be another way of referring to the sons of Annas, or it could represent the presence of some Pharisees or other legal experts who had managed to earn the trust of Annas.

Fifth, there are several references to some sort of council, *synedrion* in Greek, which is usually transliterated in its Hebraic form as 'Sanhedrin'. What, precisely, did these authors mean when they used this term? This is a crucial issue that has often proven to be a source

---

1. Mark refers to the presence of 'all the chief priests, the elders, and the scribes' (14.53). The 'all' probably refers only to the chief priests, not the elders and scribes. Technically, the 'chief priests' would have consisted of Annas, his son Eleazar (high priest in 16), Ishmael ben Phiabi (high priest in 15-16), and Shimon ben Camith (high priest in 17). By extension, the other four sons of Annas, who would serve as high priests after Caiaphas, may have been considered part of this powerful group. It is also possible, though more of a chronological stretch, that one or two of the high priests who preceded Annas were also still active as chief priests. Annas would have been at least in his sixties at the time of this inquest.

2. For further discussion, see Sanders, *Judaism*, 170-82.

of misunderstanding and has sparked scholarly controversy. It is important, therefore, that we take the time to understand this term in its historical context so that our analysis and reconstruction of the high priestly inquest of Jesus will rest on a solid foundation.

Detailed Analysis: The Role and Composition of the Sanhedrin[1]

Both Mark and Matthew refer to the presence of the 'whole *synedrion*' at the home of the high priest where Jesus was brought for his inquest, and Luke uses the same term for his abbreviated gathering placed the next morning. John uses this term in an earlier context.[2] What did these authors have in mind when employing this term? Who participated in this *synedrion* and what was their larger function in Jerusalem?

It is common and reasonable to begin this analysis from the perspective of the *Mishnah*. According to the tractate *Sanhedrin*,[3] the Great Sanhedrin of Jerusalem consisted of seventy-one members, and functioned as the supreme judicial and governing council of the Jews, with jurisdiction over a broad range of criminal, civil, religious, and logistical matters. Some modern interpreters even suggest that the Sanhedrin was a representative body of the Jewish people. It met in the 'Chamber of Hewn Stone' in the Temple precinct. The Great Sanhedrin, according to the *Mishnah*, is to be distinguished from lesser Sanhedrins of twenty-three members that seem to be regional councils. Procedures of the Great Sanhedrin were strictly regulated, including the requirement that they never meet at night or during Shabbat or holidays. The high priest presided over the Great Sanhedrin, in which role he was referred to as *nasi*, 'prince'. While it makes some sense to read the New Testament with the *Mishnah* in mind, there are many problems with this method of analysis that need to be addressed.[4]

---

1. I am indebted to my student, Mckayla Stevens, for her preliminary research on this topic.
2. 11.47.
3. Supplemented by the *Tosefta* and numerous passing Talmudic references.
4. Several scholars have provided thoughtful studies on this topic, especially M. Goodman, *The Ruling Class of Judaea*, 112-116; E.P. Sanders, *Judaism*, 472-88; J. McLaren, *Power and Politics in Palestine: The Jews and the Governing of their Land 100 BC-AD 70* (Sheffield, 1991); L.I. Levine, *Judaism and Hellenism in Antiquity: Conflict or Confluence?* (Seattle: University of Washington Press, 1998), 84-90; H.K. Bond, *Caiaphas: Friend of Rome and Judge of Jesus?* (Louisville: Westminster John Knox, 2004), 33-34. For a

First, the *Mishnah* and later *Tosefta* are late sources, though they do preserve some earlier traditions (*Mishnah* c. AD 200; *Tosefta* c. AD 300). The challenge is that it is often difficult if not impossible to distinguish earlier and later traditions. Scholars agree that these texts are rife with anachronisms and idealisations retrojected back into earlier periods, and therefore we must employ them with due caution.

Second, the *Mishnah* reflects almost entirely Pharisaic perspectives, values, and procedures, so it is natural that its depiction of the Great Sanhedrin shares those characteristics. Moreover, there was good reason in the late second or early third century for rabbinic authors to forge a link between the first-century Sanhedrin and the later rabbinic courts, for such a link would bolster the prestige of the latter. This link, however, seems to be anachronistic when judged from the perspective of first-century evidence. Despite some interesting parallels between the *Mishnah* and the New Testament on other matters, the *synedrion* of the earlier period, as it appears in the pages of Josephus and the New Testament, appears to differ in many respects from its counterpart in the *Mishnah*. *Synedria* in first-century evidence are dominated largely by Sadducees and their particular concerns, rather than the Pharisees who dominate the *Mishnah*. This difference alone suggests a substantial disconnect between earlier and later periods.[1] Moreover, the treatment of the Great Sanhedrin in the *Mishnah* may well reflect the conditions and functions of the Pharisaical leadership in Yavne after AD 90 more than those of Jerusalem much earlier in the first century.[2]

Third, while there are references to regional councils and Jerusalem *synedria* in the first century, in Josephus and the New Testament, there is not a single unequivocal reference to a seventy-one-member Great Sanhedrin of Jerusalem with the kind of jurisdiction, procedures and governing authority that is depicted in the *Mishnah*.

These and other considerations have caused a number of recent scholars to call attention to the absence of specific evidence from the last decades of the first century BC and the first decades of the first century AD that mentions the particulars evident in the *Mishnah*: a regularly

---

slightly different angle, see R.E. Brown, *The Death of the Messiah* (New York: Doubleday, 1994), 349; cf. R.H. Gundry, *The Old is Better: New Testament Essays in Support of Traditional Interpretations* (Eugene: Wipf and Stock, 2005), 98-110, who points to some detailed parallels between the *Mishnah* and the inquest of Jesus, including the charge of blasphemy and the tearing of robes.

1. Goodman, 113.
2. E. Lohse, 'synedrion', in *Theological Dictionary of the New Testament,* ed. G. Kittel and G. Friedrich (Grand Rapids: Eerdmans, 1971), Vol. VII, 863.

constituted Great Sanhedrin, consisting of seventy-one members that served either as a representative body of the Jewish people or a supreme judicial body. Rather, a detailed analysis of the term '*synedrion*' in the New Testament and the decades immediately surrounding it indicates a much more malleable usage. Both the textual evidence and the cultural and political context suggest that '*synedrion*' in Josephus and the New Testament refers to a council of a variable number of persons, or a group of advisors. In the specific context of early first-century Jerusalem, '*synedrion*' was used for a group of elite Jews, called together on an ad hoc basis by the high priest, to deal with specific issues. To avoid confusion, I have adopted the convention of using the neutral and literal transliteration of the Greek: *synedrion*, without a capital 'S'.[1]

I realise that this understanding of *synedrion* will be novel, even surprising or disconcerting to many readers. It is therefore important to take a thorough look at the evidence, in the process intentionally bracketing any ideas gleaned from the *Mishnah*. Let us then take a fresh look at how the word '*synedrion*' was used in Greek literature for many centuries before and around the time of our inquiry. In this way, we can enter into the linguistic world of the first century and attune our ears to hear the resonance of this term long before the *Mishnah* was written. In particular, we will pay careful attention to the composition and the function of the various *synedria* we will encounter.

The Greek noun '*synedrion*' means literally a 'sitting with'. It was regularly used in classical Greek for a group of people who sat together, gathered around some sort of common interest, in particular as ad hoc advisory councils called together by someone in authority.[2] Such councils regularly advised rulers, especially in the Hellenistic era. *Synedrion* appears in the writings of many authors, but those most likely to form the basis for the usage of the term in first-century Judaea are the Septuagint, Philo, Josephus, and the twenty-two times it appears in the New Testament.[3]

In the Septuagint, the ancient Greek translation of the Hebrew Bible, '*synedrion*' appears several times, referring to an otherwise undefined 'assembly', both in a literal and a metaphorical sense.[4] The two most

---

1. Most of our older Greek manuscripts were written in all capital letters. The later distinction made between sanhedrin and Sanhedrin would thus have been meaningless, at least in terms of palaeography.
2. E.g. Herodotus 8.79.2; 8.75.1; Plato, *Protagoras* 317d; Isocrates, *Oration* 3.19; Xenophon, *History* 2.4.23; cf., Strabo 14.3.3.
3. For fuller discussion, see Lohse, 860-71.
4. Psalms 25.4; Proverbs 11.13; 22.10; 26.26; 27.22; Jeremiah 15.17; 4 Maccabees 17.17 (A).

relevant passages are Proverbs 31.23 and 2 Maccabees 14.5. In Proverbs 31, the husband of the virtuous woman sits in the gate of the city, in a *synedrion* with the elders of the land. In 2 Maccabees, Demetrius, king of Syria, convenes a *synedrion*, a group of trusted advisors, to consult about his ongoing conflict with Jews.

Philo uses '*synedrion*' primarily in a metaphorical sense: referring to the mind or soul engaged in deliberation.[1] One passage, however, speaks a little more directly to our query, for Philo refers to a *synedrion* 'of friends' (*tōn philōn*), hosted by God, whose purpose is to teach the precepts of virtue.[2] This idea of a *synedrion tōn philōn* would have far-reaching implications over time.

Given their proximity to the New Testament in chronological, geographical, and cultural terms, the writings of Josephus are of primary significance for our query. More than any other author, Josephus can help us understand the nuances of '*synedrion*' in the Jewish world. Josephus mentions *synedria* several times, both with and without the definite article.[3] Some of the more important examples will suffice to clarify the range of his usage.

In his *Antiquities*, Josephus uses '*synedrion*' to refer to the seventy-two Jewish scholars who, according to the received story, translated the Hebrew Bible into Greek.[4] Gabinius, when he created his system of governance for Judaea in 57 BC, divided the realm up into five districts. He created one *synedrion* for each district, a scheme of governance that was ill-defined and short-lived.[5] Hyrcanus II convoked a *synedrion* consisting of 'leading Jews' in 46 BC, to try Herod the Great for Hezekiah's murder.[6] This *synedrion*, though it initially lodged a complaint against Herod, ultimately complied with the will of Hyrcanus (and the legate of Syria) by acquitting him. Herod later convened a *synedrion* of unknown constitution to condemn Hyrcanus on evidence of incriminating letters.[7] Augustus, upon his visit to Judaea, convened a *synedrion* to hear complaints against Herod from some Gadarenes;

---

1. *Embassy* 213; *On the Contemplative Life* 27; *Every Good Man is Free* 11; *On Drunkenness* 165; *On the Confusion of Tongues* 86.
2. *On Dreams* 1.193.
3. Analysis of the usage of *synedrion* with and without the definite article, 'the', has not demonstrated a significant difference in terms of the composition and function of the gathering in question.
4. *Antiquities* 12.103ff, based in part on the *Letter of Aristaeus*.
5. *Antiquities* 14.90-91.
6. *Antiquities* 14. 163-84.
7. *Antiquities* 15.173.

Augustus and the *synedrion* acquitted Herod of the charges.[1] When Herod wished to condemn his sons for treason, Augustus urged him to convene a *synedrion* in Berytus, this time consisting of one hundred and fifty regional rulers from multiple cities. Ultimately, this *synedrion* supported Herod's accusation and condemned the accused.[2] In addition, Herod called together a *synedrion tōn philōn*, 'a *synedrion* of friends', to try the wife of his brother, Pheroras.[3] Herod also called a *synedrion* 'of friends and relatives' to deal with accusations against Antipater.[4] Similarly, several years later, Augustus in Rome convened a *synedrion tōn philōn* to hear Jewish accusations against the misrule of Archelaus, son of Herod.[5] Ananus, high priest and son of Annas, in AD 62 convened a *synedrion* which complied with his wish to execute by stoning James, brother of Jesus.[6] Agrippa II called a *synedrion* to deal with the colour of Levites' robes. They wanted to wear white, and the *synedrion* decided to permit them to do so, as Agrippa had wished.[7]

In his autobiographical *Life*, Josephus provides two additional glimpses of *synedria*. The first comes from the outset of the Jewish revolt, in AD 66. The 'first men of Jerusalem' commissioned Josephus to organise Jewish resistance in Galilee. Josephus reported back to this group, which probably included the chief priests, and referred to them as a *synedrion*. The function of this *synedrion* seems to be unique in that it oversaw military and governance issues far from Jerusalem.[8] After establishing his position in Galilee, Josephus himself convened a *synedrion* of friends to deliberate about measures to be taken against John of Gischala, his avowed enemy.[9]

In all these cases, the *synedrion* did not have any consistent membership. *Synedria* could consist of regional rulers, friends, family members, priests, or 'first men'. The only generalisation we can make about *synedria* in Josephus is that they consisted of important persons in the realm as

1. *Antiquities* 15.358. This *synedrion* of Augustus would have consisted of the trusted Roman advisors who had travelled with him, though it is possible that he included some Jewish elites in the mix.
2. *Antiquities* 16.357-61.
3. *Antiquities* 17.46; *Jewish War* 1.571 adds that it was a *synedrion* of 'friends and relatives'.
4. *Antiquities* 17.89-131. *Jewish War* 1.620, 640 adds that this was a *synedrion* of 'friends and relatives' with Herod and Varus, legate of Syria, presiding.
5. *Antiquities* 17.301.
6. *Antiquities* 20.200.
7. *Antiquities* 20.216.
8. *Life* 62.
9. *Life* 368.

judged by the person who convened them. Second, the size of *synedria*, while seldom mentioned explicitly, seems to have varied widely, from small, intimate numbers (at one point, the number seems to be two) to a hundred and fifty regional magistrates. Third, *synedria* in Josephus were called by leaders, whether client kings or high priests, to deal with a particular issue. In each case, the function of the *synedrion* was effectively to deliberate and approve what the person who summoned it wanted in the first place.[10]

A final issue from Josephus remains to be considered. Some have suggested that the number seventy was a norm for Jewish governing institutions. This claim points back to the curious number of seventy-one for the membership of the Great Sanhedrin in the *Mishnah*, which may refer to a normal governing group of seventy plus the high priest who convenes the group. In support of this claim is an appeal to Moses and his appointment of seventy elders in Numbers 11.16-25. Josephus seems to support this claim at a couple of points. For example, the Jews of Batanea sent a delegation of seventy to Varus.[11] Josephus himself appointed a group of seventy in Tiberias who assisted in handling some legal matters.[12] The Zealots, when they took over Jerusalem, appointed a court of seventy.[13] The *Tosefta* seems to confirm this pattern by suggesting that the Jews of Alexandria had a ruling council of seventy.[14] When

---

10. Levine summarises not only the evidence of *synedria* in Josephus, but also what is absent from his pages: '. . . [the *synedrion*] never represents the people vis-à-vis Rome, either in the rebellion of 4 BCE or later on, in the course of the many events that preceded the outbreak of hostilities in 66 CE. Nowhere do we read of the Sanhedrin functioning as an autonomous legislative-judicial body, nor is it ever mentioned in any of the crises concerning the various procurators. Moreover, it appears that the *sanhedrin* was not functioning under Agrippa I, nor in Agrippa II's dispute with the Temple authorities over the wall they built (*Antiquities* 20.216-18) – an issue in which it would have been natural for such a body to have been convened had it existed, at least according to the rabbinic description of its prerogatives' (89). One additional note: Josephus does at times refer to some sort of council, either a *boulē* or a *gerousia* (see discussion in Goodman, 110). The precise meaning and function of these terms in Josephus and the New Testament is beyond the scope of this study, but these terms could refer to separate bodies. It is also possible that at certain times and places, they might have been used as synonyms for *synedrion*.
11. *Jewish War* 2.482; cf. *Life* 56.
12. *Jewish War* 2.570; cf. *Life* 79.
13. *Jewish War* 4.336.
14. *t. Sukkah* 4.6 (198). See Lohse for further discussion (863).

we put these pieces together, should we not assume that the Sanhedrin in Jerusalem consisted of seventy members plus the high priest in the early first century? While this argument seems attractive on the surface, it is both misleading and anachronistic.

The reference to the seventy from Batanea does not suggest that this group formed any sort of ruling or judicial council in that city. Rather, that number was chosen by a Roman, Varus, who summoned seventy leading citizens to appear before him. Josephus specifically says that he appointed his group of seventy from Tiberias not to function as a ruling council in its own right but quite the contrary; he did not trust them and wanted to keep an eye on them. So, he gave them the 'honour' of appointment, and then forced them to travel with him so they would not stir up trouble. The Zealots did set up a court of seventy in Jerusalem, but it was a calculated mockery. They summoned seventy leading citizens to the Temple, then forced them to preside over a show trial to condemn one Zacharias, a man renowned for his integrity. Most telling of all is the reference to the *Tosefta* and its council of seventy in Alexandria. Philo, who was an elite Alexandrian Jew, suggests that their *gerousia*, 'council of elders', included only thirty-eight people.[1] There is no question that seventy was a number used by some Jews at some times for groups of leaders, and it is reasonably probable that this number was popular (as were groups of twelve) precisely because of the Biblical precedent it evoked. The reference in the *Tosefta*, however, seems to be an intriguing anachronism which may give us some idea of the process by which the *Mishnah* developed the idea of seventy-one members for the Great Sanhedrin. Nevertheless, none of these groups of seventy was called a *synedrion*, and none of them provides a counter-balance to the more malleable usage of the term in Josephus. All of this does, however, serve to provide linguistic, cultural, and political context for understanding the constitution and function of *synedria* in the New Testament.

'Synedrion' appears twenty-two times in the New Testament in five different texts by four different authors: Matthew, Mark, Luke-Acts, and John. A brief survey of these appearances of *synedrion*, focusing on the context, participants, and functions of each, will give us a clearer picture. Translations of all twenty-two texts appear in Appendix II.

'Synedrion' appears three times in the Gospel of Matthew: 5.22; 10.17; and 26.59. In 5.22, Jesus says, 'You have heard it said. . . . Do not commit murder, but I say to you that . . . if you insult a brother or sister, you

---

1. *On Flaccus* 74. It is possible that not all elders were persecuted, though Philo does not specify.

will be liable to the *synedrion.*' This particular *synedrion*, if we are to think in literal terms, seems to be a local one and its function suggests the judgment or punishment of the person who is guilty of insulting a brother or sister. This understanding is consistent with our evidence from Josephus. On the other hand, the reference to liability to a *synedrion* for insulting a brother or sister may well be intended in a metaphorical sense. In 10.17, Jesus warns his disciples that they will face persecution; they will be handed over to *synedria* and flogged in synagogues. Note that in this context, *synedrion* appears in the plural, pointing to some sort of local councils. In this context, we receive no information about the participants in these councils, but they seem to have a punitive function. The only reference in Matthew to a *synedrion* in Jerusalem appears in 26.59, and the context is the high priests' inquest about Jesus at the home of Caiaphas. This text is Matthew's redaction of Mark 14.55, though he changes very little, primarily adding the name of the high priest.

Mark uses *synedrion* three times: 13.9; 14.55; 15.1. Two of these are close parallels of Matthew. Mark 13.9 parallels Matthew 10.17, but while Matthew places this prediction of persecution in the context of the discourse to the twelve, Mark places it within the context of his version of the discourse on the Mount of Olives. Thus, in Mark, when Jesus speaks these warnings about future persecution, he is in Jerusalem. Nevertheless, he still uses the plural, which seems to suggest that these *synedria* to which his disciples will be handed over may be local. Mark 14.55 parallels Matthew 26.59 with little variation. Mark and Matthew agree on the participants and function of this particular *synedrion* gathered at the home of the high priest, who goes unnamed in Mark. Joseph of Arimathea may also have been there, if that is what Mark intends by his reference to Joseph as *boloutēs*, 'councillor'.[1] In the same context, Mark mentions *synedrion* again in 15.1. In the early morning, the participants in this *synedrion* made a plan (*symboulion poiēsantes*), which seems to refer to the culmination of their process of determining the specific charge against Jesus they would bring before the prefect. Mark's usage of *synedrion* differs in no material way from that of Matthew; we are left with the same fluid sense of the word with respect to locality, participants, and functions.

While Matthew and Mark mention '*synedrion*' only three times apiece, John includes but a single example. By far the most frequent usage of this term in the New Testament comes from Luke-Acts, a total of fifteen occurrences.

---

1. 15.43.

Luke 22.66 is his redaction of Mark 15.1. While Mark twice mentions *synedrion* in the context of the high priests' inquest, Luke abbreviates the whole event, mentioning only that Jesus, after he was arrested, was taken to the home of the high priest.[1] Then, in the early morning, the *synedrion* gathered, consisting of the same sub-groups we saw in Matthew and Mark: high priest, chief priests, elders, and scribes. The guards 'led [Jesus] to their *synedrion*', which then interrogated him. Luke also calls this group a *presbyterion tou laou*, 'assembly of the elders of the people'. This phrase takes the place of 'elders' in Matthew and Mark. It may be that '*presbyterion*' served as a synonym for '*synedrion*' in popular usage. 'Elders of the people' in both Matthew and Luke, has a functional force; namely, this group consisted of that portion of the people who were elders (social elites) and who, as such, exercised some leadership over their social inferiors. Luke, following Mark with some additions, seems to suggest that Joseph of Arimathea was also part of this gathering, though a dissenting participant.[2]

The appearances of *synedria* in Acts are both numerous and instructive. In Acts 4.15, Peter and John have caused a stir in the Temple precinct, so the 'priests, captain of the Temple guard, and the Sadducees' arrested Peter and John and threw them into prison. The next day, the 'rulers, elders, and scribes', together with the family of Annas, gathered together, with Annas presiding. This group, called *synedrion*, questioned Peter and John and then counselled together about what they should do to stop these followers of Jesus from spreading their message. After commanding them to stop teaching in the name of Jesus, the *synedrion* released them. The parallels between this scenario and the arrest and inquest of Jesus are significant. In response to a disturbance in the Temple precinct, the high priestly family has the perpetrators arrested, the high priest gathers a similar group of people as a *synedrion*, and they engage in a sort of inquest. This time, however, it was during the day, and not at a private home. The one difference among the participants in this case is the presence of 'rulers' (*archontas*) which may, in context, refer to the high priestly family, or to some other leading individuals who were invited by the high priest. This passage is important in many ways. This gathering of what appears to be a similar *synedrion* to that which participated in the high priests' inquest of Jesus does not seem to function as a court. There is nothing resembling charges or a trial here. The purpose of this gathering is to ask a few questions, to deliberate together on how to handle some

1. 22.54.
2. Luke borrows the term *bouloutēs* from Mark: Luke 23.50-1.

men the high priestly family considers trouble-makers, and to provide opportunity for the most powerful and important men in the Jewish world to intimidate some lower-class Jews from Galilee. Note also that this episode provides important confirmation that Annas and family acted with diligence against any disturbances perpetrated by Jesus's followers.

Acts 5.21, 27, 34, 41: These four occurrences of '*synedrion*' appear in a single narrative context. Some unnamed apostles, ignoring the warning of chapter four, were arrested and brought before a *synedrion*. Who was there? In this case, there is specific reference to the high priest, 'those who were with him', 'all the elders of the sons of Israel', and the famed Pharisee, Gamliel. Presumably, 'those who were with' the high priest, are the usual family members and the chief priests, though they are not named specifically. 'All the elders of the sons of Israel' is a curious phrase. In context, it seems to be an identifiable sub-group within the larger *synedrion*. The term may well be intended as a synonym for the *presbyterion tou laou* of Luke 22.66. Both '*presbyterion*' and '*gerousian*' suggest a gathering of social elites, and both appear in genitive constructions that, in context, seem to suggest that this group consists of that portion of the sons of Israel who were of high social rank. Their social status seems to imply responsibility to provide leadership over the children of Israel. Many members of this group likely hailed from the extended family of Annas. Gamliel represents the scribes, though of course there may have been other scribes or Pharisees.[1] In this case, Peter was once again among those arrested, and he served as spokesman in his typically brusque fashion. When the high priest again attempted to intimidate him by pointing out the Apostles' violation of the specific command to stop speaking in the name of Jesus, Peter's response, 'we must obey God rather than men', caused a furore. It took the cool logic and unrivalled stature of Gamliel to cause this elite group of high-priestly relatives and allies to see beyond their family interests. He seems to have at least hinted that the Apostles should be released. In the end, however, the house of Annas prevailed. The *synedrion* had the Apostles flogged. Only then were they released, with lasting reminders of the

---

1. *Gerousia*, in broader Greek usage refers to a group of elite elders, such as the *gerousia* that was significant in the governance of Sparta. *Gerousia*, translated into Latin would be *senatus*, 'senate', though we should not read either Spartan or Roman Republican usage into the term in this context. In this context, *gerousia* seems to be synonymous with the references to 'elders' (more commonly, *presbyteroi*) we have encountered in other contexts as part of a *synedrion*. It is possible that a separate group called *gerousia* did exist in first-century Jerusalem, but if it did, we know nothing else about it.

confrontation visible on their backs. In this case, we see evidence of a *synedrion* of a similar membership and function to the one in 4.15, but while there was no formal trial, the deliberation among members of the latter *synedrion* did result in judicial punishment. This gathering of the *synedrion* looks a bit more like the Great Sanhedrin of the *Mishnah* than we have seen anywhere else, but it is still distant from the specific group of seventy-one with its very particular procedures. Everything in this context in Acts can be accounted for by a modest gathering of the family of Annas plus some other like-minded retainers. The one outlier in the deliberations was the only Pharisee explicitly included in any *synedrion* thus far. The lack of earlier references to Pharisees makes sense, given the fact that the house of Annas was inclined toward the Sadducees.

Acts 6.12 and 6:15 deal with the ministry of Stephen, who engaged in debate with some diaspora Jews. They seized him and brought him before a *synedrion*. Who was there? The only person mentioned is the high priest. There is also a mention of Saul at the end of this narrative, but there is no specific reference to his participation in the *synedrion*. In this case, the *synedrion* seems more clearly to have a judicial function: Stephen is brought to them with specific charges against him, and the high priest begins his inquiry by asking Stephen to answer the charges. This meeting of the *synedrion* also seems to be open to the public. Stephen answers the high priest by launching into a long sermon on the history of Israel, concluding with some strong and provocative language that elicited an infuriated response, not only from the high priest and his *synedrion*, but also from the people who heard the sermon. Rather than complete their inquiry and render judgment, the *synedrion* appears to have lost control, and the scene degenerated into a lynch mob who stoned Stephen on the spot, with the approval of Saul.

Acts 22.30; 23.1, 6, 15, 20, 28; 24.20. The context of these six references to *synedrion* is the arrest of Paul in Jerusalem when he was accused of bringing a Gentile into the Temple court of Israel. The year was around 57. A riot ensued, and Paul was taken into custody by the Roman guards. The Roman commander asked the 'chief priests' to convene a *synedrion* to inquire into the matter. Much had changed in the intervening years since our last encounter with a *synedrion*. There was a new high priest who, though his name was Ananus, was not from the house of Annas (who may well have died by that time). Who was there? The high priest, Ananus ben Nedebaeus.[1] He was joined by the

---

1. Ananus was appointed by Herod of Chalcis in 47. He was renowned for his corruption and his favouritism toward Rome at a time when tensions

chief priests, who in all probability, continued to be dominated by the sons of Annas. Later in the context, there is a reference to scribes and elders. This *synedrion* included a substantial group of both Sadducees and Pharisees. When Paul noticed this composition, he sided with the Pharisees, claiming that he stood before them because of his belief in the resurrection of the dead. Predictably, the Pharisees supported him while the Sadducees opposed him. They began to fight among themselves so violently that the Roman guards intervened and took Paul back into custody. Subsequently, the Roman commander transferred Paul to the custody of the procurator, Felix, in Caesarea. In this group of references, the same patterns remain, even under a new high priest. The same constituents appear when the *synedrion* is called, the high priest still presides, the house of Annas probably still has considerable influence, and the *synedrion* still seems to function as a deliberative body inquiring into disruptions in the Temple precinct. There are, however, two differences. In this case, the Pharisees seem to be present in significant numbers, and the respectful but guarded interplay between *synedrion* and Roman guards is something that has not been present in earlier contexts.

'*Synedrion*' appears only once in the Gospel of John (11.47), and the context is unique. Jesus has just resuscitated Lazarus and, as a result, many of 'the Jews' put their faith in him. The 'chief priests and Pharisees' responded by calling a *synedrion*. Who was there? Caiaphas is specifically named as the high priest, and he is joined by the chief priests and some Pharisees. There is no specific mention of scribes or elders. In this case, no person was being questioned; the participants in this *synedrion* were alone to deliberate. The question before them was how they could stop people from believing in Jesus for, they feared, if too many people followed him, the Romans would come and destroy their 'place (the Temple?) and nation'. In response, Caiaphas famously replies, 'It's better for one man to die for the people. . . .' From that point forward, 'they', presumably the *synedrion*, or at least its leaders, considered how they might kill Jesus. In this context, we see a membership of the *synedrion* that most closely resembles that of Acts 22, with Pharisees playing a significant role. Otherwise, Caiaphas presides as high priest and the house of Annas is prominent.

between Jews and Romans were elevated. At one point, he was thrown into chains and hauled off to Rome to face charges before the Emperor Claudius concerning his involvement in a conflict between Jews and Samaritans. Ananus was subsequently cleared and returned to his high priestly duties about five years before Paul was arrested (Josephus, *Antiquities* 20.131-6).

In this case, the function of the *synedrion* is purely deliberative, not presiding over an inquest or a trial: the accused is not there; there are no charges (other than popularity); there are no witnesses; and there is no reference to any sort of defence.

When we gather together all the evidence from the final years of the first century BC and the early decades of the first century AD, a consistent if murky picture emerges that does not easily conform in its particulars with the portrait of the Great Sanhedrin in the *Mishnah*, with its formal judicial and ruling council of seventy-one in Jerusalem that operated by prescribed rules and procedures. Rather, we see evidence of local *synedria* with ill-defined functions, as well as *synedria* that met on occasion in Jerusalem. In Jerusalem, they were convened by rulers or high priests as needed for various ad hoc functions as determined by the needs of the leaders. The participants and size of *synedria* in Jerusalem varied from meeting to meeting, depending on the invitation of the one who convened them, but the high priest, chief priests, scribes and elders are the most common constants.

We should also note that any idea of a large *synedrion* would create logistical problems that would not escape at least some notice in our sources (like the *synedrion* of a hundred and fifty called by Herod). Imagine the implications of trying to gather and deliberate with seventy-one elites in all the circumstances noted above. Imagine, in particular, trying to gather seventy-one elites at the home of the high priestly family in the middle of the night (our earliest evidence claims that the 'whole' *synedrion* was there). Imagine trying to get such a group to come to unified decisions and getting them to keep confidence on delicate matters. I have attended enough faculty meetings to get a chuckle out of imagining such things. It is just possible to imagine such large and cumbersome gatherings but there is nothing in the early evidence that compels us to do so and the logistical problems would be significant. To be clear, it is possible to read at least some of these gatherings through the lens of the *Mishnah* without doing injustice to the evidence. It is possible that at least some of these gatherings consisted of seventy-one members, but we need to bring the late evidence from the *Mishnah* to bear on the first-century evidence to cause us even to consider such interpretations. Such a methodology always creates the danger of anachronism or eisegesis. It is possible that at least some of the particular attributes of the Great Sanhedrin of the *Mishnah* were present in the first century. The earlier evidence alone, however, suggests a much more fluid situation. It is possible that the *synedrion* that participated in the high priests' inquest consisted of seventy-one members, but I suspect

Annas would be discomfited by such a prospect, for his objective was to exercise control over his domain. For him and the family dynamics that were his chief concerns, the smaller the *synedrion*, the better. Based on the earliest evidence, over the course of more than a century, it is also possible, perhaps even probable, that the *synedrion* that met at the home of Annas and Caiaphas was considerably smaller than the *Mishnah* would lead us to suppose.

In many ways, the structure and function of a *synedrion* in the pages of Josephus and the New Testament resembles the *consilium* of a senator in Rome, which served as a small, relatively informal body, called together on occasion to provide advice to the senator who convened it. It was a mark of honour to be invited to participate in a *consilium*. Indeed, *synedrion* would be a reasonable translation of the Latin *consilium*.[1]

It is important to note that we have not a word in the evidence that 'members' were elected to *synedria*, nor is there any hint that these groups functioned as representatives of the Jewish people.[2] Quite the contrary. In every case, the *synedrion* consisted of elites who virtually always confirmed the will of the elite leader who called it together and presided over it.[3] So far as our evidence is concerned, every *synedrion* in Jerusalem,

1. Goodman, 115.
2. The concept of a political or judicial body representing the will of the people is a modern idea that sometimes creeps, anachronistically, into discussions of antiquity. Even in a system which included elections, such as the Roman Republic, elected magistrates were not expected to represent the people. Rather, they were to lead Rome, and in the process, they represented the interests of their families, their patrons, their classes, and their political factions. There was no theory or even pretence that they were expected to represent the interests of the people. All the more so in the Roman province of Judaea, with its personally appointed prefect, who in turn appointed the high priest, who in turn invited participants in *synedria*. The closest idea in our evidence is the reference to the participation in *synedria* of the 'elders (*presbyterion*) of the people' (Luke 22.66) and 'the group of elders (*gerousian*) of the sons of Israel' (Acts 5.21). Both of these phrases refer to that portion of the people, or the sons of Israel, who held the highest social status. There is also a functional connotation to these phrases, namely that those of high status are expected to provide local leadership appropriate to their rank. As social elites, the interests they represent, and the nature of their leadership has little to do with, and may often have been in conflict with, the broader interests of common Jewish residents in Judaea.
3. There are three possible exceptions: Acts 5, 6-7, and 22-23. The context of Acts 5 suggests that Caiaphas called together a *synedrion* with the objective of punishing the Apostles for disobeying their gag order. 'They' (presumably Caiaphas and the chief priests) seem to have favoured a death penalty (33),

from AD 6 until at least the late 50s, was dominated by the interests of the house of Annas. Thus, the function of such *synedria* as existed in Jerusalem in the first half of the first century was, almost exclusively, to affirm the will of the house of Annas. Participants in these *synedria* could not have been farther removed from the plights and perspectives of the Jewish populace.[1] Because of these considerations, and to avoid confusion, I will continue to employ the simple Greek transliteration, *synedrion*.

If we put these pieces together and read the Gospel accounts again, an unexpected picture begins to emerge which looks very different and much more realistic than the traditional view. We notice that this gathering at the home of the high priestly family, at night, by invitation only, was the 'whole' *synedrion*, an advisory group called by the high priest. It would have consisted largely of the house of Annas. We need to think here of the extended family and the network of alliances that grew within it. Annas had five sons, all of whom would have been married to daughters of other aristocratic families in Jerusalem. His daughters-in-law had brothers and fathers and other relatives who were attached

---

while Gamliel seems to have favoured releasing them. In the end, they compromised on flogging before release. The will of the high priest that they be punished thus prevailed, even if his possible desire for the death penalty did not. The second is Acts 6-7, the hearing or trial of Stephen. In this case, we do not know the will of the high priest initially, for the allegations were brought to him rather than by him. Before the hearing or trial had gotten far, Stephen's sermon caused an uprising and lynching that effectively dismissed the *synedrion*. As a result, we have no way of judging whether or not the *synedrion* supported the high priest. In the case of Acts 22-23, it is unclear what the high priest wanted to happen when he convened this *synedrion*, for the meeting was requested by the Roman commander. Moreover, the high priest quickly lost control of the situation when Paul divided the Pharisees and Sadducees by appealing to the resurrection. This *synedrion* did not reach a final conclusion, but rather degenerated to such an extent that the Roman commander intervened. If the high priest wanted the *synedrion* to support some punishment of Paul, his will was thwarted by factional strife within the *synedrion*. If, however, he was simply launching an inquiry at the request of the Roman commander, the most we can conclude is that the inquiry did not get very far. He may have been frustrated at the behaviour of his *synedrion*, but his will was not thwarted by them.

1. The few specific references to the involvement of Pharisees in *synedria* might suggest the participation of non-elites, since many Pharisees were not necessarily of privileged status. This is possible, but given the consistent theme in the sources that *synedria* in Jerusalem were convened by the high priest, it is more plausible that only Pharisees of elite social standing would receive invitations.

to the house of Annas and honoured by the marriage alliance. Annas also had at least one daughter, though he may well have had others. That daughter married into the elite family of Caiaphas, thus creating another set of allies won at the altar. Further, Annas likely had in-laws and brothers and cousins that he could call upon for such a gathering. All the adult males in this extended family would have been considered elders, and some might also have been scribes. Even this brief glimpse would account for a significant number from whom Annas could have chosen the most loyal.

At a minimum, then, this *synedrion* consisted of nine people: Annas, Caiaphas, the five sons of Annas, and the two former high priests who may still have been alive. All the essential groups are accounted for in this number, so long as at least one of them had the appropriate learning and stature to be designated a scribe. These nine may well constitute a 'whole' *synedrion*. Beyond this minimal number, it is reasonable to imagine the issuing of invitations to a larger group of trusted members of the extended house of Annas, as well as some loyal allies from other important families. Given the fact that many scribes were associated with the Pharisees, it is possible that Caiaphas also invited some trusted elite members of the rival Jewish sect. It is not difficult to imagine such a group of thirty to forty people, consisting largely of family members. It is even possible, though more difficult, to imagine a gathering of seventy-one, if the number designated in the *Mishnah* was in force at this time, with proper allowances for the logistical difficulties of gathering and controlling such a large group. In any case, regardless of the size of the gathering, a significant portion of the group consisted of members of the house of Annas, and all were his loyal supporters.[1] From my perspective, the size of this particular *synedrion* is significant, but the evidence is not conclusive. Given the unique circumstances, the short notice, the meeting at night, and the setting in the private home of Annas and Caiaphas, the most important thing to understand is that the participants

---

1. Two other possible participants should receive their due: Joseph of Arimathea and Nicodemus. According to Mark and Luke, Joseph was '*bouloutēs*', 'a participant in a council'. It is unclear in Mark whether the 'council' refers to the *synedrion*, but Luke makes the equation specific, by suggesting that Joseph 'had not agreed to their plan or action' (Mark 15.43; Luke 23.51). If Luke is correct, Joseph seems to have been a lone dissenting voice at the high priestly inquest, if he spoke at all. According to John, Nicodemus was both a Pharisee and an 'archōn', a 'ruler' of the Jews (3.1). It is possible, though less probable, that Nicodemus also participated in the *synedrion* at the high priests' inquest.

in this *synedrion* were anything but representatives of the Jewish people. Rather, this gathering consisted of wealthy, powerful, well-connected, hand-picked, by-invitation-only elites focused on the interests of the most powerful family in the land.

The High Priests' Inquest

In light of the detailed evidence above, the inquest of Jesus was conducted before a gathering of the extended house of Annas and its elite supporters, hosted by Annas and Caiaphas, to deal with family business. Family business, in their minds, was indistinguishable from the business of protecting the interests of the Temple and the greater interests of Israel itself.

Importantly, whatever the precise size and composition of this *synedrion*, Annas and Caiaphas had every reason to keep it focused and well-controlled, for they needed good advice from their most trusted and like-minded allies. Moreover, as mentioned repeatedly in our sources, they had a healthy fear of Jesus's popular following. The last thing they wanted was to incur popular wrath by calling attention to their proceedings. All their actions, from the hiring of Judas to the arrest of Jesus in a quiet place, to the hosting of the inquest in their own home, point in the same direction. They needed to keep their dealings with Jesus quiet and private. When Annas and Caiaphas, separately or together, presided over this *synedrion*, it appears that they did so in an alcove or a room that opened onto their courtyard where guards, slaves, Peter, and perhaps another unnamed disciple gathered around a fire warming themselves – the fire appears in all accounts.[1]

As for the proceedings themselves, it is difficult to call this a trial. There were no formal charges until the conclusion, and even then they can only be inferred. There was no attempt to determine guilt or innocence. There was no attempt to impose any sort of judicial punishment. On the other hand, there are some references to witnesses. It appears that, rather than a trial, this gathering was what moderns would call an inquest, a hearing whose aim was to determine the nature of the charges the high priestly family could bring to a trial before the prefect. According to our best evidence, Annas and his family had already determined that Jesus was guilty. He had threatened their leadership of the Temple Mount, he had threatened their livelihood, and he had said

---

1. Only John mentions Annas; the synoptics mention only Caiaphas by name (Matthew) or by title (Mark and Luke). Both were probably present.

things that from the high priestly perspective were unforgiveable, not to mention bordering on blasphemous. Moreover, according to Mark, and corroborated by John, they wanted to execute him before they even arrested him.[1] They did not need evidence to determine either the guilt of Jesus or what penalty they sought. They themselves were witnesses of what he had done and said in the Temple precinct.

The issue they hoped to resolve was simple on the surface: how to articulate a charge that would be meaningful to a Roman prefect. They wanted to find a way to get Pilate to handle the execution, for Jesus had too many followers for Annas and Caiaphas to risk offending them.[2] Annas and Caiaphas were savvy political power brokers. They were not foolish enough to consider executing Jesus on their own authority, even if they wished to claim that authority. There has been much debate over whether the high priest and his *synedrion* had the authority to execute criminals at this time. While many of these discussions are interesting and informative, they may be inconclusive and, in this case, immaterial. From the perspective of Annas and Caiaphas, there was a much better way to deal with this issue: let the prefect handle it.[3] That is why they needed to call together their trusted *synedrion* in private. Involving Pilate required careful deliberation. If they and their *synedrion* could determine a way to convince Pilate to execute Jesus, they would protect the status of their family, reassert their control over the Temple precinct, ensure their considerable sources of income, and protect the Jewish people from what they viewed as a dangerous influence. If they could come up with just the right charge, they would be able to deflect any public anger over the execution of a popular teacher and healer away from the house of Annas and onto the Roman authorities. The inquest was therefore not an attempt to press charges and convict but to determine the nature of the charges that they, in turn, could bring to the prefect. For these reasons, this chapter is not titled 'The Trial of Jesus', but instead the 'High Priests' Inquest'. The trial of Jesus will have to wait until the next chapter.

---

1. Mark 11.18; 14.1; cf. John 7.1; 11.53.
2. There is a persistent refrain in the evidence that the chief priests feared the large following of Jesus (Mark 11.18; 12.12; 14.2; Matthew 26.5; Luke 20.19).
3. Luke 20.20 says explicitly that the scribes and chief priests sent spies to question Jesus with the express purpose that they might 'seize on his words' and thus be able to 'hand him over to the governor' – not to condemn and execute him themselves. For discussion, see Sherwin-White, 35ff.

Now to the proceedings themselves. According to John, Jesus was taken first to Annas, and then bound over to Caiaphas, which may simply mean that they moved across the courtyard to Caiaphas's quarters. This reference makes sense if Annas and Caiaphas lived in separate portions of a single home with a central courtyard, such as the palatial mansion, as seems plausible.[1]

According to Mark, followed by Matthew, Caiaphas invited a few witnesses to testify, but the testimony was confused and inconsistent. Finally, one theme emerged: that Jesus threatened to destroy the Temple. That theme had some promise for their objectives, but upon examination, even the high priest had trouble taking forward such a threat from Jesus. After some time, expressing frustration at the silence of Jesus, Caiaphas stood up, taking on the role of chief interrogator, and began to question Jesus directly.[2] The focus of that line of questioning reveals the agenda of this inquest. The final question was thoughtfully engineered, for any response would be advantageous to the house of Annas. 'Are you the Christ [Greek for Messiah], the son of the Blessed One?' This is really two questions and both are loaded. The first seeks to ferret out the political pretentions and ambitions of Jesus, for many hoped for a Messiah who would come and liberate Israel. Any such liberation would come at the expense of Rome (not to mention the house of Annas). A Messiah, a 'king of the Jews', could therefore be viewed as a threat to Roman governance.[3] The second

---

1. In John, there was an initial round of questioning by the 'high priest' focusing on general matters – Jesus's disciples and his teaching. It appears that John applies the title of high priest to Annas, though the phrasing is a bit ambiguous. Caiaphas, however, is unambiguously referred to by that title. It is possible that Caiaphas presided over all of the questioning. On the other hand, it is possible that Annas presided over the initial round of questioning. Whoever presided, the existence of this initial round of questioning must be considered of lower probability since it comes from a single source.

2. Our sources call our attention to the relative silence of Jesus and his apparent unwillingness to defend himself. This language seems to echo the silence of the suffering servant of Isaiah 53.7.

3. Scholars and popularisers often make the claim that there were many messianic pretenders in Judaea at the time of Jesus and, further, that this context may help explain the reason for this question. The claim is misleading. While many Jews imagined the Messiah as a king, they certainly did not consider all Jewish kings Messiahs. Herod was king indeed, but it would take an unusual Jew to suggest that he was the Messiah. Neither does royal pretension a Messiah make. While some diversity of perspective is to be expected of our sources, the Messiah was not just a king, but *the* king, sent

part was designed to test whether that hint of blasphemy the high priest had detected earlier grew out of something more substantial.[1]

According to Mark, Jesus's response was more than Annas and Caiaphas could have hoped for: he admitted to both identifications without qualification. Then he gave them even more, '. . . and "you will see the Son of Man seated at the right hand of the Power," and "coming with the clouds of heaven."'[2] This response, conflated from Psalm 110.1 and Daniel 7.13, made several claims at once. The reference to being seated at the right hand of the power, from the perspective of Annas and Caiaphas, was pretentious beyond all measure, especially when one considers that 'of the power' was, in context, a euphemism for 'Yahweh', the sacred, covenant name of God never to be uttered in vain. Jesus's reply reinforced the high priests' suspicion of blasphemy – he was insulting the dignity of God by claiming divine prerogatives for himself. Moreover, the reference to the Son of Man coming with the clouds of heaven was a remarkable claim of enormous eschatological significance, for this Son of Man in the apocalyptic vision of Daniel not only traverses the heavens, but enters the presence of the Almighty from whom he is 'given dominion and glory and kingship, that all peoples, nations, and languages should serve him. His dominion is an everlasting dominion that shall not pass away, and his kingship is one that shall

---

by God. In fact, Josephus never uses the term *christos* ('Messiah') for any Jew in Judaea other than Jesus, and that reference to Jesus was almost certainly a Christian interpolation. From the perspective of our best source for the period, therefore, there were no messianic pretenders to provide such a social and political context. Josephus does mention, however, three would-be kings who gathered modest and short-lived followings just after the death of Herod the Great in 4 BC: Judas son of Ezechias, Simon the slave, and Athrongaeus the shepherd (*Jewish War* 2.55-65). After 4 BC, even would-be kings are absent from the evidence for nearly half a century. Later, in the two decades leading up to the Jewish revolt, Josephus mentions a couple of others, though he may have been reluctant to use this title, given his context and audience. In the second century, some thought Bar Kokhba might be the Messiah (*P. Ta'anit* 4.5). It is possible that, despite the silence of the sources, some of these various pretenders to the Jewish monarchy or their followers may have made messianic claims, but we should be very cautious about generalising from any such conjecture. For detailed discussion of the meaning of 'Messiah', see N.T. Wright, *Jesus and the Victory of God*, 477-539.

1. There are also overtones here of the Jewish conception of Israel, and even Messiah, as the son of God: e.g. Exodus 4.22; Jeremiah 3.19; Wisdom 9.7; 18.13; *Jubilees* 1.24.
2. Mark 14.62; cf. Matthew 26.64, with modest redaction.

never be destroyed.'[1] This text also clarifies a curious habit of speech Jesus commonly employed, referring to himself in the third person as the 'Son of Man'. While it may by itself seem an innocuous reference to his ties with common humanity, when viewed through the lens of this quotation of Daniel it appears striking if not audacious. At the very least, in this context, Jesus suggests that, despite his arrest and the suffering he expects to endure as a result, he also expects his words and actions to be vindicated by God.

One can well understand Caiaphas's response. Jesus had just spoken in his presence words that were shocking. From his perspective, Jesus had, almost casually, admitted that he was guilty of one of the worst offences any Jew can commit: blasphemy.[2] Upon Jesus's words, Caiaphas tore his tunic in outrage, and his loyal *synedrion* likely joined him. In one accord, they 'all judged him to be deserving of death'. Then they handed Jesus over to their guards to sport with him a bit.[3]

Concerning the abuse and mockery of Jesus in association with the high priests' inquest, there are two interesting parallels from ancient sources. The first is evidence of an ancient game which included blindfolding a person who was then struck by others. The blindfolded person was challenged to guess with which hand his assailant had struck

---

1. Daniel 7.14. For further discussion on the vexed question of 'Son of Man', see W. Horbury, 'The Messianic Associations of "Son of Man"' (*Journal of Theological Studies* 36, 1985), 34-55; cf. N.T. Wright, *Jesus and the Victory of God*, 510ff.

2. In rabbinic literature, blasphemy is often associated with vain pronunciation of the sacred name of God. It is possible that, at his inquest, Jesus did pronounce the sacred name, but Mark or his source has substituted the euphemism. Another possibility is evident in Mark 2.5-7, which offers a broader definition which may be reflected in the inquest. In context, some scribes accused Jesus of blasphemy for usurping a divine prerogative by claiming to forgive sins. John 10.33 offers yet another definition: 'you, though only a human being, are making yourself God.' It seems that the words of Jesus at times had a way of provoking the charge of blasphemy, so this charge resurfacing at his inquest should occasion no surprise.

3. In context, 'some' began to spit on him, blindfold him, beat him, and mock him by urging him to prophesy. Who are the 'some'? In grammatical context, the most reasonable referent would be backward to the 'all' of the previous sentence – that is, the *synedrion*, though such behaviour among such elites seems a bit bizarre. On the other hand, it is possible that the 'some' should be construed forward, to refer to the servants or guards who 'received him with slaps', though such a construction is a grammatical stretch. The language of the narrative above reflects this ambiguity.

him.[1] The second concerns another Jesus, son of Ananias, who in the AD 60s predicted the destruction of the Temple in Jerusalem. He was arrested by the Jewish authorities, who gave him 'many bruises' before they handed him over to the Romans for judgment.[2] This later Jesus suffered the abuse from his fellow Jews in silence. These two parallels are at least suggestive. It is not implausible that Jesus of Nazareth suffered some sort of abuse after the inquest.

The job of the high priestly *synedrion* was not yet complete. Jesus may have been worthy of death in their eyes because of his blasphemy, but such a charge would hardly be convincing to a polytheistic Roman prefect. For him, there would always be room for one more god, so blasphemy would not even be meaningful, much less offensive or worthy of punishment. The *synedrion* needed to come up with a more substantial charge from a Roman perspective, one that would convince the prefect to take responsibility for ridding Jerusalem forever of this man who was the source of so much vexation to them.

This is where the genius of Caiaphas's question becomes evident. Jesus's admission that he was the 'Christ, the son of the Blessed One' gave the *synedrion* something to work with, but they needed to consider it carefully.[3] They could try to make a case that Jesus's claim to be Messiah made him guilty of treason (*maiestas*, as the Romans called it), but that charge was one of the most serious in Roman law, reserved for those who represented clear, present and viable threats to the emperor himself. For the most part, charges of *maiestas* were levelled against Roman elites in Rome, people like Sejanus, the praetorian prefect. Tiberius had just recently executed him, along with several of his close associates. Since Sejanus was likely the patron of Pilate, from Annas's perspective it was probably better not to broach the subject of treason. Alternatively, they could charge Jesus with insurrection, but that would be hard to substantiate, for the only time Jesus had showed a violent streak was when he attacked their tables. It took a while, but finally they figured out a way to approach the prefect.

---

1. Pollux, *Onomasticon* 9.113, 123, 129.
2. Josephus, *Jewish War* 6.302.
3. Many historical Jesus scholars doubt that Jesus ever himself made messianic claims, though those doubts may be alleviated to some extent by this evidence. Jesus's affirmative to the question of Caiaphas, and the charge of 'King of the Jews' fits both with the cultural and textual context. The so-called 'Triumphal Entry' that began the week also set a messianic tone with its overt imitation of the messianic prophecy of Zechariah 9 (Mark 11.1-11 and parallels). Reports of this event may have informed the question of Caiaphas, who may also have seen messianic pretentions in Jesus's symbolic action in the Temple.

First thing in the morning, the chief priests, the elders, and the scribes – the whole *synedrion* – settled upon a plan. They decided to charge Jesus with claiming to be 'King of the Jews'. That charge captured the nuances of the case. It made the whole situation personal – personal for the house of Annas and personal for Pilate. If they brought forward a charge that Jesus claimed to be King of the Jews, that claim would call into question Pilate's entire position in Judaea. Such a charge would be personally threatening, portraying the prefect as an illegitimate usurper rather than a legitimate governor, making the whole situation less a matter of law and more a matter of loyalty – and loyalty was something very much on Pilate's mind. His loyalty to the emperor, not to mention his competence, was already suspect. He was in no position to take chances on such matters. Moreover, there was another dimension of loyalty at stake: loyalty of the prefect to the fledgling alliance with the high priestly family.

For Romans, the granting and seeking of personal favours made the empire go round. Annas knew this as well as Pilate. Annas also knew that, when the high priestly family of Jerusalem asks the prefect for a favour, he would do well to take notice. Pilate would have much to lose by failing to grant their request. There was also the matter of tone: the specific charge, 'King of the Jews', carried with it an implicit threat. If the prefect were to release the prisoner, the high priestly family could easily send a letter of complaint to the emperor in Rome, suggesting that Pilate was not a loyal supporter of Tiberius, instead tolerating the presence in the province of a king other than the emperor. Annas knew that any such threat was potent in the eyes of Pilate. He knew that any such complaint would likely result in Pilate losing his prefecture, and quite possibly his life, for Tiberius had become exceedingly suspicious of disloyalty in the aftermath of the execution of Sejanus. Pilate simply could not take any chances, and Annas knew it. The charge that Jesus had called himself the 'King of the Jews' effectively cornered Pilate. In the chess game that was the politics of first-century Judaea, this was a brilliant move. Pilate was in check before ever he woke on the morning of April 3, AD 33.

So it was that the sun rose on 14 Nissan, and Annas, fatigued from his long night of exertion, immersed himself in his *miqveh* (ritual bath) and changed into a new, untorn linen tunic. Over this he fitted his richly embroidered purple *me'il*, the high priestly ceremonial robe, held together by a sash of purple, crimson, and blue embroidered with gold. The robe reached his feet, and featured tassels to which were attached alternating bells and pomegranates. Donning his elaborate turban of fine linen encircled in purple, he ate his kosher breakfast from his stone bowl while reclining on his scarlet cushions. Then he offered up his morning prayers, and prepared for the long day ahead.[1] Not to be outdone, Caiaphas followed suit in every detail. Even from a great distance, the regal figures of Annas and Caiaphas were unmistakable. Nobody would dare question their piety, their sanctity, or their authority. Annas was confident as he gathered his *synedrion* and gave the order that the prisoner, Yeshu ha-Notsri, be bound and marched under guard to the *praetorium* of Pontius Pilatus, prefect of Judaea. He sent a servant ahead to make proper arrangements.

Just a few more hours and Annas would be free to return to his family, having secured their well-earned place at the pinnacle of Jewish society. He would then join them in the celebration of the great feast of God's deliverance of the Jewish people. The double irony was not lost on Annas. The name Yeshua meant 'salvation', and some of his followers believed he would save Israel. Annas considered it a greater service to save Israel from Yeshua.

---

1. This description is based on Exodus 28, with details elaborated by Josephus (*Jewish War* 5.231ff.). My description assumes that Annas continued to wear the robes of the high priest, though only Caiaphas would wear the sacred Ephod, breastplate, and triple-tiered gold crown. According to *Ezekiel* 42.14, 44.19, priests were to remove their sacred vestments when leaving the holy place in the Temple. It is not clear whether or to what extent this practice was in force in the first century. I am assuming that the Ephod, breastplate, and crown, as the most distinctive vestments of the high priests, may have been so reserved, but am allowing Annas and Caiaphas use of their robes for formal occasions when they wanted to dress to impress. It is possible, of course, that they had alternative vestments for public formal occasions.

Evidence from the Gospels about the High Priests' Inquest[1]

Mark 14-15	Matthew 26-7	Luke 22-3	John 18
53 **They took Jesus to the high priest**; and all the chief priests, the elders, and the scribes were assembled.	57 Those who had arrested **Jesus took him to Caiaphas the high priest**, in whose house the scribes and the elders had gathered.	54 Then they seized him and led him away, bringing him into the high priest's house. But Peter was following at a distance.	12 So the soldiers, their officer, and the Jewish police arrested Jesus and bound him.

13 First they took him to Annas, who was the father-in-law of Caiaphas, the high priest that year.

14 Caiaphas was the one who had advised the Jews that it was better to have one person die for the people.

15 Simon Peter and another disciple followed Jesus. Since that disciple was known to the high priest, he went with Jesus into the courtyard of the high priest, |

1. Areas of substantive agreement are in bold. I have excised the narratives of the denials of Peter in the interests of space and clarity since they are not germane to the inquest itself, even though they are integral to the respective Gospel accounts. Accounts of Peter's denials agree in substance, but conflict in some points of detail. Analysis of these issues is beyond the scope of this study, and best handled by biblical scholars.

Mark 14-15	Matthew 26-7	Luke 22-3	John 18
54 Peter had followed him at a distance, right into the courtyard of the high priest; and he was sitting with the guards, warming himself at the fire.	58 But Peter was following him at a distance, as far as the courtyard of the high priest; and going inside, he sat with the guards in order to see how this would end.	55 When they had kindled a fire in the middle of the courtyard and sat down together, Peter sat among them.	16 but Peter was standing outside at the gate. So the other disciple, who was known to the high priest, went out, spoke to the woman who guarded the gate, and brought Peter in.
55 Now the chief priests and the whole council were looking for testimony against Jesus to put him to death; but they found none.	59 Now the chief priests and the whole council were looking for false testimony against Jesus so that they might put him to death,	65 They kept heaping many other insults on him.	17 The woman said to Peter, 'You are not also one of this man's disciples, are you?' He said, 'I am not.'
56 For many gave false testimony against him, and their testimony did not agree.	60 but they found none, though many false witnesses came forward. At last two came forward		18 Now the slaves and the police had made a charcoal fire because it was cold, and they were standing around it and warming themselves. Peter also was standing with them and warming himself.
57 Some stood up and gave false testimony against him, saying,	61 and said, 'This fellow said, "I am able to destroy the temple of God and to build it in three days."'	66 When day came, the assembly of the elders of the people, both chief priests and scribes, gathered together, and they brought him to their council.	
58 'We heard him say, "I will destroy this temple that is made with hands, and in three days I will build another, not made with hands."'			

Mark 14-15	Matthew 26-7	Luke 22-3	John 18
59 But even on this point their testimony did not agree.		67 They said, 'If you are the Messiah, tell us.' He replied, 'If I tell you, you will not believe;	19 Then the high priest questioned Jesus about his disciples and about his teaching.
60 Then the high priest stood up before them and asked Jesus, 'Have you no answer? What is it that they testify against you?'	62 The high priest stood up and said, 'Have you no answer? What is it that they testify against you?'	68 and if I question you, you will not answer.	20 Jesus answered, 'I have spoken openly to the world; I have always taught in synagogues and in the temple, where all the Jews come together. I have said nothing in secret.
61 But he was silent and did not answer. Again the high priest asked him, 'Are you the Messiah, the Son of the Blessed One?'	63 But Jesus was silent. Then the high priest said to him, 'I put you under oath before the living God, tell us if you are the Messiah, the Son of God.'	69 But from now on the Son of Man will be seated at the right hand of the power of God.'	21 Why do you ask me? Ask those who heard what I said to them; they know what I said.'
62 Jesus said, 'I am; and "you will see the Son of Man seated at the right hand of the Power," and "coming with the clouds of heaven."'	64 Jesus said to him, 'You have said so. But I tell you, From now on you will see the Son of Man seated at the right hand of Power and coming on the clouds of heaven.'	70 All of them asked, 'Are you, then, the Son of God?' He said to them, 'You say that I am.'	22 When he had said this, one of the police standing nearby struck Jesus on the face, saying, 'Is that how you answer the high priest?'
63 Then the high priest tore his clothes and said, 'Why do we still need witnesses?	65 Then the high priest tore his clothes and said, 'He has blasphemed! Why do we still need witnesses? You have now heard his blasphemy.	71 Then they said, 'What further testimony do we need? We have heard it ourselves from his own lips!'	23 Jesus answered, 'If I have spoken wrongly, testify to the wrong. But if I have spoken rightly, why do you strike me?'

Mark 14-15	Matthew 26-7	Luke 22-3	John 18
64 You have heard his blasphemy! What is your decision?' All of them condemned him as deserving death. 65 Some began to spit on him, to blindfold him, and to strike him, saying to him, 'Prophesy!' The guards also took him over and beat him.	66 What is your verdict?' They answered, 'He deserves death.' 67 Then they spat in his face and struck him; and some slapped him, 68 saying, 'Prophesy to us, you Messiah! Who is it that struck you?'		24 Then Annas sent him bound to Caiaphas the high priest. 25 Now Simon Peter was standing and warming himself. **28 Then they took Jesus from Caiaphas to Pilate's headquarters. It was early in the morning.**
15.1 As soon as it was morning, the chief priests held a consultation with the elders and scribes and the whole council. They bound Jesus, led him away, and handed him over to Pilate.	27.1 When morning came, all the chief priests and the elders of the people conferred together against Jesus in order to bring about his death. 2 They bound him, led him away, and handed him over to Pilate the governor.	23.1 Then the assembly rose as a body and brought Jesus before Pilate.	
2 Pilate asked him, 'Are you the King of the Jews?' He answered him, 'You say so.'	11 Now Jesus stood before the governor; and the governor asked him, 'Are you the King of the Jews?' Jesus said, 'You say so.'	3 Then Pilate asked him, 'Are you the king of the Jews?' He answered, 'You say so.'	33 Then Pilate entered the headquarters again, summoned Jesus, and asked him, 'Are you the King of the Jews?'

VI

Cognitio Extra Ordinem:[1]
The Trial of the Millennium

From the sumptuous second-story bedroom of his palace in Jerusalem Pontius Pilatus, prefect of Judaea, could look out his eastern window and see the great Temple, its white stone and gilded trim glowing in the first light of dawn. The view was spectacular – another triumph of that great builder, Herod. From his southern window he could survey his lovely courtyard, park-like, with gardens, olive trees and cedars of Lebanon, punctuated by the pinks and lavenders of roses of Sharon, reflecting pools, bronze sculptures, and bubbling fountains, all flanked by porticoes whose columns were expertly crafted out of exotic stone from throughout the empire.[2] The serenity of his vision was only slightly disturbed by the scent of the Hinnom valley, just outside the wall of his courtyard, acrid with smoke and decay, for it had served for long years as Jerusalem's city dump. His room was lighted by two snub-nosed Herodian oil lamps, guttering on their lamp stands protruding from the wall, their light glinting off golden *accoutrements.* Soon he would not need the lamps, as the first rays of the sun stretched their fingers into the palace. He donned his *tunica angusticlava*, a tunic with the thin purple stripes that marked his equestrian rank. Then he would have called in a slave to help him with the oft-challenging task of properly folding around his body his *toga virilis*, the elaborate off-white toga worn only by adult male citizens. It was a cumbersome thing, but Pontius Pilatus wore it with pride. It was strange living in a place where the striped tunic and toga were such rare sights.

---

1. *Cognitio extra ordinem* means 'investigation beyond the [normal legal] order'. Roman trials either worked according to the 'order' which dictated rules of procedure, crimes and associated punishments rooted in precedent as collected by the great legal scholars of the empire, or they were 'beyond the order', which allowed broad latitude in terms of procedures, crimes, and punishments. Provincial trials were most commonly *extra ordinem*.
2. This description is based on recent archaeological excavations and Josephus, *Jewish War* 5.176-181.

As he finished getting dressed and gazed over his gardens, he heard voices in the courtyard. It was early, even by Roman standards, when a slave delivered a message: the high priest requested an urgent audience to consult on a legal matter. He would be joined by his personal entourage. This was odd, but from a Roman perspective what was not odd about the high priestly family? Pilate resisted the temptation to make the priests wait until after his morning meal, for he had learned from hard experience that Annas and Caiaphas were important not just to Jews but to him as well. Late in his career, Pilate had come to understand that nothing in Judaea was as important as his relationship with the house of Annas. That relationship was crucial to his future.

This morning's request for an audience was awkward in another way, for it was not permissible for the high priest to enter the home of a Gentile during or just before a great Jewish festival, for fear of defilement. Any such defilement would render him unfit to carry on some of his most important duties of the year. The high priest thus requested that they meet in an official capacity somewhere that was not within the Roman headquarters (*praetorium*). It also needed to be a secure space, under the control of the prefect, where Pilate could set up his tribunal, his *sella curula*, the ornate chair that represented his office and his authority to render judgment and impose punishment. Pilate knew just the place. The courtyard of his *praetorium* was bordered on the west by the city wall. Part way down was a private gate, small in size and likely seldom used, and then only by those in Pilate's household. Its security was assured by Roman guards. Pilate sent word that he would meet the high priests shortly in the open air courtyard of that private gate, between the inner and outer doors.

Pilate knew that this was likely to be a long day, even a long week, given the fact that the Passover celebration had just begun, but he had no idea it would start this early. Nor did he have any idea that this early audience would sorely test his political acumen.

The Nature of the Evidence for the Trial of Jesus

Much of what we have discussed in previous chapters about the evidence applies here. We need not rehash our discussion of the nature, date, and interrelationships among the Gospels of the New Testament, for their value as evidence does not change appreciably. We still have evidence from all four Gospels, and we still have the material from Matthew and Luke primarily derived from Mark.

We should also recall here the *Testimonium Flavianum* of Josephus:

> About this time there lived Jesus, a wise man, if indeed one
> ought to call him a man. . . . When Pilate, upon hearing
> him accused by men of the highest standing among us, had
> condemned him to be crucified, those who had at first come
> to love him did not abandon their affection for him.[1]

While most scholars believe that this text contains scribal interpolations
by later Christian copyists, the style of most of the text is consistent
with Josephus. For our purposes, there can be little doubt that Josephus
corroborates two things: that accusation against Jesus was brought by
'men of the highest standing among us', and that Pilate presided over
his trial and condemned Jesus to crucifixion.

It is also important to recall the later evidence from Tacitus.[2] He
too corroborates the claim that Jesus was 'executed in Tiberius's reign
by the Procurator of Judaea, Pontius Pilatus'. We should also note that
several other texts of the New Testament corroborate Jesus's encounter
with Pilate.[3]

In sum, for the trial under Pilate, our evidence is even stronger than
the very strong evidence for the high priests' inquest. Our evidence
is early, multiple, includes both strong and weak corroboration, and
provides opportunity for cross-examination. That there was a trial of
Jesus before Pontius Pilate is supported by at least six different sources.
It is the highest probability event of anything under consideration
in this study and one of the most probable events in all of ancient
history.

One more line of evidence is worthy of our attention: the recent excavations of the Herodian palace in Jerusalem and the private gate (called
today the Hidden Gate or the Essene Gate) which has been proposed
as the site of the trial of Jesus.[4] I must admit to having been sceptical of
this identification at first, but since I have examined the evidence as a
whole, I have become convinced that it is probably correct. As is evident
from the photograph, the reconstruction drawings, and the map overleaf,
this gate was a modest construction providing access through the
western city wall from the praetorium in which Pilate resided, allowing

---

1. *Antiquities* 18.63-4. For detailed discussion of sources, see Chapter II.
2. *Annals* 15.44.
3. Acts 3.13; 4.27; 13.28; I Timothy 6.13.
4. First discovered in the 1970s by Magen Broshi. For details, see S. Gibson,
   The Final Days of Jesus: The Archaeological Evidence (New York: Harper
   Collins, 2009), 96 ff.

The 'Hidden' or 'Essene' gate into the praetorium *of Pilate as viewed in 2014
from outside the old-city wall. The stone steps in the foreground represent the outer
staircase, providing approach to the outer door and small courtyard of the gate
complex just above those steps. In the background the three small steps that disappear
into the much later Ottoman wall originally led to the inner door providing access
to the courtyard of Pilate's* praetorium. *The trial would have taken place within
the small courtyard of the gate between the inner and outer doors, once paved with
stones, now the flat area covered with grass.*[1]

passage from the courtyard to the region outside the city near the
northern end of the Hinnom valley. This gate, probably constructed by
Herod, consists of parallel walls approached by an outer staircase, eight
metres wide, flanked by two perpendicular walls, leading to an outer
door. Inside that door was a small courtyard, then an inner staircase,
three metres wide, rising up through the inner wall to an inner door, and
thence into the *praetorium* of the prefect. The whole space of the inner
courtyard of the gate was thirty metres north-south by eleven metres
east-west. Most of the northern area between the inner and outer walls
is, however, taken up by a large natural rock outcropping, so only a small
portion of that space was available for the courtyard. The reconstruction
drawing overleaf shows a couple of steps rising to the north inside the
courtyard to a raised platform built on top of the rock outcropping. If

---

1. Photo by the author.

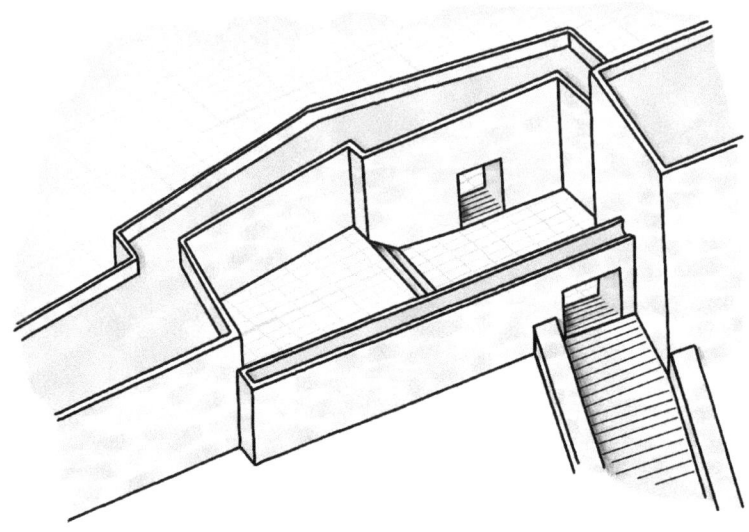

Reconstruction of the gate.[1]

this conceptual reconstruction is correct, it would extend the capacity of
the courtyard. The area of the courtyard, bounded by the inner and outer
gates and the tower to the south and the rock outcropping to the north
is about eight by eleven metres; that is, about the same size as my living
room. Here is where I think it is probable that the 'crowd' gathered for
the trial of Jesus.[2] This courtyard was likely paved with cut stones, and
fits the description of the '*lithostrotos*' or '*gabbatha*' of the Gospel of John.[3]

My reasons for accepting the probability of this identification have
to do with a problem not addressed in the synoptic Gospels, but which
the Gospel of John appropriately raises. It was Passover and therefore
the high priests needed to retain the highest level of purity as they led
the corporate worship of Israel and offered sacrifice at the Temple. The
Gospels agree that Jesus was tried in the *praetorium* of the prefect. The
problem is that the *praetorium* was a Gentile home.[4] How was it possible

1. Drawing by Alice Vinson, by permission, based in part on Gibson, 102.
2. The term usually translated as 'crowd' in the context of Jesus's trial, is *ochlos*
   (e.g. Mark 15.8, 11, 15). This Greek word can refer to gatherings ranging
   from a relatively small group (e.g. Mark 14.43), to a large crowd of thousands
   (e.g. Mark 6.34-45).
3. 19.13. Unfortunately, these paving stones were removed in later centuries.
4. John 18.28.

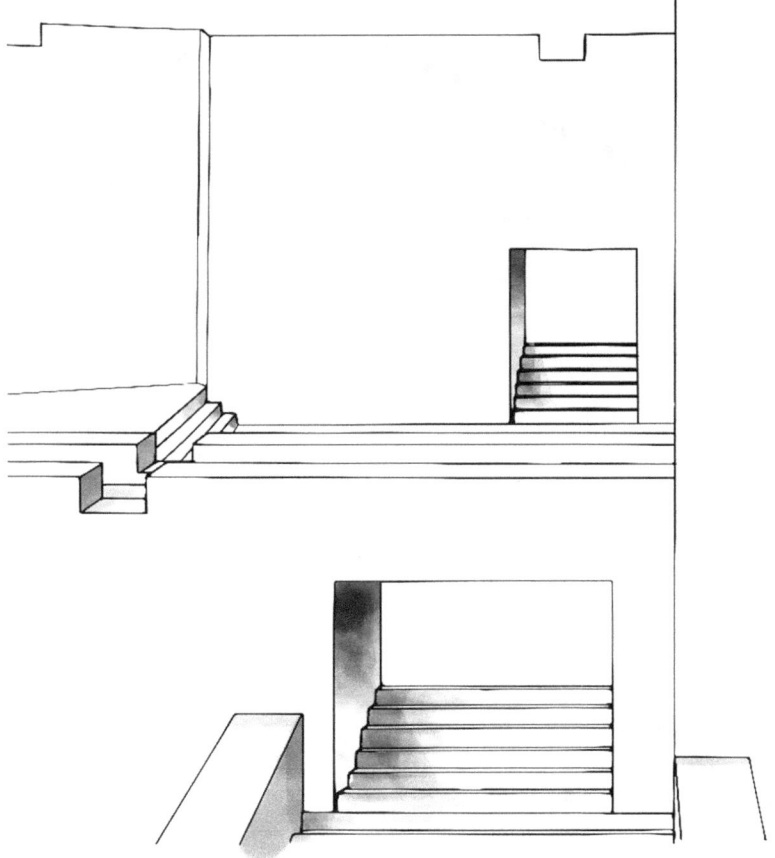

An expanded view of the inner and outer gates.

for Jesus to be tried in the Gentile *praetorium*, and for the high priest and chief priests to be present, and yet for the priests not to run the risk of defilement? The trick was to find a space, controlled by the prefect, attached to and yet not inside the *praetorium*. This modest gate is the only viable candidate thus far discovered, and it helps make sense out of several other pieces of relevant evidence. The Gospel of John is replete with detailed and accurate references to the geography of Jerusalem, and includes important incidental details, including several times when Pilate 'went out' of his *praetorium* and then 'went in' to it during the course of the trial.[5] These references make perfect sense if Jesus was just inside the inner gate, in the *praetorium*, while the high priestly retinue was outside that door in the courtyard of the gate. Pilate would therefore

5. John 18.29, 33, 38; 19.4, 9, 13. See Gibson for detailed discussion.

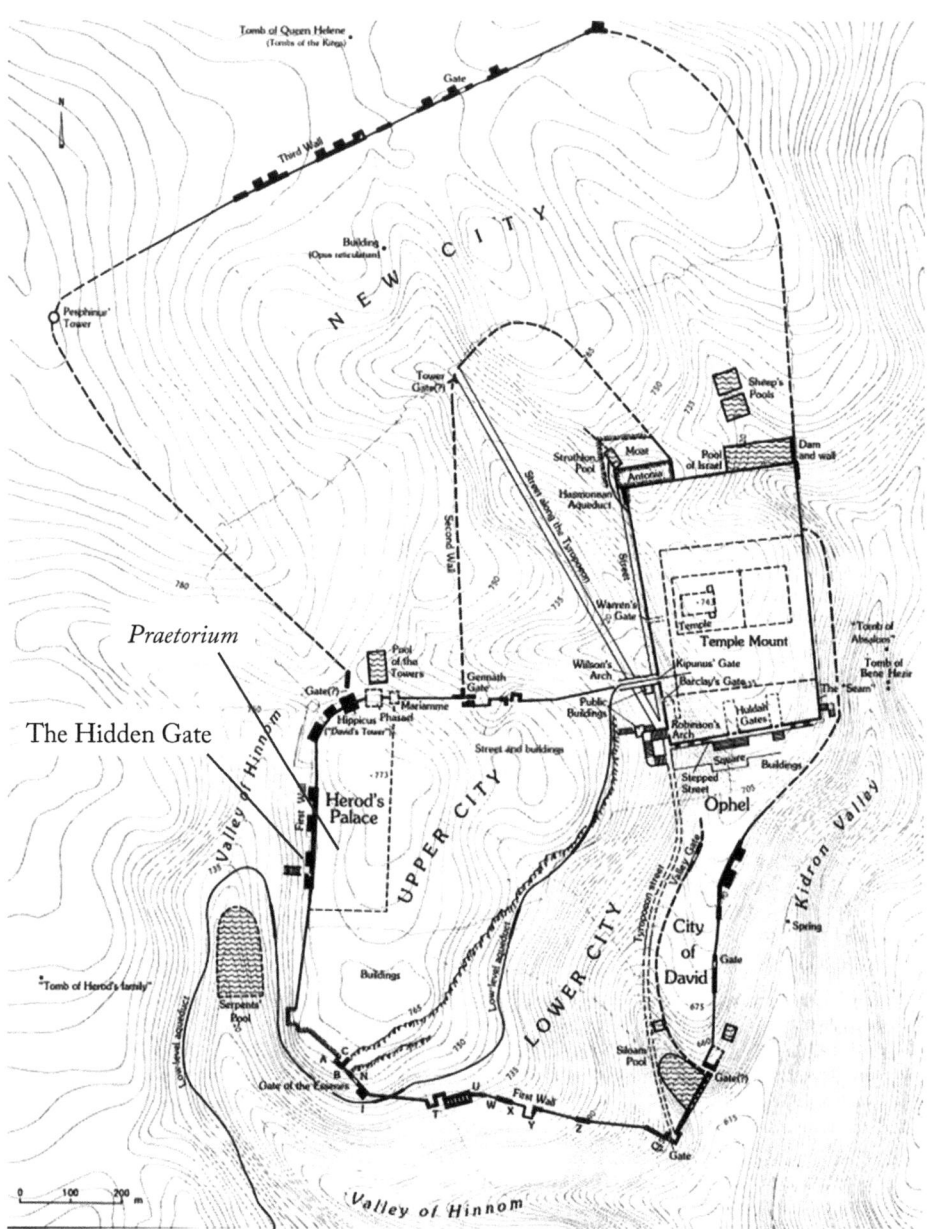

Map of Jerusalem showing the probable locations of the
praetorium *and the 'Hidden Gate'.*[1]

---

1. From *New Encyclopedia of Archaeological Excavations in the Holy Land*, 718.
   Reproduced by permission of the Israel Exploration Society.

Expanded view of the inner gate. Pilate's tribunal would have sat at the top of the stairs, with Jesus in the courtyard of the praetorium just behind him. The high priestly entourage would have stood in the small courtyard of the gate in the foreground, with Pilate presiding above them, and between them and Jesus.[1]

have to go in through the inner door to talk with Jesus and come back out to talk with the priests, and he could have done so in this place while only moving a couple of metres. The size of the courtyard also makes sense of the nature of this trial. It was very early in the morning, and the high priestly family had every reason to want to keep the proceedings private. The Gospels mention several times that the house of Annas feared the large number of followers of Jesus.[2] The last thing Annas (or Pilate) wanted was for some of those followers of Jesus to get wind of legal proceedings involving their leader. Their presence could result in a protest, or an uprising, or disruption during the course of the trial. The early hour, the security provided by the prefect to prevent trespassing into his quarters, and the small size of the courtyard would combine to ensure that only the house of Annas, together with their faithful supporters, their *synedrion*, guards, and hangers-on would be present in the space available. This crowd was modest in size. It could have been as few as twenty to thirty, though if the *synedrion* numbered seventy-one,[3] the crowd may have been a bit larger than that. In any case, space was

1. Expanded drawings are from Alice Vinson, by permission.
2. E.g. Matthew 21.46; Mark 11.18; 11.32; 12.12; Luke 20.19; 21.38.
3. *m. Sanhedrin.*

severely limited. No more would fit, and no more were wanted. This space would accommodate the needs of both the high priestly family and Pilate perfectly.

For all these reasons, it is probable that the specific place of the trial of Jesus has been identified. If this is true, then Pilate would have placed his *sella curula*, his official seat of judgment, at the top of the stairs leading to the inner door, above the group gathered in the courtyard. Jesus would have been held just inside the threshold of the inner door, with Pilate presiding between the accusers and the accused. The inner door would have remained open so that those present in the courtyard could see and perhaps hear the proceedings.

Before we turn to the narratives of the New Testament, there is one additional and fascinating piece of evidence that parallels the trial of Jesus of Nazareth: the trial of another Jesus, son of Ananias (not the Annas of the New Testament). It appears in the pages of Josephus's *Jewish War*. The year was AD 62, twenty-nine years after the trial of the other Jesus. I quote Josephus's account in full, for it is instructive on many levels:

> One Jesus, the son of Ananias, an uncouth peasant, came to the feast at which every Jew is expected to set up a tabernacle for God; as he stood in the Temple courts, he began to cry out: 'A voice from the east, a voice from the west, a voice from the four winds, a voice against Jerusalem and the sanctuary, a voice against the bridegroom and the bride, a voice against the whole people.' Day and night he uttered this cry throughout the city. Some of the leading citizens [of Jerusalem], exasperated at these ominous pronouncements, laid hold of the man and beat him savagely. But he, without uttering a word in his own defence . . . persisted in uttering the same imprecations over and over again. Finally, the Jewish magistrates, concluding that some supernatural impulse was responsible for his behaviour, took him before the Roman procurator. There, although he was flayed to the bone with scourges, he neither begged for mercy nor shed a tear, but rather raised his voice in a mournful cry, answering every stroke with 'Woe, woe to Jerusalem!' When Albinus, the procurator, asked him who he was, whence he came, and why he cried out as he did, he made no reply, but continued to repeat his imprecation over the city, until Albinus released him because he judged him insane.[1]

---

1. 6.300-305.

In Josephus's context, the words of Jesus son of Ananias serve as the capstone to a whole series of portents and apparitions by which God warned his people about the consequences of armed rebellion against Rome. For Josephus, the legal processes involved are incidental. For our purposes, however, it is these legal processes that give us a glimpse of the ways in which Jewish and Roman authorities worked together in response to a perceived threat. It is important to be clear that there is no evidence that Josephus was familiar with the Gospels of the New Testament, nor their accounts of the trial of Jesus of Nazareth. He is not in any form re-shaping Gospel material. In addition, Josephus was an adult priestly aristocrat when Jesus son of Ananias was around, soon to be commissioned as general for the Jewish resistance in Galilee. Josephus may well have met the later Jesus and heard his lament. That is, Josephus may have been an eyewitness to this as so many incidents in the Jewish War. Even if he was not, his evidence is very early and falsifiable, meaning that we have good reason to think that the incidental processes he describes are reasonably authentic.

Given the nature of this evidence, the parallels with the proceedings against the earlier Jesus are striking. Jesus son of Ananias was perceived as threatening the sanctity of the Temple. He was arrested by 'leading citizens', who, given the Temple context and the nature of the Judaean aristocracy of the time, may well have been the chief priests. This group of Jewish leaders had him beaten, while Jesus chose not to defend himself against their accusations. Then, the Jewish leaders handed him over to the Roman governor who held a trial, interviewed him personally, and subjected him to a brutal scourging. All the while Jesus son of Ananias did not contest the charges, but merely recited his woes. While these details are striking, there is one crucial difference between the two Jesus trials: Jesus son of Ananias was released because the governor deemed him mentally unbalanced. Josephus concludes the story: Jesus continued to proclaim his message of woe against Jerusalem for more than seven subsequent years, until Roman armies under Titus besieged the city. In the process they launched massive stones over the walls. One of those stones struck Jesus as he spoke his final words: 'Woe, woe to the city . . . and also to me.' He spoke his final prophecies of destruction just a few weeks before Roman legions fulfilled them.

All our detailed and early evidence for what happened during the trial of Jesus of Nazareth comes from the Gospels of the New Testament, whose accounts are placed in parallel columns at the end of this chapter for ease of analysis. The level of corroboration among these sources is remarkable. What are the areas of agreement?

1. Who was there: Pilate, Jesus, the high priest, chief priests, and their invited supporters.
2. Pilate presided over the trial (also corroborated by Josephus and Tacitus).
3. The chief priests brought the charges against Jesus (corroborated by Josephus).
4. The primary charge: Jesus claimed to be 'King of Jews'.
5. Pilate asked Jesus: 'Are you King of the Jews?'
6. Jesus did not contest the charge.
7. Pilate offered a holiday pardon.
8. The accusers asked for Barabbas to be pardoned, which Pilate granted.
9. Pilate asked the accusers what they wanted him to do with Jesus, and they responded with some energy that he should be crucified.
10. Pilate expressed reluctance to grant their request.
11. The accusers responded with increased passion that they wanted him crucified.
12. Pilate acquiesced to the demand of the accusers.
13. Pilate gave the order that Jesus be crucified (corroborated by Josephus and Tacitus).

Such abundant corroboration at this level of detail is extraordinary in ancient history. Virtually all of Mark, our earliest evidence, is corroborated in some fashion by the other sources. Moreover, there are no overt disagreements among the sources, though there are unique redactions and some additions in Matthew, Luke, and John.

Matthew adds a reference to Judas, the infamous words, 'His blood be on us and our children', and the vivid portrayal of Pilate washing his hands. Matthew's redactions of Mark's text introduce subtle changes to suit his rhetorical purposes; their cumulative effect is to make Pilate appear reticent about his condemnation of Jesus.

Luke's most important change from Mark's account is the addition of a hearing before Herod Antipas, tetrarch of Galilee, who appears to have been in Jerusalem for the festival. It is probable that this addition came from a source other than Mark and thus it may have some historical probability. Because it is nowhere corroborated, however, its probability is considerably lower than the strongly corroborated details above. Luke's pervasive understanding of details of Roman governance does lend some credence when he raises the problematic issue of jurisdiction: Jesus is from Galilee; should he not be tried by the ruler of Galilee,

Herod Antipas, rather than Pilate? Roman law was not consistent about whether a criminal should be tried where the crime was committed or at his place of residence, though in this period, it tended toward the former.[1] If Luke's evidence does point to an historical event, then it would make sense that Pilate would latch onto the issue of jurisdiction in order to extricate himself from his delicate situation. There is nothing inherently improbable about such a manoeuvre, even if the evidence itself lacks corroboration.

The Gospel of John is much longer than the other accounts, with most of the additions consisting of dialogue between Jesus and Pilate. John alone includes the almost certainly authentic detail that the chief priests were concerned about ritual purity and therefore did not wish to enter the *praetorium* proper. John concurs with the details of the mockery of Jesus, his purple robe and crown of thorns, but he moves these forward into the midst of the trial proceedings in a manner that does not fit well with normal Roman practice. Perhaps he did so for dramatic effect, as a parody of the Jewish leaders before him, as if to say, 'Here's a king worthy of you.'[2] Once again, we encounter incidental details in John's account that smack of an eyewitness source, in particular, the references to purity concerns, the space where the principals gathered, and the several goings in and comings out of the *praetorium*. At the same time, the text of John places almost all the extensive dialogue between Jesus and Pilate inside the *praetorium*, so the audience was not well positioned to hear the conversation. Predictably, that dialogue is written in the typical style of John. There is therefore good reason to consider the incidental details probable, even though most scholars retain some scepticism about the words exchanged between Pilate and Jesus.[3]

The overall effect of the differences among the accounts is that Mark emphasises the fulfilment of Jesus's prediction of his suffering in detail, while Matthew's narrative portrays a more reluctant Pilate and a more virulent group of accusers, and Luke's account is more concerned with administrative and legal detail, matters of jurisdiction, and heightening the protestations of Jesus's innocence. John is more interested in the personal encounter between Pilate and Jesus, while

1. For discussion, see Sherwin-White, 28ff.
2. Matthew and Mark place the mockery, the robe and the crown of thorns after the trial, when Jesus was in the custody of the Roman soldiers (Matthew 27.28-30; Mark 15.17-19). The agreement of three of the Gospels on these details is significant, even if the timing is inconsistent.
3. The words of Jesus in John's trial narrative have the effect of exculpating him, and even placing him in authority over Pilate.

supplying those important incidental details. The similarities and differences among these accounts are evidence of the varying biases and agendas of the individual writers, but these differences, because they are not corroborated, represent a lower level of probability and need not occupy our attention. Despite these differences, the evidence, bolstered by multiple levels of corroboration, is remarkably detailed and places our whole reconstruction at a level of probability that is exceedingly rare in ancient history. The following analysis and reconstruction will focus on the strongest areas of corroboration, relying primarily on Mark, our earliest source (though we will at points note additional evidence from other sources where relevant). We are now prepared to consider the trial of Jesus in context.

The Trial of the Millennium

It was early in the morning, and the city of Jerusalem was only beginning to stir. The night before saw the beginning of the great Passover feast and many, sated from the night's festivities, were late to rise. Pilate set up his tribunal at the top of the steps inside the 'Hidden' gate attached to his *praetorium*. This was not a public affair, but a private tribunal, specifically requested by the high priest, Caiaphas. Pilate looked down on the gathered crowd in the small courtyard between the inner and outer gates. It was necessarily a modest group, somewhere between twenty and ninety people, but it was an important one, consisting of Annas and Caiaphas, resplendent in their high priestly attire, the aristocratic elders and chief priests, the sons of Annas and members of his extended family, some scribes, and other loyal retainers. These made up the trusted *synedrion* commonly called together by Annas or Caiaphas when they dealt with matters of import. Beyond that, there were likely a few guards, slaves, and hangers-on who had witnessed the high priests' inquest the night before, perhaps including Peter and another unnamed follower of Jesus.[1] Only these people, on this morning, had any idea that anything interesting was happening at the *praetorium*, and the unusual venue and cramped space made it unlikely that these proceedings would become public knowledge. That was just as the high priestly family wanted it, and Pilate concurred. Because the modest crowd consisted largely of the family of Annas and their closest allies, the dynamics of this trial consisted primarily of a delicate dance between the most powerful Jew in the world and the most powerful Roman in the province. Stuck in the middle was the dishevelled

---

1. John 18.15-16.

prisoner, his hands bound together, his tunic soiled, remnants of blood streaking his face. We have no evidence that Pilate had ever seen this man, but he might well have heard reports of a teacher and healer from Galilee who fancied himself something of a social and moral critic.

Provincial trials were common, and it was important that the prefect act with due regard to Roman law and accepted Roman procedure. Provincial trials usually operated under the rules of *cognitio extra ordinem*, according to which governors had a relatively free hand to inquire into matters of fact and to apply Roman law broadly with specific objectives in mind. Above all, the objective of such a trial was to uphold the *Pax Romana*. In addition, every Roman trial was a display of Roman *dignitas*. It was therefore essential to act with the kind of justice and propriety that made the Roman legal system the envy of the ancient world. Pilate understood all of this, but the purple robes before him made it clear that this was not a normal trial, for the stakes were much higher. Before a word was said, Pilate was on his guard, for he knew that the high priestly family did not lightly undertake such legal action. Before the proceedings even began, Pilate understood that there was more than one person on trial here; Pilate was also on trial, for his alliance with the high priestly family would stand or fall based upon how he handled this situation and with it his career. He was vulnerable on multiple fronts and he had little in the way of political capital. One word to Rome from the high priestly family, and Pilate would be removed from office. Pilate might have sat on the judge's tribunal, but he knew that the real judge in this case stood before him in colourful vestments. His situation was thick with irony, especially given the prisoner he was to try. Pilate knew, before he asked for the charges to be presented, that it would take extraordinary circumstances for him to deny the request of the house of Annas. In a sense, the verdict in this case was determined from the moment the prisoner stepped into the *praetorium*. Pilate had expected this day to be challenging, but he had not anticipated anything this momentous.

Despite the angst that accompanied his political position, Pilate knew that he needed to adhere to proper legal procedure. He would have begun, as Roman trials should, with the formal *interrogatio* (request for an official statement of charges), which is not mentioned in the synoptics, but is captured in John's words: 'What accusation do you bring against this man?' In response, Annas, probably the spokesman for the chief priests, stated the charges.[1] The details are not consistent in the sources,

---

1. John 18.29. One might expect that the primary voice for the prosecution would be the high priest, Caiaphas. It is therefore instructive that Mark, followed by Matthew and Luke, indicates that the 'chief priests', rather

but they all agree that the principal charge was that Jesus claimed to be 'King of the Jews'. Doubtless, Pilate was immediately alarmed, for he understood the implications. This charge was pregnant with negative possibilities; he needed to proceed with extreme caution.

The next proper step in a Roman *cognitio* was the examination of the accused, seeking clarification on matters of fact, and providing ample opportunity for the accused to answer to the charges. According to Mark, Pilate turned to Jesus and asked him directly, 'Are you the king of the Jews?' Jesus's response was surprising: 'You say that I am.'[1] This answer may seem evasive, as if to say 'your words, not mine', but most important is the fact that Jesus did not deny the charge. He certainly did not protest his innocence, but he also hedged on an admission of guilt. From a Roman perspective, this statement may be similar to the *nolo contendere*, the 'no contest' plea in modern American law which, while not technically an admission of guilt, does not challenge the charge, and therefore has a force similar to a guilty plea. Read in light of the detailed discussion of the Gospel of John, Jesus seems to be saying something like, 'Your words are not mine, but you are onto something important, even if we differ on the meaning of "king."' Regardless of how one treats the discussion in John, all narratives of the trial suggest that both Jesus and Pilate understood Jesus's response as a tacit admission of guilt relative to the charge. At the very least, Jesus never contested the charge and, therefore, from a Roman legal perspective, it was not necessary for Pilate to call witnesses or pursue additional matters of fact.

Jesus's response to Pilate's question could have been the end of it, for the trial began with a request by the high priestly family which Pilate was in no position to resist. The charges were alarming, and the defendant did not contest them, even if with some ambiguity. Pilate had every reason to accede to the request of Annas. This scenario, however, assumes too little of Pilate's political acumen. Not for nothing had Pilate survived for seven years as prefect, despite several missteps. He may not have been very perceptive about Jewish sensibilities, but he did understand the dynamics of patronage. He also understood the stakes. He needed to play this right, or the results could be catastrophic.

---

than the high priest, brought the charges and presided over the ensuing proceedings (Mark 15.3; Matthew 27.12 [who adds 'elders']; Luke 23.3-5). We should think of Annas whenever we read 'chief priests' for, as the elder statesman and patriarch of the high priestly family, he was very probably the leader and spokesman for this powerful group.

1. Mark 15.2.

What followed was a delicate dance, rife with posturing and indirection, designed by Pilate to extricate himself from his vulnerable position. Jesus was guilty; of that Pilate had no doubt, but guilty of what? And what is the appropriate penalty for one who claims to be king of the Jews, who has shown no penchant for revolutionary violence and poses no visible threat to the *Pax Romana?* Just as the prefect had broad latitude in terms of his application of Roman law, he also had broad latitude when it came to exacting penalties. In my judgment, the statements in the sources, hinting that Pilate found Jesus innocent, represent not summary judgment but posturing, as subsequent events demonstrate. That posturing had in part to do with determining the appropriate penalty, but it was much more than that. The delicate dance had two other objectives which, from the perspective of Pilate, were far more important than the fate of the prisoner. First, Pilate needed to assert his position in his fragile alliance with the house of Annas. Second, Pilate needed to anticipate the responses of his Jewish subjects. One false step could be deadly: socially, politically, and perhaps literally.

Pilate still had vivid memories of the Aqueduct Riot. That the house of Annas did not step forward to support him in that situation was a lesson learned; Pilate needed to ensure that such a thing would not happen again. If and when he granted the request of Annas to convict Jesus, Pilate needed to be sure that the high priestly family would stand by him. This objective was crucial for Pilate, for he knew from experience the pressure an angry Jewish mob could put on the prefect and he never wanted to experience again the bared necks at Caesarea or the trampled corpses in Jerusalem. His challenge was that, if he were to release Jesus, Annas would have every reason to turn his base of elite supporters against Pilate. Annas could also send a complaint to Tiberius. This combination would be fatal, at least to his career, if not his life. Pilate well understood the potency of the threat. Whether or not the words were ever spoken, Pilate did not need Annas to explain: 'If you release this man, you are no friend of the emperor. Everyone who claims to be a king sets himself against the emperor.'[1]

On the other hand, if Pilate were to condemn Jesus, Annas would be satisfied, but Jesus had many followers in Jerusalem and it was Passover. It would not take much to ignite that volatile situation, and Pilate would be left to cope with the consequences. Any failure to uphold the *Pax Romana* would also likely end his career. Pilate was damned if he released Jesus and damned if he did not. It would take all his skill to escape impalement on the horns of this dilemma.

---

1. John 19.12.

These considerations help make sense out of what follows in the evidence available to us. The first thing Pilate did was to look for an avenue of escape. It is at this point that Luke alone inserts into his narrative the hearing of Jesus before Herod Antipas, who happened to be in the neighbourhood celebrating the Passover. Because of the singular nature of the evidence, this event is not as probable as other portions of the trial; nevertheless, it would be sensible from Pilate's perspective to make this particular move. If it worked, Pilate could extricate himself from his dilemma on legal, jurisdictional grounds, suggesting that, because Jesus was from Galilee, Antipas should properly judge the case. It was a weak legal argument, for Romans commonly heard cases where crimes were committed rather than arranging for extradition to the place of residence, but the political relationship between the prefect and the Herodian client kings was complex enough that Pilate's legal expertise would not be questioned. In the end, if there were a hearing before Antipas, it did not go as Pilate had hoped, and Jesus was returned to his custody.[1]

When Pilate's first move failed, another possible solution presented itself in the form of the 'Passover Pardon'. Whether the prefect offered this pardon regularly or only on this occasion is immaterial for our reconstruction.[2] The important point for the delicate dance with Annas is that Pilate offered to release Jesus as an act of magnanimity. This expedient would have solved Pilate's problem nicely, for he could theoretically have granted the request of Annas by declaring Jesus guilty, while at the same time preventing any mob action on the part of Jesus's followers by releasing him. So long as Jesus himself did not later create a riot, and Pilate seems not to have feared that eventuality, Pilate would have extricated himself gracefully. Of course, Annas knew exactly what Pilate was trying to do, and he was prepared to make his counter-move. 'The chief priests stirred up the crowd.' This was a modest crowd consisting

---

1. There is historical precedent for Roman governors delegating cases or preliminary investigations to local magistrates, such as *Papyrus Oxyrinchus* II.237. The idea that a Roman governor might invite a Herodian prince to examine a Jewish prisoner may seem a stretch on the surface, until we consider Acts 25.13-26.32 where the governor Festus invited the Herodian prince Agrippa II to examine Paul.

2. There is some evidence for such pardons on occasion in the Roman provinces, but no specific evidence of a regular, annual, Passover pardon in Judaea. Some examples include Livy 5.13.8; Josephus, *Antiquities* 17.204; *P. Florence* 61; Pliny the Younger, *Epistle* 10.31; *m. Pesachim* 8.6; Philo, *On Flaccus* 83.

predominantly of Annas's family, allies, and loyal retainers, so that was not difficult. The stirred up crowd, under Annas's leadership, asked for Barabbas, a convicted murderer, to be released rather than Jesus.[1] The first two moves by Pilate had failed. Annas still had him in check. It could have ended there: Barabbas released and Jesus condemned, but that did not solve Pilate's problem, and he was not out of moves.

Pilate's next step was crucial. He could at this point have decided upon the appropriate penalty for Jesus and been done with the proceedings, but such a move could have threatened his alliance with the family of Annas and left Pilate vulnerable to any mob action by the followers of Jesus. His next move was the most important. Rather than decide upon the penalty himself, which was his right and responsibility, Pilate took the bold and counterintuitive step of asking the crowd of Annas partisans to propose a penalty. Under the leadership of Annas, they shouted, 'crucify him!'

At this point, Pilate may have become a bit concerned, for he seems to have favoured a penalty of scourging. Crucifixion was a relatively harsh penalty for such an anomalous crime, but Pilate was not terribly

---

1. It is important to note that, in Mark, the 'crowd' asks only that Pilate honour the 'Passover pardon'. Pilate offers only to release Jesus. The chief priests first introduce Barabbas into the discussion, as they 'stir up the crowd' to reject the offer of clemency for Jesus. Only in Matthew does Pilate offer the 'crowd' a choice between Jesus and Barabbas. Luke abbreviates the whole account. John confirms this aspect of the account of Mark, which also seems more likely from a Roman perspective. According to Mark, 'Barabbas [literally, 'son of the father'] was in prison with the rebels who had committed murder during the insurrection' (NRSV). The words here translated as 'rebels' and 'insurrection' are *'stasiastōn'* and *'stasei'*, both from the same root, *stasis*, which refers to conflict or discord of any sort. John refers to Barabbas as *'lēstēs'*, a robber or brigand (whether criminal, social, or political) or even, in Josephus, a Zealot. The translation 'insurrection' assumes that the particular kind of conflict Barabbas caused was political in nature, but that is only one possibility. He may have fancied himself something of a freedom fighter, but he may also have been merely a local thug who got himself into conflict (such as a robbery, as described in the parable of the Good Samaritan) and killed someone in the process. It is also possible that the two who were crucified with Jesus were somehow affiliated with Barabbas, but that is mere speculation based on Mark's use of the term *'lēstēs'* to refer to them. If we speculate that there was some sort of insurgency, the fact that Josephus does not mention it suggests that it was of little moment. So far as Josephus is concerned, there were no significant anti-Roman uprisings among Jews between Yehuda of Gamla in AD 6 and well after the death of Jesus (unless one counts the Aqueduct Riot).

reluctant to crucify a potential trouble-maker. If he was concerned, he also knew that his strategy was working for, at long last, he had taken the lead in the delicate dance. Now that Annas had spoken openly before his family and his group of retainers, he had declared himself, and he would need to stand by his word or squander his reputation. Just in case, Pilate engaged in one more round of posturing, suggesting that he saw no cause for capital punishment, thus forcing Annas and his supporters to declare themselves with the utmost clarity.

It is here that Matthew alone inserts those horribly misinterpreted and misapplied words: 'His blood be on us and our children.' If these words were uttered (and this statement is nowhere corroborated), they were uttered by Annas and his family and allies, *not* by the Jewish people.

Whether or not Annas and his followers spoke such words, Pilate had evened the score, and established for himself a formidable position relative to the house of Annas. Now he could grant the favour sought by Annas and, in the best tradition of ancient Roman patronage, make Annas beholden to him. Moreover, the fact that he had deftly forced Annas to declare himself before his strongest allies guaranteed that there would be no repeat of the Aqueduct Riot. If the followers of Jesus were to rise up against Pilate after the crucifixion of their leader, Pilate had every assurance that Annas would stand by him and handle the situation. Moreover, while Pilate won the chess game, he also found a way for Annas to feel satisfied at its conclusion. For all his blundering in his early years, from the perspective of Roman governance this was Pilate's finest hour.

In the event, the followers of Jesus did not disband, and Annas was true to his word. He did support Pilate, and took on with persistence the task of suppressing the fledgling Jesus movement, as aptly chronicled in the pages of Acts and Josephus. A short while after the execution of Jesus, when Peter and John gathered a crowd in the Temple courts to hear them proclaim the 'good announcement' about Jesus, Annas, Caiaphas and their *synedrion* had them arrested and brought in for questioning. They concluded by warning Peter and John to stop their public speaking.[1] A short while thereafter, Peter and the Apostles returned to teaching in the Temple courts and, once again, the high priest had them arrested and brought before his *synedrion* for more questioning, followed by flogging.[2] When Paul was persecuting infant Christian churches, he did so under some sort of authority granted by the 'chief priests'.[3] In 62, Ananus son

---

1. Acts 4.1-23.
2. Acts 5.18-40.
3. Acts 9.14, 21.

of Annas became high priest and the first item on his agenda was the execution by stoning of James, brother of Jesus.[1] When we view the evidence chronologically, it becomes clear that, for nearly thirty years after the trial of Jesus, the house of Annas was vigilant in its commitment to quash the nascent Jesus movement. All of this makes perfect sense in light of the trial of Jesus. Pilate and Annas were true to the terms of their partnership struck in the Hidden Gate on April 3, AD 33.

Scholars have quite often gotten caught up in the most interesting trees that make up this trial, while missing the fact that these trees grew up in a Roman forest. Too often, interpreters have taken literally Pilate's protestations of the innocence of Jesus and his attempts to release him, and thus arguments have centred on the purported whitewashing of Pilate, which is attributed to the theological biases, anti-Jewish tendencies, and political considerations of the Gospel writers. Certainly these writers had theological agendas and biases, and there are certainly delicate relationships in the New Testament between Christians and 'the Jews',[2] but all these discussions fail to deal adequately with the fact that this was a Roman trial. Moreover, the evidence is extremely strong and consistent with other Roman provincial practices and the centrality of alliances between Roman governors and local elites. When we examine in a Roman context the puzzle that is the trial of Jesus, we discover that we have many more puzzle pieces than usual, and they add up to a reasonably clear picture: the proceedings had far less to do with Jesus, and far more to do with Annas and Pilate than most analysts realise.

---

1. Josephus, *Antiquities* 20.197-203.
2. Accusations that New Testament authors were anti-Semitic are anachronistic. There are, however, statements in the New Testament that are critical of some Jews – most of them written by Jews. 'The Jews' as the term appears in the New Testament is a case in point. It is a confusing term, primarily as it appears in the Gospel of John and Acts. A quick look at a concordance will reveal that, at times, the term can be used positively, but often it has negative overtones. Interpretation is further confused when one considers that many Jews, including Jesus and most of the early Christian leaders, are treated positively, even while these Jews occasionally suffer criticism or persecution at the hands of 'the Jews'. In context, when 'the Jews' is used in a negative sense, it refers to a specific small group of Jews that is hostile to Jesus or his followers. Never does 'the Jews' mean in the New Testament what the phrase seems on the surface to mean to some modern readers, namely as a general reference to the Jewish people as a whole. Unfortunately, these nuances have been lost on many readers and, as a result, the negative use of 'the Jews' in the New Testament has been used to bolster Christian anti-Semitism.

As we come to the end of the Trial of the Millennium, and before we proceed to the gory details of Roman capital punishment, we need to address a final question: was Jesus guilty, or was the trial of Jesus a grand miscarriage of justice? My considered answer would be, 'Yes, on both counts.'

Much the same can be said of the trial of the previous millennium, that of Socrates. He was charged with impiety and corrupting the youth. From a legalistic perspective, one could argue that he was guilty, in the sense that some of his youthful followers, according to Plato and Xenophon, went on to do terrible things, and some of the things he said about the traditional gods of Greece challenged the views of many important Athenians. Socrates's ethical philosophy called into question the foundation of the prestige of the elite of Athens and some of their most cherished assumptions. On the other hand, these charges masked a grave miscarriage of justice. Socrates was arguably the greatest moral philosopher in the history of Western civilisation. He spent his life seeking wisdom and justice: these were the realities of his life and his relationships with his fellow Athenians. In the process of seeking these things, he offended powerful people and faced the consequences, suffering execution at the age of seventy – a grave injustice indeed.

Similarly, for Jesus: he was guilty, in a sense, of challenging the status quo. He had a significant number of followers and he did lay claim to inaugurating a kingdom. Moreover, he did, with his actions in the 'cleansing of the Temple', create a potential threat to the peace and stability of the province by challenging the social hierarchy and the power of the high priestly family. Annas, Caiaphas, and Pilate, even if they did not understand the nuances of Jesus's Kingdom of God, did rightly understand that that kingdom undercut the foundation of their lofty positions. When Jesus had the chance, he failed to contest the charge of claiming to be the 'King of the Jews'. On the other hand, from the perspective of who Jesus was and what he stood for – with his grand announcement of the Kingdom of God, his non-violent approach to personal, social, and political transformation, his emphasis on ethics, integrity, and devotion to fulfilling the long-cherished hopes of Israel – this trial was a grave miscarriage of justice indeed. Moreover, the probability that this trial consisted more of posturing and patronage than a quest for justice could itself be considered unjust, even if such proceedings were not unusual from a Roman perspective.

Pilate might have washed his hands that day, but he also gave the order for Jesus to be crucified. Any adequate analysis must do justice to both actions. He chose crucifixion, not because he was sadistic, but because it was the standard form of capital punishment for any serious crimes among non-Roman citizens.[1]

Local legend has it that Mount Pilatus, overlooking Lucerne in Switzerland, was the final resting place of the former prefect. Every Good Friday, the guilt-ridden spirit of Pilate rises over nearby Lake Pilatus and strives vainly to wash his hands of the blood of Christ. It is a story sure to inspire tourism, but from the perspective of history it is upside-down. Pilate did not leave his tribunal that day wracked by guilt. Rather, he likely returned to his sumptuous palace with a sense of satisfaction he had not felt in seven long years. As a Roman, he would not have joined the Jews in celebrating Passover, but he might well have had a celebration of his own, breaking the seal on an amphora of rich Falernian wine and rejoicing with his friends and family over the rebirth of his prefecture. He was blissfully unaware that his actions over the past couple of hours would make him one of the most infamous men in history. Meanwhile, less than a Roman mile away, outside the wall of Jerusalem, the merciless machinery of Roman capital punishment operated with efficiency.

---

1. Many scholars have made the confusing claim that Jesus was crucified because this was the normal Roman punishment for insurrectionists. This claim makes some sense if one only considers the evidence from Josephus and the New Testament. When, however, one examines the broader evidence for the empire as a whole, crucifixion of insurrectionists is only a small part of the history of this form of capital punishment. In the period of the Republic, the victims of crucifixion are largely slaves (some of whom, indeed, were involved in dereliction or rebellion). In the imperial period we have a number of cases of crucifixion, still mostly of slaves and non-citizens who had in some way angered those in power, but outside of Josephus, very few of these cases involved insurrection. Of course, the images of the thousands of Jews crucified by Titus, or the Spartacan slave rebels crucified by Crassus create memorable if distorting images. For further discussion, see my 'Capital Punishment and Burial in the Roman Empire'.

Gospel Accounts of the Trial of Jesus

Areas in bold indicate agreement in all accounts.

Mark 15	Matthew 27	Luke 23	John 18-19
1 As soon as it was morning, the chief priests held a consultation with the elders and scribes and the whole council. **They bound Jesus, led him away, and handed him over to Pilate.**	1 When morning came, all the chief priests and the elders of the people conferred together against Jesus in order to bring about his death. **2 They bound him, led him away, and handed him over to Pilate the governor.**	**1 Then the assembly rose as a body and brought Jesus before Pilate.** 2 They began to accuse him, saying, 'We found this man perverting our nation, forbidding us to pay taxes to the emperor, and saying that he himself is the Messiah, a king.'	**28 Then they took Jesus from Caiaphas to Pilate's headquarters.** It was early in the morning. They themselves did not enter the headquarters, so as to avoid ritual defilement and to be able to eat the Passover. 29 So Pilate went out to them and said, 'What accusation do you bring against this man?' 30 They answered, 'If this man were not a criminal, we would not have handed him over to you.' 31 Pilate said to them, 'Take him yourselves and judge him according to your law.' The Jews replied, 'We are not permitted to put anyone to death.'

Mark 15	Matthew 27	Luke 23	John 18-19
2 Pilate asked him, 'Are you the King of the Jews?' He answered him, 'You say so.' 3 Then the chief priests accused him of many things. 4 Pilate asked him again, 'Have you no answer? See how many charges they bring against you.' 5 But Jesus made no further reply, so that Pilate was amazed.	11 Now Jesus stood before the governor; and the governor asked him, 'Are you the King of the Jews?' Jesus said, 'You say so.' 12 But when he was accused by the chief priests and elders, he did not answer. 13 Then Pilate said to him, 'Do you not hear how many accusations they make against you?' 14 But he gave him no answer, not even to a single charge, so that the governor was greatly amazed.	3 Then Pilate asked him, 'Are you the king of the Jews?' He answered, 'You say so.' 4 Then Pilate said to the chief priests and the crowds, 'I find no basis for an accusation against this man.' 5 But they were insistent and said, 'He stirs up the people by teaching throughout all Judaea, from Galilee where he began even to this place.' 6 When Pilate heard this, he asked whether the man was a Galilean. 7 And when he learned that he was under Herod's jurisdiction, he sent him off to Herod, who was himself in Jerusalem at that time.	32 (This was to fulfil what Jesus had said when he indicated the kind of death he was to die.) 33 Then Pilate entered the headquarters again, summoned Jesus, and asked him, 'Are you the King of the Jews?' 34 Jesus answered, 'Do you ask this on your own, or did others tell you about me?' 35 Pilate replied, 'I am not a Jew, am I? Your own nation and the chief priests have handed you over to me. What have you done?'

Mark 15	Matthew 27	Luke 23	John 18-19
		8 When Herod saw Jesus, he was very glad, for he had been wanting to see him for a long time, because he had heard about him and was hoping to see him perform some sign. 9 He questioned him at some length, but Jesus gave him no answer. 10 The chief priests and the scribes stood by, vehemently accusing him. 11 Even Herod with his soldiers treated him with contempt and mocked him; then he put an elegant robe on him, and sent him back to Pilate. 12 That same day Herod and Pilate became friends with each other; before this they had been enemies.	36 Jesus answered, 'My kingdom is not from this world. If my kingdom were from this world, my followers would be fighting to keep me from being handed over to the Jews. But as it is, my kingdom is not from here.' **37 Pilate asked him, 'So you are a king?' Jesus answered, 'You say that I am a king.** For this I was born, and for this I came into the world, to testify to the truth. Everyone who belongs to the truth listens to my voice.' 38 Pilate asked him, 'What is truth?' After he had said this, he went out to the Jews again and told them, 'I find no case against him.

Mark 15	Matthew 27	Luke 23	John 18-19
6 Now at the festival he used to release a prisoner for them, anyone for whom they asked.	15 Now at the festival the governor was accustomed to release a prisoner for the crowd, anyone whom they wanted.	13 Pilate then called together the chief priests, the leaders, and the people,	39 But you have a custom that I release someone for you at the Passover. Do you want me to release for you the King of the Jews?'
7 Now a man called Barabbas was in prison with the rebels who had committed murder during the insurrection.	16 At that time they had a notorious prisoner, called Jesus Barabbas.	14 and said to them, 'You brought me this man as one who was perverting the people; and here I have examined him in your presence and have not found this man guilty of any of your charges against him.	40 They shouted in reply, 'Not this man, but Barabbas!' Now Barabbas was a bandit.
8 So the crowd came and began to ask Pilate to do for them according to his custom.	17 So after they had gathered, Pilate said to them, 'Whom do you want me to release for you, Jesus Barabbas or Jesus who is called the Messiah?'	15 Neither has Herod, for he sent him back to us. Indeed, he has done nothing to deserve death.	19.1 Then Pilate took Jesus and had him flogged. 2 And the soldiers wove a crown of thorns and put it on his head, and they dressed him in a purple robe.
9 Then he answered them, 'Do you want me to release for you the King of the Jews?'		16 I will therefore have him flogged and release him.'	3 They kept coming up to him, saying, 'Hail, King of the Jews!' and striking him on the face. 4 Pilate went out again and said to them, 'Look, I am bringing him out to you to let you know that I find no case against him.'

Mark 15	Matthew 27	Luke 23	John 18-19
10 For he realised that it was out of jealousy that the chief priests had handed him over.	18 For he realised that it was out of jealousy that they had handed him over.	18 Then they all shouted out together, 'Away with this fellow! Release Barabbas for us!'	5 So Jesus came out, wearing the crown of thorns and the purple robe. Pilate said to them, 'Here is the man!'
11 But the chief priests stirred up the crowd to have him release Barabbas for them instead.

12 Pilate spoke to them again, 'Then what do you wish me to do with the man you call the King of the Jews?' | 19 While he was sitting on the judgment seat, his wife sent word to him, 'Have nothing to do with that innocent man, for today I have suffered a great deal because of a dream about him.'

20 Now the chief priests and the elders persuaded the crowds to ask for Barabbas and to have Jesus killed. | 19 (This was a man who had been put in prison for an insurrection that had taken place in the city, and for murder.)

20 Pilate, wanting to release Jesus, addressed them again;

21 but they kept shouting, 'Crucify, crucify him!' | 6 When the chief priests and the police saw him, they shouted, 'Crucify him! Crucify him!' Pilate said to them, 'Take him yourselves and crucify him; I find no case against him.'

7 The Jews answered him, 'We have a law, and according to that law he ought to die because he has claimed to be the Son of God.'

8 Now when Pilate heard this, he was more afraid than ever.

9 He entered his headquarters again and asked Jesus, 'Where are you from?' But Jesus gave him no answer. |

Mark 15	Matthew 27	Luke 23	John 18-19
			10 Pilate therefore said to him, 'Do you refuse to speak to me? Do you not know that I have power to release you, and power to crucify you?'
			11 Jesus answered him, 'You would have no power over me unless it had been given you from above; therefore the one who handed me over to you is guilty of a greater sin.'
13 They shouted back, 'Crucify him!' 14 Pilate asked them, 'Why, what evil has he done?' But they shouted all the more, 'Crucify him!' 15 So Pilate, wishing to satisfy the crowd, released Barabbas for them; and after flogging Jesus, he handed him over to be crucified.	21 The governor again said to them, 'Which of the two do you want me to release for you?' And they said, 'Barabbas.' 22 Pilate said to them, 'Then what should I do with Jesus who is called the Messiah?' All of them said, 'Let him be crucified!' 23 Then he asked, 'Why, what evil has he done?' But they shouted all the more, 'Let him be crucified!'	22 A third time he said to them, 'Why, what evil has he done? I have found in him no ground for the sentence of death; I will therefore have him flogged and then release him.' 23 But they kept urgently demanding with loud shouts that he should be crucified; and their voices prevailed.	12 From then on Pilate tried to release him, but the Jews cried out, 'If you release this man, you are no friend of the emperor. Everyone who claims to be a king sets himself against the emperor.'

Mark 15	Matthew 27	Luke 23	John 18-19
	24 So when Pilate saw that he could do nothing, but rather that a riot was beginning, he took some water and washed his hands before the crowd, saying, 'I am innocent of this man's blood; see to it yourselves.'	24 So Pilate gave his verdict that their demand should be granted.	13 When Pilate heard these words, he brought Jesus outside and sat on the judge's bench at a place called The Stone Pavement, or in Hebrew Gabbatha.
	25 Then the people as a whole answered, 'His blood be on us and on our children!'	25 He released the man they asked for, the one who had been put in prison for insurrection and murder, and he handed Jesus over as they wished.	14 Now it was the day of Preparation for the Passover; and it was about noon. He said to the Jews, 'Here is your King!'
	26 So he released Barabbas for them; and after flogging Jesus, he handed him over to be crucified.		15 They cried out, 'Away with him! Away with him! Crucify him!' Pilate asked them, 'Shall I crucify your King?' The chief priests answered, 'We have no king but the emperor.'
			16 Then he handed him over to them to be crucified.

VII

Summmum Supplicium:[1]
The Death and Burial of Jesus

It is disconcerting to come to terms with the historical probability that the trial of Jesus had as much to do with the relationship between prefect and priests as it did with Jesus. Immersion in the text of the Gospels causes the reader to view the Roman world through a wide-angle lens set firmly in Jerusalem. In the foreground stands Jesus, with all other actors shrinking into the background. This makes perfect sense given the nature of the evidence, but the view from Rome is precisely the opposite. It is difficult to imagine just how unimportant Jesus was in Roman eyes, even those of the prefect of Judaea. The evidence does not support the numerous imaginative reconstructions of ministers and scholars that suggest Pilate or any Roman authorities were interested in Jesus, or concerned about him, or looking for him, or out to get him. So far as the evidence indicates, Pilate knew little of Jesus before April 3, AD 33. He may have received some reports from Galilee or heard something concerning Jesus's earlier visits to Jerusalem, but that is mere conjecture. If Pilate was a small cog in the machinery of the Roman Empire, Jesus was a tiny Judaean pebble. Only after the trial was over and the penalty exacted did Jesus become the centre of attention, as the Roman machine sought to grind that pebble into dust.

As Annas returned from the trial to his sumptuous home to celebrate the festival with his family, and Pilate returned to his palace to celebrate the restoration of his *dignitas*, Roman soldiers took Jesus to their quarters to create their own form of entertainment. There, the morbid mechanisms of Roman capital punishment began to turn. An understanding of what happened next requires a broader discussion of capital punishment in the Roman Empire.

---

1. *Summum supplicium* means 'supreme penalty', a term Roman authors regularly applied to crucifixion.

Roman Capital Punishment

The primary Roman methods of capital punishment were decapitation, burning alive, condemnation to the arena or wild beasts, casting from the Tarpeian Rock, 'the sack', enforced suicide, and crucifixion, with the last considered the extreme penalty (*summum supplicium*). In the ancient world, punishments were relatively sensational and intended to be exemplary, perhaps to make up for the relative inefficiency of the government's ability to apprehend criminals.[1] For Romans, punishment should not only fit the crime, but the criminal. On the positive side of Roman law, as well as the negative, Romans remained elitist. There were grades of crimes, and grades of punishments, but the relationship between a particular crime and the punishment exacted depended primarily on the social standing of the condemned. The most important distinction was whether or not the person was a Roman citizen, for citizens had special privileges, including that of appeal to the emperor. Moreover, citizens often faced lighter punishments than non-citizens, who had few privileges and were subject to the worst of penalties. A thorough examination of Roman capital punishment requires detailed analysis of hundreds of pieces of textual, epigraphical, and archaeological evidence. I have analysed all of this evidence in an earlier publication, so here I will summarise.[2]

Decapitation was the most merciful way the Romans executed people. If Roman citizens were to be executed, it was almost always by axe or sword. Both beheadings and the fate of the beheaded appear seldom in the sources, but the evidence we possess suggests that their bodies were commonly buried.[3]

Burning alive was not very common and seems largely to have been used in persecutions of early Christians, such as those Nero burned on stakes to illuminate his garden parties. The only evidence we possess indicates that mortal remains of the victims of fire, if there were any, were buried.[4]

---

1. For detailed discussion, see C.J. Fuhrmann, *Policing the Roman Empire: Soldiers, Administration, and Public Order* (Oxford: Oxford University Press, 2012).
2. 'Capital Punishment and Burial in the Roman Empire', in *Bethsaida in Archaeology, History, and Ancient Culture: A Festschrift in Honor of John T. Greene,* ed. J. Harold Ellens (Newcastle: Cambridge Scholars, 2014), 395-436.
3. E.g. Dio Cassius 49.22.6; 30-35 fr. 109.4ff.; Seneca, *On Anger* 2.5.5; Josephus, *Jewish War* 2.242; Eusebius, *Ecclesiastical History*, 2.25.5-8; Mark 6.14-29; Josephus, *Antiquities* 18.119.
4. Tacitus, *Annals* 15.44.4; cf. *Martyrdom of Polycarp*.

Criminals condemned to the arena could, depending on size and skill, end up as gladiators or as soldiers in mock naval battles staged in flooded amphitheatres, but more commonly, they were simply thrown to wild beasts for what little entertainment value they had to offer. We do not know the fate of most of their bodies, except for the few gladiators who received honourable cremation or burial, whose names were celebrated on inscriptions in Roman cemeteries.[1]

The Tarpeian Rock at the edge of the Capitoline Hill was an infamous place of shame from which notorious criminals were thrown down into the Forum Romanum in the heart of Rome. We know of only a few such executions, and we are never told of the fate of those bodies after they hit the rocky ground.[2]

'The sack' was a ritualistic and rare form of execution, usually reserved for parricides. The condemned was tied into a leather sack and thrown into the River Tiber. Animals, such as an ape and an adder, were sometimes added to the sack. By definition, the victims of the sack were not buried.[3]

Enforced suicide seems to have been a favourite form of capital punishment, especially for elite political enemies of such embattled emperors as Tiberius, Caligula, Nero, and Otho. In most cases, we learn nothing of the fate of the bodies, though some were buried.[4]

Crucifixion was the most brutal form of Roman capital punishment. Assyrians, Scythians, Carthaginians, Persians, Greeks, and even Jews had made use of crucifixion for centuries, but most of our evidence comes from Rome. Crucifixion was brutal and, by its nature, the suffering it imposed was both highly visible and long-lasting. Without doubt, crucifixion had significant value as a deterrent, with the result that it became a common topic of discussion, humour, and threats among the lower classes, at least as they are depicted in Roman sources.

---

1. E.g. Apuleius, *Metamorphoses* 10.28, 34; Seneca, *On Anger*, 2.2.4; *Epistle* 7.3-5; Josephus, *Jewish War* 6.418; 7.23-4, 37-8, 40, 96; Pliny, *Epistle* 10.31.2; *Digest* 48.19.29, 31; Seneca, *Epistle* 93.12; Augustan History, *Commodus* 18.3, 5, 19.1, 3; Suetonius, *Claudius* 34.1; *Corpus Inscriptiones Latinae (CIL)* 14.3041 = *ILS* 6252; *CIL* 6.10171; Dio 78 (77).6.2; *CIL* 5.563; http://www.yorkarchaeology.co.uk/headless-romans/index.htm.

2. Tacitus, *Annals* 6.19; Josephus, *Jewish War* 7.154-55; Seneca the Elder, *Controversies* 1.3; Festus 458L; Aurelius Victor, *On Illustrious Men* 24.6; 66.8; Appian, *Civil War* 3.3; Dio 42.29-33.

3. Juvenal, *Satire* 8.213-4. Valerius Maximus 1.1.13; Dionysius of Halicarnasus, *Roman Antiquities* 4.62.4; Orosius 5.16.23; Suetonius, *Claudius* 34.1; Seneca, *On Clemency* 1.23.1; *Theodosian Code* 9.15.1.

4. E.g. Tacitus, *Annals* 15.60ff;16.17ff; Tacitus, *Histories* 1.72; Suetonius, *Nero* 37; Tacitus, *Annals* 16.10-14; Suetonius, *Tiberius* 56; *Caligula* 23.

The Jews of Judaea were well-acquainted with crosses. In the first century BC, their own Hasmonaean king, Alexander Jannaeus, had crucified a significant number of Pharisees who had opposed him.[1] In 4 BC, when the Syrian legate Varus stepped in to quell the uprisings that followed upon the death of Herod the Great, he crucified many Jews in Jerusalem.[2] We know nothing about the frequency with which Romans used this punishment, and our sources do not preserve a great number of occurrences, but we can get some idea from the trial and execution of Jesus. On that day alone, four people had probably received this sentence, though one of them received a pardon. While that one day may be anomalous, it does suggest that Golgotha, the place of execution outside the wall of Jerusalem, was a relatively busy place over time. Romans demonstrated little reluctance to impose crucifixion on non-citizens in the name of keeping the peace.

The Process of Crucifixion

Just as the Roman prefect had a good deal of latitude concerning how to handle trials and what sentences to impose, so too with the implementation of those penalties. The Roman mechanisms involved in the crucifixion of Jesus may seem strange or even perverse from a cultural distance, but the process described in the Gospels fits well with other evidence of Roman executions. Once again, our evidence from the Gospels is very strong. Although the sources demonstrate the kinds of detailed variation any careful investigator would expect given the nature of their interrelationships, the level of agreement is quite significant. All four Gospels agree that the Romans included the following procedures in their execution of Jesus:

1. Mockery
2. The carrying of the cross
3. A placard stating the charge
4. Soldiers dividing up the victims' clothes
5. Two others on crosses
6. The crucifixion proper

Mark, Matthew, and John further agree that Jesus was flogged, though John places the flogging in the midst of the trial. Even though Luke does not include it, flogging seems to have been a common form of Roman punishment. It could be inflicted as a punishment in its own

---

1. Josephus, *Jewish War* 1.97-8; *Antiquities* 13.380.
2. *Jewish War* 2.75; cf. *Antiquities* 17.295

right, and sometimes it could be fatal. It also served as a prelude to other punishments. According to Roman law and common practice, flogging was a standard precursor to crucifixion.[1] Josephus describes this process in action at the hands of Florus, Procurator of Judaea.[2] The instrument Roman soldiers used to flog prisoners was called in Latin *flagrum* or *flagellum*. The *flagrum* consisted of a handle to which were attached multiple leather straps or light chains. Toward the end of those straps, small lead balls with holes in them could be slid over the leather thongs and held in place by knots, like so many slip sinkers on a fishing line. Pieces of bone could similarly be attached.[3] The result was a fearsome weapon that could flay the victim to the bone, as Josephus describes in lurid detail.[4] Anyone who suffered a Roman flogging would be severely traumatised by the experience.

According to our sources, the next step consisted of mockery: the purple robe, the sceptre, and the crown of thorns. In fact, mockery of condemned criminals in antiquity seems to have been common. We see one instance of it at the home of Annas when Jesus was beaten and asked to demonstrate his prophetic ability to identify the assailant.[5] Mockery at the hands of soldiers had a long pedigree. We see evidence among Greeks in their mockery of the Maccabean martyr Eleazar.[6] Plutarch relates the story of some pirates who mocked a prisoner who claimed the rights of a Roman citizen. They responded by dressing him in a faux-toga.[7] Roman soldiers mocked the deposed emperor Vitellius, humiliating him as

---

1. E.g. *Digest* 48.19.8.3; Josephus, *Jewish War* 2.308; 5.449; 7.154, 200, 202, 450; *Antiquities* 12.256; Livy 22.13.9; 28.37.3; 33.36.3; Cicero, *Against Verres* 5.62; Dionysius of Halicarnassus, *Roman Antiquities* 5.51.3; 7.69.1-2; Philo, *On Flaccus* 72, 84. On flogging in general: *Jewish War* 2.612; 6.304; *On Flaccus* 75, Ovid, *Metamorphoses* 10.227; Zosimus 5.2.7; *Theodosian Code* 1.9.35.2.

2. *Jewish War* 2.306.

3. For details and drawings, see H. Leclercq, 'Supplice de la flagellation' in *Dictionnaire d'archéologie chrétienne et de liturgie*, Vol. 5 (Paris: Letouzey et Ané, 1923), 1637-44, which claims to have evidence from the excavations in Herculaneum. See also A. Rich, 'Flagellum', in *A Dictionary of Roman and Greek Antiquities* (New York: D. Appleton, 1874), 288-9. He includes a drawing based on an engraving from the handle of a bronze jug discovered at Pompeii.

4. *Jewish War* 6.304.

5. Mark 14.65. See Josephus, *Jewish War* 6.300-305 for a parallel case of the beating of a Jewish prisoner under the auspices of Jewish leaders.

6. 4 Maccabees 6.1-30.

7. *Life of Pompey* 24.7-8.

much as possible before executing him.[1] Philo describes an event during the prefecture of Flaccus, where a group of Alexandrians engaged in the public mockery of a local victim of mental illness who was often the butt of humiliating jokes. In this case, the mockery consisted of giving him a mock crown, a rug for a royal robe, and a stem of papyrus to serve as a sceptre; then they bowed before him and fawned on him as if he were a king. In this case, the victim of mockery was deemed harmless and not executed.[2] There is also evidence that Romans made a game of mockery.[3] While there is little doubt that the Gospel accounts of the mockery of Jesus echo the language of the mockery of the suffering servant of Isaiah 50.6, that does not diminish the historical probability that Jesus was mocked. The mockery of Jesus, while humiliating, fits well in its broader cultural context. The particular use of a crown of thorns, beaten upon by rods, would likely cause substantial blood loss, for the scalp is heavily vascularised and head wounds often bleed profusely. This injury would only exacerbate the trauma already experienced as a result of flogging.[4]

All four Gospels make reference to carrying the cross to the place of execution. John says that Jesus carried it, while the synoptics mention that another man, Simon of Cyrene, carried it. The reference to Simon is anomalous, for it was common for Romans to require the condemned to carry their own crosses. This anomaly has caused some scholars to suggest that Simon may be a fictitious character, created to make a theological point. Mark's incidental references to Simon's sons, Alexander and Rufus, and his 'coming in from the country', however, point in the opposite direction, meaning that it is more likely that John's *omission* of the role of Simon was theologically motivated.[5] Simon's role in Mark,

---

1. Dio 64.21-1.
2. *On Flaccus* 36-39.
3. E.g. Pollux, *Onomasticon* 9.110; Horace, *Odes* 1.14.8. The *Gospel of Peter* intensifies the mocking scene and attributes it to Jews rather than Roman soldiers.
4. Some scholars have suggested that the crown of thorns was modelled on the radiate crowns featured on the busts of emperors that appear on many imperial coins, representing the rays of the sun beaming out from the emperor's head. Such crowns were a symbol sacred to the sun god, Sol Invictus. If this is so, then the thorns would have pointed primarily outward, not inward toward the scalp, and thus would not cause further bleeding. While this theory is plausible, most emperors who issued coins that featured radiate crowns came from a much later period, primarily the later third century.
5. A dominant theme of John's passion narrative is that Jesus lays down his own life; it is not taken from him. He needs no help from Simon or anyone else to fulfil his mission.

both historically and literarily, is intrusive unless there was some specific reason for his involvement. The Roman soldiers would not likely excuse a condemned criminal from carrying his own cross unless they were concerned that the act of carrying the cross might cause the criminal to expire before suffering the full brunt of Roman punishment. If this is true, it is a measure of the toll the earlier flogging and other abuse had taken on Jesus. It may also help explain why he died so quickly. Moreover, the mention of the names of Simon's two sons without any explanation may suggest that Mark assumed that his audience would be familiar with them.

Of course, Jesus carrying the cross and Simon carrying the cross are not mutually exclusive alternatives. In this case, the later tradition embedded in the medieval 'Stations of the Cross' may well be correct. Jesus may have carried it part of the way, collapsed under his weakened state, and Simon was conscripted to carry it the rest of the way. The reality is, however, that none of our sources tells that particular story, so we do not have sufficient evidence to determine who carried the cross along the route of the Via Dolorosa. Despite these differences in detail, the practice of having victims carry their crosses is attested in Roman sources, but it appears that they did not carry the whole cross, which would have been too heavy, but rather just the *patibulum*, the cross bar.[1] This practice was also a matter of convenience; the vertical post could already be planted firmly in the ground before the victim arrived. Once again, the procedure of Jesus's execution fits well with other Roman sources.

A note of explanation is in order concerning the Via Dolorosa. 'Via Dolorosa' refers to the 'way of suffering', which during the Middle Ages became the basis for the spiritual exercise of the Stations of the Cross. One can engage in meditations on the Stations of the Cross anywhere, but the medieval tradition of pilgrimage to the Holy Land demanded identification of the original route Jesus walked on his way to Golgotha. Local guides complied, and for a thousand years or more, Christian pilgrims have walked the crowded streets of Jerusalem, from just inside St Stephen's Gate to the Church of the Holy Sepulchre, meditating at the fourteen Stations of the Cross along the way. The route of this medieval Via Dolorosa is based on two primary identifications: the Fortress Antonia as the *praetorium* of Pilate and the Church of the Holy Sepulchre as the place of both the crucifixion and burial of Jesus. Careful examination by historians and archaeologists over the past couple of centuries has increasingly challenged the former while confirming the

---

1. Plautus, *Carbonaria* 2; *Miles Gloriosus* 2.4.6-7; Plutarch, *Moralia* 554 a-b.

latter. Most scholars now believe that the *praetorium* of Pilate was not at the Fortress Antonia, but at the opposite end of Jerusalem, at the Upper City Herodian palace that served as the residence of prefects and procurators when they came to Jerusalem.

At the other end of the Via Dolorosa, analysis of the Church of the Holy Sepulchre and the nearby city walls suggests that, at the very least, there was an ancient tradition associating that particular rock quarry on which the church was built with the place of Jesus's execution and burial. In addition, there is ample archaeological evidence that this site may corroborate the descriptions in the written evidence as a place outside the city wall where there were new tombs. Both were confusing for a time. Today, the Church of the Holy Sepulchre is well inside the walls of the old city, but excavations have revealed that at the time of Jesus the city wall was just five hundred feet to the south and three hundred and fifty feet to the east of the present church, placing the site outside the walls. During the time of Herod Agrippa, shortly after the death of Jesus (41-44), the walls of Jerusalem were extended to the north and west, thus enclosing the site within their circuit. When, in the early fourth century, the Emperor Constantine commissioned the construction of the Church of the Holy Sepulchre, locals identified the site as the place of Jesus's execution and burial, despite the fact that it did not match the Biblical description, for it was inside the wall at that time and housed a pagan temple. This identification suggests a very old and conservative oral tradition associated with that site, one that pre-dated the relocation of the wall. According to Eusebius of Caesarea, who lived nearby and was the keynote speaker at the dedication of the church, the Emperor Hadrian had intentionally built a temple of Venus on the site. This temple, whose remains Constantine cleared to make way for the new church, may well have served as a long-term marker, helping to preserve local memories over the intervening centuries. Based on this local identification of the site, Constantine constructed the first Church of the Holy Sepulchre, which was finally dedicated in 335.[1]

A second line of inquiry concerns whether this area was a burial ground within the right period. Within the church, archaeologists have discovered several tombs and burial niches (*kokhim* in Hebrew), of the

---

1. There is also later evidence that Helena, the mother of Constantine, in her famed pilgrimage of 326, discovered at the site the 'true cross', though that evidence is problematic because Eusebius, who was bishop of Caesarea at the time, and gave the inaugural address at the dedication of the Church of the Holy Sepulchre, never mentions it. For further discussion, see H.A. Drake, 'Eusebius on the True Cross,' *Journal of Ecclesiastical History* 36 (1985), 1-22.

type that was typical only of Jewish tombs in the first century. Four of them are still visible in a rear alcove of the church, behind the ornate Edicule commemorating the site of Jesus's tomb. These *kokhim* are now referred to as the tombs of Nicodemus and Joseph of Arimathea.[1] These *kokhim* are significant because they are very old, predating modern archaeological analysis of the nature of first-century Jewish rock-cut tombs. This makes it vanishingly unlikely that someone in the Middle Ages cut these *kokhim* into the rock, for they would have known nothing about the dating of this style of tomb. It went out of fashion shortly after the time of Jesus. At least three other tombs from the first century have been found within the area of the church.[2] One additional piece of evidence is worthy of note. Under the elevated chapel dedicated to Stations 10 and 11, commemorating Golgotha, one can see through plexiglass a substantial vertical rock outcropping that was excavated around the edges when the church was constructed. Visualise the removal of the church building, and one can well imagine how this rocky knoll would have stood out as the most visible geological feature in the area.[3]

The most famous alternative is the Garden Tomb (with adjoining Gordon's Calvary, purported to be a potential site of the crucifixion), just outside the modern Damascus gate. This site was first identified in the mid-nineteenth century and has long provided a welcome solace for Christian pilgrims. The site is beautiful, the tomb is impressive, and Gordon's Calvary looks like a stony skull from the right angle, not to mention that the whole site is outside the modern wall of the old city. In contrast to the dank, crowded, and ornate confines of the Church of the Holy Sepulchre, this site, along with the friendly and hospitable people who run it, is refreshing and invigorating. There are so many things to commend this site that one wants it to be authentic but, alas, archaeologists will not be so easily distracted. The tomb is of the wrong type and from the wrong period.

Although we cannot be certain where Jesus was executed and buried, the evidence pointing to the authenticity of the Church of the Holy Sepulchre is quite significant. It was in the right location, with tombs dating from the right time, with a significant rocky knoll as a prominent

---

1. These *kokhim* were once open to the public, but the doors have recently been locked.
2. D. Bahat, 'Does the Holy Sepulchre Church Mark the Burial of Jesus?' *Biblical Archaeology Review*, May/Jun 1986, 26-45.
3. Alternatively, some have suggested that 'Golgotha' refers not to the shape of the topography, but rather to a place of polling, where heads were counted. Such an interpretation may point to a location on the Mount of Olives.

The Church of the Holy Sepulchre. [1]

Ancient kokhim *in the Church of the Holy Sepulchre. These are now called the Tombs of Nicodemus and Joseph of Arimathea.*[2]

1. Photos by permission of www.holylandphotos.org.
2. Photo by author.

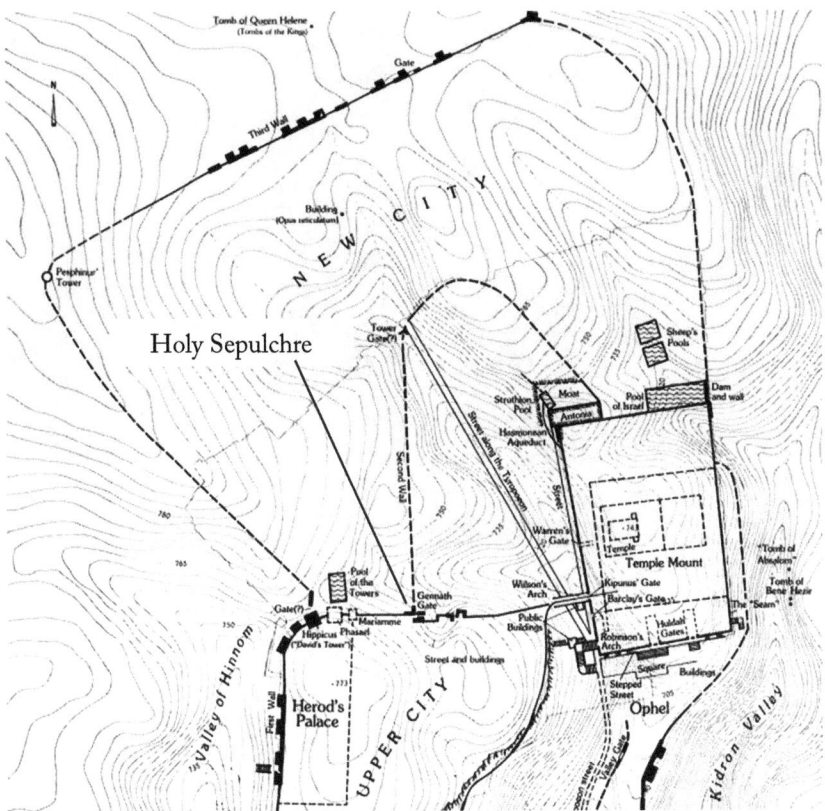

Partial map of Jerusalem spotlighting the location of the Church of the Holy Sepulchre. The 'Second Wall' served as the western city wall at the time of Jesus's execution. The 'Third Wall' was built within a few years afterward, enclosing the site of the Holy Sepulchre inside the wall.[1]

feature, and it is supported by a very early local tradition that enabled the identification of the site for Constantine at a time when the features that commend it were not visible. This evidence points to the reasonable probability that the Church of the Holy Sepulchre is the correct site.[2]

If the Holy Sepulchre is the place of Jesus's execution and burial, and if the *praetorium* was at the Herodian Palace to the southwest rather than the Fortress Antonia to the northeast, then we will need to invent a new route for the historical Via Dolorosa, proceeding in almost the

1. Map from *The New Encyclopedia of Archaeological Excavations in the Holy Land*, p. 718, reproduced by permission of the Israel Exploration Society.
2. The recent suggestion that the family tomb of Jesus has been discovered in East Talpiot has not gained much traction among historians and archaeologists. For discussion, see Gibson, 175ff.

The Edicule commemorating the tomb of Jesus.[1]

opposite direction of the medieval route, along something similar to the small roads that now lead from the modern Citadel, from near the Jaffa gate to the Holy Sepulchre.

Once Jesus arrived at Golgotha, according to all four Gospels, a placard was placed on his cross, stating the charge for which he was being executed: 'King of the Jews.' John explains, in what seems to be an authentic note, that this placard was trilingual, in Hebrew, Latin and Greek. This particular detail fits with the linguistic diversity of Jerusalem. The INRI that is common on Roman Catholic crucifixes is one way to imagine the Latin portion of the placard; it is an abbreviation of *Iesus Nazarenus Rex Iudaeorum*, 'Jesus the Nazarene, King of the Jews'. This placard, which the Romans called a *titulus*, was sometimes hung around the neck of the convicted before being affixed to the cross.[2] Eusebius cites the story of a group of Christians who were persecuted in Lyons in the late second century. One of them was led around the amphitheatre with a placard that said, in Latin, 'This is Attalus, the Christian.' He was ultimately sentenced to 'the beasts'.[3]

All four Gospels agree on another seemingly minor detail: that the soldiers overseeing the crucifixions divided up among themselves the clothes of their victims. According to Roman practice, victims of

1. Photo by permission of www.holylandphotos.org.
2. Suetonius, *Caligula* 32; Dio 54.3.6-7.
3. Eusebius, *Church History* 5.1.44

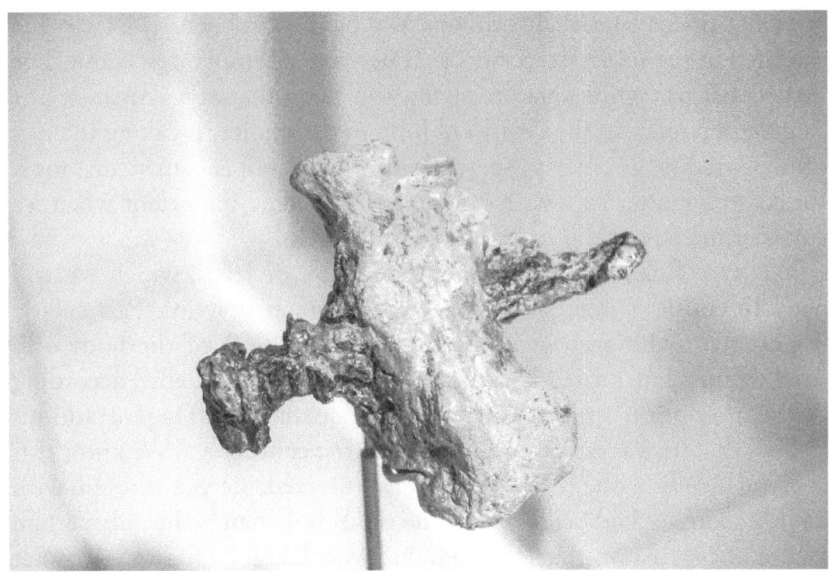

The Crucified Heel of Yehohanan, now in the Israel Museum.[1]

execution often forfeited their property. Then, as now, the victims of capital punishment tended to be poor; it is therefore not surprising that their clothing was all they had that was of any value to the soldiers. Once again, this depiction is consistent with Roman practice.[2] It may be a bit shocking to some readers, but the loincloth that commonly covers the Jesus who appears on crucifixes may be a concession to modest eyes. It is possible that Jesus was crucified naked – yet another component of the humiliation of death on a Roman cross.

Another relatively small detail upon which all our sources agree is that two others were executed at the same time as Jesus. The Gospel writers variously refer to them as 'robbers', 'evil doers', or 'others'.[3] Whatever their crime, they may have been involved with the incident for which Barabbas had been convicted and subsequently pardoned. The presence of these two additional victims suggests that Pilate often employed crucifixion as a punishment. Moreover, these two individuals provide opportunity in the text of the Gospels for dialogue with Jesus, which Luke in particular uses to great effect. Mark seems to emphasise the irony that Jesus, who sought to purify the Temple and referred to

---

1. Photo by permission of www.holylandphotos.org.
2. *Digest* 48.20.1; Tacitus, *Annals* 6.29.
3. Matthew 27.38 and Mark 15.27 (*lēstai*); Luke 23.33 (*kakourgous*); John 19.18 (*allous*).

the chief priests and their minions as a band of robbers, is now being executed in the midst of robbers as if he were a Temple-desecrator. The final detail of significance involving the two others on crosses is the singular reference in the Gospel of John to the soldiers breaking the legs of their victims in order to speed death. This detail is convincing, for it speaks to a matter of Jewish law that will become important when we consider the fate of the crucified corpses.

We have finally arrived at the crucifixion of Jesus, which we will need to consider in light of the larger Roman practice. Particularly important in this respect is the discovery, in 1968, of the body of a first-century Jew buried in a tomb in Jerusalem. His name, according to the inscription on his ossuary, was Yehohanan ben Hagkol, and his fame is that he was crucified in the early first century AD. We know this because his heel bone (calcaneum) was preserved, pierced through with an iron nail that had been bent at the tip. Yehohanan is the only certain victim of crucifixion that has been discovered, and he has caused quite a stir among scholars.[1]

For our purposes, the nail and its placement tells us a good deal about crucifixion around the same time and place as Jesus. First, Yehohanan was nailed to the cross. Victims could be attached to crosses by ropes, nails, or both. In this case, there is no clear evidence that nails were used on the hands or wrists of Yehohanan, but the feet were nailed. The use of ropes would likely prolong the agony of the death, while nails would amplify the pain. The strange fact of the placement of the nail in the heel bone of Yehohanan has caused some scholarly controversy, but there is now some consensus that his heels were nailed into the sides of the vertical wooden beam. The nail had, between its head and the bone, a fragment of wood, which suggests the presence of a wooden plate, serving as a sort of washer to prevent the foot from tearing free under pressure. It appears that the piercing of the heel bone was the work of an unskilled guard who had the ill-fortune of hitting a bone and then a knot when driving the nail into the wood, thus bending the nail and making it difficult to remove it from the bone when taking the body down. Of course, Yehohanan is only one example, but the

---

1. E.g. V. Tsaferis, 'Crucifixion – The Archaeological Evidence', *Biblical Archaeology Review*, Jan/Feb, 1985, 44-53; cf. H. Shanks, 'Scholars' Corner: New Analysis of the Crucified Man', *Biblical Archaeology Review*, Nov/Dec 1985; cf. J.D. Crossan, *Who Killed Jesus? Exposing the Roots of Anti-Semitism in the Gospel Story of the Death of Jesus* (San Francisco: Harper, 1985), 167ff; cf. J. Magness, *Stone and Dung, Oil and Spit: Jewish Daily Life in the Time of Jesus* (Grand Rapids: Eerdmans, 2011), 168-70.

evidence he provides is instructive. While the Gospels of the New Testament do not mention the specifics of how Jesus was affixed to the cross, one can infer from John that he was nailed.[1]

Other configurations have been imagined, both of the cross and of the attachment of the body to the cross. Josephus tells us that, during the siege of Jerusalem in 70, Roman soldiers entertained themselves by experimenting with a variety of configurations.[2] Some have imagined T shaped crosses, X shaped crosses, and other varieties of the traditional Latin cross. Some have imagined arms tied with elbows over cross beams, wrists, or elbows tied at full extension, or nails through palms or wrists, though wrists are more probable on anatomical grounds. Some evidence suggests that the feet of the crucified could be placed on a sort of stand, nailed or tied, sometimes with a single nail penetrating both feet from the top. It is interesting, however, that few if any, before 1968, imagined a configuration such as Yehohanan experienced. Some evidence suggests that, on occasion, a cross might be equipped with a sort of seat, even a pointed one that would prolong and distribute the agony. Some of these reconstructions are speculative. What we can say with certainty, however, is that crucifixion was a horrible way to die. Cicero was doubtless right: crucifixion was the *summum supplicium*, the supreme punishment.[3] It was humiliating, it was brutalising, it was agonising, and it could take a long time for the victim to die.

The trial of Jesus may have been private, but his execution was ruthlessly public. Naked, humiliated, and riven with agony, Jesus was lifted up to public scrutiny and public ridicule. Some of the sources mention the presence of some of his friends and family members, as well as mockers, including the 'chief priests'. All four Gospels mention the presence of Mary Magdalene and other women from Galilee.

For many years, scholars have speculated about the manner in which crucifixion finally causes death. In 1953, Pierre Barbet, a medical doctor, published his famed reconstruction, suggesting that the position of a crucified body would ultimately cause a person to die of suffocation. He made this judgment based upon his extensive knowledge of anatomy, physiology, and kinesiology. That said, he had no experimental evidence supporting his claims – for good reason.

---

1. Thomas, according to John, said: 'Unless I see the mark of the nails in his hands, and put my finger in the mark of the nails and my hand in his side, I will not believe' (20.25; cf. Colossians 2.14).

2. *Jewish War* 5.446-51.

3. For details, see M. Hengel, *Crucifixion* (London: SCM, 1977); Cicero, *Against Verres* 2.5.168.

This absence, however, concerned F.T. Zugibe, a biomedical researcher, who figured out a way to provide experimental evidence, with a little voluntary help from his graduate students. His experiments, while relatively humane, may no longer pass the Institutional Review Boards at most modern institutions of higher learning. We can, nevertheless, appreciate his research while not envying his students. He carefully tied his subjects in various positions on crosses, imitating crucifixion for a short period of time, while hooking them up to medical monitors. The result was a surprising discovery: problems with breathing were rare, happening only when the arms were extended upward behind the victim at a sharp angle. Zugibe therefore posited an alternative explanation: hypovolaemic shock. In layman's terms, the combination of trauma from the scourging, beating, and the crucifixion itself, with blood loss and dehydration, created the optimum conditions for a large-scale shock reaction. Such a massive shock, argues Zugibe, was the probable cause of death.[1]

Whatever the precise cause of death, Jesus seems to have died quickly and in great agony. He seems to have uttered some words while on the cross, but the Gospels do not agree on what they were. Mark, our earliest source, corroborated by Matthew, has Jesus call out in Aramaic (transliterated roughly into Mark's Greek): *Eloi, Eloi, lema sabachtani*; 'My God, my God, why have you forsaken me?' These words, echoing Psalm 22, are a bit shocking coming from the mouth of Jesus. Considering that they are quoted in Aramaic, they preserve a strong ring of authenticity. Luke does not include this cry of abandonment, but rather quotes Jesus as saying the words, 'Father, forgive them for they know not what they do.' This is, of course, wholly consistent with Jesus's teachings, so it may well be authentic. Luke also has Jesus say to one of those crucified with him, 'Today you shall be with me in paradise' and, at the end, 'Father, into your hands, I commend my spirit.' Luke's portrayal of Jesus on the cross is much more serene than that of Mark and Matthew. John portrays Jesus as speaking to his mother and commending her to the 'disciple whom he loved'. John's Jesus also says, 'I am thirsty,' and dies uttering the words, 'It is finished.' Together, these sayings make up the famed 'Seven Last Words of Christ'. They are not mutually exclusive sayings; none is

---

1. Other proposed causes of death include: cardiac failure or rupture, syncope, acidosis, pulmonary embolism, arrhythmia. For a more recent review of the theories, see M.W. Maslen and P.D. Mitchell, 'Medical Theories on the Cause of Death in Crucifixion', *Journal of the Royal Society of Medicine* 99.4 (April 2006), 185-88.

hard to imagine under the circumstances, but the words of Mark and Matthew are the most probable. Some scholars have suggested that the quotation of the first line of Psalm 22 should point to the whole content of that Psalm. If that is true, while that text begins with a note of despair, it concludes on a note of hope in God's love for and deliverance of his people.

Mark's chronology makes good sense, not only concerning the Passover, but also concerning the timing of the crucifixion on Friday, which he places at the 'third hour' (9 AM).[1] He then has Jesus on the cross for about six hours, until the 'ninth hour'. Somewhere around three o'clock in the afternoon, perhaps three hours before sunset, Jesus died.

As sunset approached and the two who were with Jesus breathed their last, it was time for the soldiers to finish their work for the day, taking down and disposing of the bodies. It was awkward, distasteful, and grisly work.

At this point in their narratives, all four Gospels of the New Testament and the Gospel of Peter converge: Jesus was buried. In recent decades, however, some scholars have called into question the historical probability of that burial because, they assert, when the Romans crucified someone, part of the penalty and part of the strength of the deterrent was to forbid burial, leaving the bodies exposed on their crosses as foul carrion for birds and dogs, to serve as a lasting warning for anyone who would dare challenge Roman authority. If Roman standard procedure was to deny burial to victims of crucifixion, then the probability is that Jesus's body was left hanging on the cross for an extended period, and the burial stories in the textual evidence represent mere wishful thinking. These conclusions, however, depend

---

1. 15.25, 35. The references to the time of day in Mark make perfect sense, but there is a discrepancy with John. While Mark has Jesus crucified at the third hour, around 9 am (assuming a common starting-point of 6 am), John has Jesus condemned at the sixth hour (19.14), and therefore crucified somewhat after that. On the other hand, both Mark and John agree that the trial of Jesus began early on Friday morning, and he was buried before sunset. It seems feasible in that case that John begins counting hours at midnight rather than dawn, which would place the conviction of Jesus around 6 am (cf. 1.39; 20.19). John is thus emphasising just how early in the morning this trial was. Ample time therefore remained between conviction and crucifixion. While this is a reasonable solution, is it likely to be accurate? Many scholars argue to the contrary that John's chronology for everything on this day is irreconcilable with Mark's – that John's chronology is theological rather than temporal and any attempt to reconcile the evidence misses the point.

on the viability of the premise that standard procedure among the Romans was to deny burial to the victims of crucifixion. Testing this premise requires a detailed examination of Roman crucifixions in light of Roman law, values, practices, and attitudes toward the dead and the disposal of bodies. As an advisory, I should warn the reader that the next few pages contain material that is both complex and gruesome.

Crucifixion and Burial in the Roman Empire

A detailed, if not exhaustive examination of the evidence for Roman crucifixions reveals both chronological development and circumstantial application. In terms of chronology, in the Republican period, the Romans utilised this punishment almost exclusively for slaves who were engaged in some sort of revolt. The most spectacular of these was the slave revolt led by Spartacus in 73-71 BC.[1] In the Imperial period, the punishment was expanded to apply to freedmen, non-citizens and even, on rare occasions, to citizens. What about the fate of the crucified bodies? The evidence indicates that under some circumstances they were buried or cremated, while under other circumstances they were most likely left exposed for some period of time. The most vivid example of the latter was the case of the six thousand Spartacan rebels who were crucified up and down the Via Appia after the revolt. It is a reasonable inference that these bodies were left exposed on their crosses for at least a few days, for this, of all cases of crucifixion, was meant for display, a warning to any slaves who might dare consider following in Spartacus's footsteps. In a similar manner but for different reasons, some hundred and forty years later, the Roman general Titus crucified hundreds if not thousands of Jews before the walls of Jerusalem in hopes of breaking the spirit of the besieged. These also were probably left exposed for some time, given Josephus's note that they ran out of wood for the crosses. It is important to note that both of these examples occurred in a context of war.[2]

---

1. Evidence of crucifixions in the republican period c. 100-27 BC: Dionysius of Halicarnassus, *Roman Antiquities* 5.51.3; Livy 22.33.2; 33.36.3; Orosius 5.9.4; Florus, *Epitome* 2.7 = 3.19.8; Diodorus Siculus 37.5.3; Valerius Maximus 8.4.2; Appian, *Mithridatic War* 29; Cicero, *Against Verres* 2.5.9-13; *Hispanic War* 20.5; Appian, *Civil War* 1.119-20; Livy 33.36.3; Valerius Maximus 6.3.5; Quintillian 4.2.17; Cicero, *Against Verres* 2.5.165-9.
2. Evidence of crucifixions in the imperial period 27 BC-c. AD 100: Dio 49.12.4; Josephus, *Antiquities* 18.79ff.; Seneca the Elder, *Controversies* 3.9; 7.6; Philo, *On Flaccus* 72ff., 83; Suetonius, *Caligula* 12.2; Dio 60.24.4; Tacitus, *Annals* 15.44; Eusebius, *Ecclesiastical History* 2.1; Josephus, *Jewish War* 2.253;

We do have some evidence of occasional Roman corpse abuse and exposure of bodies, such as the former tribune whose body was affixed to a cross to be publicly displayed during the proscriptions of Sulla, or Octavian's exposure of some of the enemy dead after the Battle of Philippi in 42 BC, or the abuse of the bodies of Sejanus, former Praetorian Prefect, and the former emperor Vitellius, both of whom were subsequently thrown into the Tiber at the hands of tyrannical emperors. It is important to note, however, that evidence for such practices, while memorable, is rare, and in all of these latter cases, the victims were elites. A strong negative tone concerning exposure and corpse abuse pervades the sources, suggesting an attitude that the authors think their Roman audience is likely to share.[1]

Not only is this negative perspective pervasive among Roman sources, but it also shared by Jewish sources, such as Philo and Josephus. Philo devotes one entire work to a description of and commentary on the virulent persecution of Alexandrian Jews in AD 38 under Aulus Avilius Flaccus, the Roman prefect, during which mobs of Alexandrians attacked Jewish businesses, forced Jews into a ghetto, confiscated and destroyed their property, installed idols in their synagogues, and assaulted and murdered them in the streets, leaving their bodies strewn about in public. Philo's primary complaint is that it had long been Alexandrian custom for Roman governors to prevent such things, treating the Jews with respect and deference, even giving them a degree of autonomy under a council of Jewish elders whose local authority was recognised by Rome. From Philo's perspective, not only did Flaccus fail to fulfil his traditional role as keeper of the *Pax Romana* and purveyor of Roman justice, but he exchanged protection for pogrom, exacerbating the persecution by arresting the thirty-eight elders, stripping and beating them in the theatre, and crucifying those who survived the scourge, all during the holiday celebrating the birthday of Augustus. In an exceedingly opaque passage, Philo acknowledged that, while Romans sometimes might expose executed bodies, they had a long custom, especially during holidays, of allowing the families of the executed to claim their bodies for proper burial in accordance with their own customs (in context, this seems to refer to burial before sunset).

2.293-308; 3.321; 5.289; 5.446-51; *Life* 420ff.; John 19.31-2.

1. E.g. Valerius Maximus 9.2.3; Suetonius, *Augustus* 13; Plutarch, *Tiberius Gracchus* 19.6, 20.2; *Gaius Gracchus* 3.3; Appian, *Civil War* 1.16; Plutarch, *Gaius Gracchus* 17.5; Velleius Paterculus 2.6; Dio 58.11.1ff.; Suetonius, *Vitellius* 17.1ff.

Philo expects his audience to be repulsed by Flaccus's violence and violations of Roman mores. Indeed, even so unstable an emperor as Caligula, in the aftermath of this violence, had Flaccus arrested, exiled, and ultimately executed for his misrule. Note that Philo does not say how Flaccus in fact treated the bodies of those Jews crucified in the theatre. Did he leave them up on the crosses for an extended period of time to be eaten by Egyptian vultures? Or did he have them cremated or buried along with other criminals and indigents in unmarked graves, their remains to be mixed with those of Gentiles and unclean animals? Or something else? The text does not inform us, but any of these alternatives would be abhorrent. All of these cases of corpse abuse take place in a context of violence: rebellion, war, or tyrannical cruelty.[1]

Although we do have some evidence of Roman corpse abuse, we also have considerable evidence to the contrary beyond the several examples already cited. For example, both Horace and Varro make reference to mass burial sites for the indigent outside the Esquiline Gate in Rome.[2] Other sources mention the same site as a place of execution and cremation.[3] The connection between execution, cremation and burial is at least suggestive and consistent with the numerous examples already cited in which the executed received burial. Recent discoveries of Roman burial sites of gladiators and some victims of beheading in England, while preliminary, are consistent with this pattern.[4]

Jewish sources further support this pattern, while adding a twist, for they seem to have a consistent concern with not only the burial but the timing of the burial of victims of execution. This concern grows directly out of Deuteronomy 21.22-23:

> When someone is convicted of a crime punishable by death and is executed, and you hang him on a tree, his corpse must not remain all night upon the tree; you shall bury him that same day, for anyone hung on a tree is under God's curse. You must not defile the land that the LORD your God is giving you for possession.

---

1. One piece of evidence does not fit well with this larger historical pattern: the *Satyricon* by Petronius. This fictional satire, characterised by humour and exaggeration to the point of absurdity, includes a ribald tale that mentions a soldier and a grieving widow enjoying an entombed tryst next to the corpse of the widow's husband, while corpses hung on crosses outside of the tomb. Whether there is any historical value concerning capital punishment in this comedic piece is doubtful (*Satyricon* 111-112).
2. Horace, *Satire* 8.6ff; Varro, *On the Latin Language* 5.25
3. Tacitus, *Annals* 2.32.3; Suetonius, *Claudius* 25.
4. http://www.yorkarchaeology.co.uk/headless-romans/index.htm.

In practice, this injunction seems to have been applied with considerable consistency. One example is the Temple Scroll, discovered near Qumran. One of the longest of the Dead Sea Scrolls, it deals largely with purity regulations fit for a new and purified temple. This text applies the Deuteronomic command to even the worst of traitors to the Jewish people:

> If a man informs against his people, and delivers his people up to a foreign nation, and does harm to his people, you shall hang him on the tree, and he shall die. On the evidence of two witnesses and on the evidence of three witnesses he shall be put to death, and they shall hang him on the tree. And if a man has committed a crim[e] punishable by death, and had defected into the midst of the nations, and has cursed his people [and] the children of Israel, you shall hang him on the tree, and he shall die. And their body shall not remain upon the tree all night, but you shall bury them the same day, for those hanged on the tree are accursed by God and men; you shall not defile the land which I give you for an inheritance.[1]

In sum, executed criminals are to be buried, and that before sundown. Philo seems to suggest something similar, claiming that the Romans regularly honoured this practice.

This Roman deference to these local Jewish customs seems to be confirmed by a piece of evidence we did not discuss when exploring the crucifixion of Jesus. Because it is attested in a single source, the Gospel of John, this evidence may represent lower probability, but its description is remarkably consistent with other evidence concerning Jewish and Roman practice.[2] As John tells it, 'the Jews' (in context almost certainly a reference to the chief priests of the house of Annas) asked the Roman prefect, Pilate, to break the legs of the crucified. They did not make this request because they were sadistic; rather, this was an act of mercy growing out of their central concerns with purity and legality. The request to break the legs was intended to shorten the suffering and hurry the

---

1. 11QT 64:7-13a = 4Q524 frag. 14, lines 2-4. Translation from Charlesworth: J. Zias and J.H. Charlesworth, 'Crucifixion: Archaeology, Jesus, and the Dead Sea Scrolls,' in *Jesus and the Dead Sea Scrolls*, ed. J.H. Charlesworth (New York: Bantam Doubleday Dell, 1992), 278. While this text does not specifically use the common vocabulary for crucifixion, most scholars believe that this particular usage of the verb *tlh*, 'to hang', refers in context to the specific hanging done on a cross.
2. John 19.31-2.

death of the crucified so that their dead bodies (themselves a source of impurity) could be removed and buried before sunset and the beginning of the great Shabbat of the Passover. John's claim that Pilate granted this request is both probable and instructive. Why would the Romans be willing to hurry the death of the crucified if their objective, as some have suggested, was to prolong the agony, not only of the death, but also of the exposure of the corpse after death? That 'the Jews' made this request, and Pilate granted it, fits with the evidence thus far encountered.[1]

This impression is reinforced when we turn to Josephus, who provides more evidence of Roman executions of Jews than any other author. In his *Jewish War*, in the early stages of the revolt, Josephus discusses the turmoil in Jerusalem where Idumaeans, allied with Jewish Zealots, engaged in widespread slaughter of those who opposed them, including the chief priests, whose bodies they 'threw out' without burial. Josephus, disgusted by this behaviour, comments: 'Jews have so much regard for funeral rites that even malefactors who are justly crucified are taken down and buried before sunset.'[2] Since only Romans had the authority to crucify, Josephus is referring to his knowledge of normal Roman practice, in deference to Jewish culture. Josephus is particularly illuminating when taken together with Deuteronomy, the Temple Scroll, the Gospel of John, and Philo. All concur that the executed, even the crucified, must be properly buried by sunset. Josephus and Philo further concur that Romans regularly honoured this Jewish expectation, which is consistent with the cultural deference Romans commonly accorded to provincials. As we have seen, Josephus did not hesitate to describe the many victims of crucifixion before the walls of Jerusalem whose bodies were likely exposed on crosses. Here he seems to be drawing an important distinction between ordinary executions and extraordinary ones which took place in the context of war.

Thus far, our investigation has revealed a number of cases in which the bodies of those who suffered capital punishment were buried, and other cases in which the bodies were left exposed for at least a little while. For the most part, however, silence about the bodies prevails among the sources. The most reasonable inference from the silence is likely that the

---

1. There is little probability that early Christians would have invented such an incidental reference. The legs of Yehohanan were also broken. The original forensic report suggested that these breaks were pre-mortem, though there has been controversy since then over whether those breaks might not have been post-mortem after all. N. Haas, 1970, 58; J. Zias and E. Sekeles, 'The Crucified Man from Giv'at ha-Mivtar – A Reappraisal', *Israel Exploration Journal*, 35 (1), 1985, 22-27 consider the evidence inconclusive.
2. *Jewish War* 4.317.

Romans did not deal with these unmentioned bodies in a remarkable way, but rather followed their standard procedures in accordance with their cultural values. If this inference has any value, then the next step in our inquiry should be an examination of those Roman values, practices, and attitudes toward the dead and the disposal of bodies.

Roman Burial Practices

From a Roman perspective, burial may do away with the corpse, but not the dead. Disembodied souls were believed to experience shame, restlessness, dishonour – or peace, depending on how their bodies were treated. Romans practiced a cult of the dead, including grave gifts, feasts in family tombs, and festivals in honour of the ancestors. Death brought pollution, which demanded proper purification and burial rites, all manifestations of that most central of Roman virtues, *pietas*: piety or duty toward the gods, the family, and Rome itself. Sacred custom told Romans not to molest corpses, to permit proper burial by relatives or others claiming the body, and failing that, to provide minimal burial. Only three handfuls of dirt were required. Both cremation and inhumation were practiced in the first century, with the former more common.[1]

While some philosophers might suggest that we are all equal in death, the archaeology of mortality in the Roman Empire was anything but an egalitarian enterprise. Who was buried and how depended on social status. Elites staged elaborate funerals and erected monumental mausoleums. The humble were laid to rest in urns, simple columbaria or graves. The destitute were buried in pits or mass graves with minimal dirt or burnt on mass pyres of up to eleven bodies at a time. Plutarch counselled that it is wise to burn one female body for every ten male bodies to add some heat to the flames![2] Some of these mass graves have been unearthed outside the Esquiline Gate in Rome. The Romans even had a shadowy infrastructure of professional undertakers (*libitinarii*) whose job it was to remove putrefying corpses from the streets, to ensure proper burial of the indigent, and the removal of pollution and stench from the city.[3]

---

1. D. Kyle, *Spectacles of Death in Ancient Rome* (London: Routledge, 1998), 129. On the minimum burial requirements, Cicero, *On the Laws* 2.22.57; cf. J. Toynbee, *Death and Burial in Ancient Rome* (Baltimore: Johns Hopkins, 1971), 49.
2. *Moralia* 651B.
3. R. Lanciani, *Ancient Rome in the Light of Recent Discoveries* (London: Macmillan, 1888); Plutarch, *Moralia* 651B; J. Bodel, 'Graveyards and Groves: A Study of the *Lex Lucerina*', *American Journal of Ancient History* 11 (1994), 1-117.

According to Roman law, criminals condemned to death must be buried. Only in the case of the highest form of treason (*maxime maiestatis causa*) was denial of burial permitted (but not required).[1] Roman cultural values combined with Roman law to demand that even the destitute and abandoned, even executed criminals, most of whom, then as now, were from the lower classes, would not rot in the streets or at the places reserved for executions, but would receive at least the minimal proper burial or cremation.

From Ephesus: some of the finest Roman public toilets in the empire.[2]

To these cultural values, we need to add another: sanitation. Anyone who has travelled to the lands once ruled by Rome has come to appreciate their spectacular baths, whose massive water needs were supplied by Roman aqueducts. Another reason for the need for so much water was their invention of some of the finest continuous flush toilets in the ancient world. It is clear that the Romans were willing to invest much money and effort to live in a relatively clean environment. In addition, evidence of professional undertakers and dung-collectors bear fragrant witness to Roman aversion to unsightly messes and strong odours in public places.

Surprisingly, contemporary Jewish burial practices and values were in some ways similar to those of the Romans. Most Jews agreed with their Roman contemporaries that human life outlasted death, that the dignified handling of the dead with proper rites and burial was a sacred duty, and that the living were obligated to treat the dead in accordance with traditional and sacred law. On the other hand, their views of ritual purity diverged significantly, and official Judaism opposed any cult of the dead (even if some individuals seem to have ignored this prohibition).

1. *Digest* 48.24.1.
2. Photo by author.

For Jews, the victims of capital punishment were to be treated with appropriate dignity. As we have seen, Deuteronomy required the burial of the executed before sundown. Both written and archaeological evidence suggests that Jews seldom if ever practiced cremation, corpse abuse, exposure of bodies, or dumping of bodies into rivers. Burial methods were determined by wealth, with Judaea and its environs hosting many necropoleis, monumental tombs, cave tombs, and ossuaries.

Those lower in the social hierarchy were often buried in trench graves, either with no coffin or in simple wooden coffins, accompanied by few grave goods, as we see at such burial sites as Qumran, the Judaean desert, around Jerusalem, and at Bethsaida.[1] Among Jews, we do not find, in the Roman period, mass graves like those outside of the Esquiline Gate. It seems, as Jodi Magness put it, that 'the majority of the ancient Jewish population must have been disposed of in a manner that left few traces in the archaeological landscape'.[2] Given the simplicity and obscurity of the graves of commoners, combined with the consistent value of burial, even for the executed, it is probable that some of the Jewish burials thus far unearthed contained the bodies of executed criminals, including victims of crucifixion. The state of preservation of simply buried bones makes it difficult to identify with any confidence whether execution was the cause of death, with the occasional exception of decapitation.

---

1. **Qumran:** R. de Vaux, *Archaeology and the Dead Sea Scrolls* (London: British Academy, 1973), 46-7; R. Freund, *Digging Through the Bible* (Lanham, MD: Rowman and Littlefield, 2009), 247-93; R. Freund, 'New Insights on the Cemetery at Qumran', http://uhaweb.hartford.edu/QUMRAN/history. pdf, Originally presented at the International Brown University Qumran Conference, November, 19, 2002; J. Zangenberg, 'Bones of Contention: "New" Bones from Qumran Help Settle Old Questions (and Raise New Ones) – Remarks on Two Recent Conferences', *Qumran Chronicle*, 9 (1), 2000, 67-70; **En Gedi:** N. Avigad, 'Expedition A – The Burial Caves in Nahal David', *Israel Exploration Journal*, 12, 1962, 181-2; **Dura Europos:** N.P. Toll, *The Necropolis in the Excavation of Dura Europos, Ninth Season 1935-36 pt. III* (New Haven: Yale University Press, 1946), 20, 99; **Jericho:** R. Hachili and A. Killebrew, 'Jewish Funerary Customs during the Second Temple Period, in the Light of the Excavations at the Jericho Necropolis', *Palestine Exploration Quarterly*, 115, 1983, 109-139; '**En el-Ghuweir and Hiam el-Sagha:** H. Eshel and Z. Greenhut, 'Hiam El-Sagha, A Cemetery of the Qumran Type, Judean Desert', *Revue Biblique*, 100-102, 1992, 252-259; **Jerusalem:** A. Kloner and B. Zissu, *The Necropolis of Jerusalem in the Second Temple Period* (Leuven: Peeters, 2007), 95-99; **Bethsaida:** Verbal Report by Rami Arav.
2. J. Magness, 'What Did Jesus' Tomb Look Like?', *Biblical Archaeology Review*, Jan/Feb 2006.

All these factors, combined with the traditional Roman respect for the autonomy of the cultural practices of provincials, suggest that standard Roman procedure would be to allow Jews to handle their dead as they wished, including those who were executed. While Romans often found Jewish cultural practices curious if not incomprehensible, in this particular area, Romans would have had little trouble appreciating the care with which Jews handled their deceased loved ones. It should come as no surprise, therefore, that Philo expressed such outrage when Flaccus threatened to deny burial to crucified Jews, or that Josephus condemned the cavalier treatment of Jewish bodies by the Idumaeans, or that the legs of those crucified with Jesus were broken by Roman soldiers. From a Roman perspective, Philo and Josephus had just complaints, and the Jews who asked for the legs of the crucified to be broken to ensure death and burial before sunset had a just request.

In sum, the Romans seem to have practiced a 'situational thanatology'.[1] Extant evidence for the disposal of the executed bodies demonstrates that, in some situations, the Romans engaged in corpse abuse, exposure of bodies, and dumping of bodies into the Tiber. In other situations, they handed the bodies over to family and friends for proper disposal, whether by cremation or burial, or carted them off to places reserved for mass burial or cremation.

Perhaps most important is the discovery that every historical narrative of execution followed by non-burial took place in a violent context. Conversely, over the course of two centuries, we do not have evidence of a single case of corpse abuse or exposure of executed bodies under peaceful circumstances, save for the few victims of the sack wending their way down the Tiber. We can draw an important conclusion from this: non-burial of the victims of capital punishment might have happened in the context of mass violence, but burial is far more probable in a context of peace. When we consider this conclusion together with our discussion of the Roman values of piety and sanitation, and a broad commitment to practical efficiency, in times of peace, the Romans were most likely to follow their own law, handling executed corpses in the most efficient manner that guaranteed both a minimal standard of dignity and that the stench of rotting corpses would not waft its way into the city. Whether that meant handing them over to friends or relatives, or assigning them to undertakers, or cremating them, or disposing of them in mass or individual graves, made little difference from a Roman perspective. It took unusual circumstances,

---

1. I owe this phrase to my colleague, Jeff Snyder-Reinke.

such as war and violence, for the Romans to engage in corpse abuse or exposure. This should occasion no surprise, for such inconsistencies are commonplace throughout history.

We can take this conclusion a step further by combining the evidence from Philo, Josephus, and the victims of execution in Jewish tombs with the crucifixion and burial of Jesus as depicted in various texts in the New Testament. From the perspective of over two centuries of evidence concerning the Roman Empire, there is nothing unusual about how Pilate handled Jesus's execution or his burial, for unlike the slave rebellion of Spartacus or the homicidal rage of Nero this execution took place in a context of peace.

We are now in a position to take another look at Yehohanan and his heel. Was his burial the result of normal procedure or was it exceptional? Based on our analysis, the most probable answer that accounts for all of the evidence is 'it depends'. Was Yehohanan crucified in a time of relative peace or in a context of violence, war, rebellion, or tyrannical cruelty? Since most scholars date his execution around the 20s to 30s AD, a period of comparative stability in the region, the most probable conclusion is that Yehohanan was one of many victims of Roman capital punishment whose body the Romans handed over to his family. In this respect, the discovery of his ossuary provides significant corroboration for our literary evidence concerning the burial of Jesus.

What Did Jesus's Tomb Look Like?

Our evidence consistently supports the conclusion that Jesus was buried in the new family tomb of Joseph of Arimathea. What did this tomb look like? Thankfully, we are on solid archaeological ground when addressing this question.[1] The limestone hills around Jerusalem host a large necropolis, with a great many tombs dating from the first century. The tomb of Jesus would not have been appreciably different from that of Caiaphas or Yehohanan. Most first century tombs in the Jerusalem necropolis were cut into the limestone, with low cave-like entrances, a central room, often with a depression in the floor to allow a person to stand inside. A large stone was often rolled in front to close off the entrance. The walls surrounding the central room usually had burial niches (Hebrew: *kokhim;* Latin: *loculi*) cut into them at ground level, like drawers in a morgue. These burial niches were usually rectangular, wide enough to accommodate shoulders and long enough to hold a body length-wise. More *kokhim* could be added to a tomb over time, and

---

1. See the detailed discussion in J. Magness, *Stone and Dung*, 145ff.

the desiccated bones of the deceased were often gathered and placed in ossuaries or in pits to provide more room for future family members. Ossuaries were commonly stored in some unoccupied *kokhim*. A relatively rare alternative is found in some tombs from the period which had a semi-circular niche cut into the wall, with the flat side at the bottom (in Latin an *arcosolium*) forming a bench upon which bodies could be laid until they decomposed and the bones were collected. Other types of carved benches have also been unearthed. All rock-cut tombs were expensive and thus they were limited to the elite. Commoners and the indigent were buried in simple pit or shaft graves. The photograph below gives a very good idea of what the tomb of Jesus probably looked like.

First-century tomb with kokhim, from the Convent of the Sisters of Nazareth.[1]

The Gospels agree that Joseph wrapped the body of Jesus in linen cloth. The fourth Gospel adds the realistic detail that the burial cloth was not singular, but plural. In 2000, a case of grave robbery resulted in the chance discovery of a first-century Jewish burial shroud in a tomb in the Akeldama necropolis in Jerusalem. Unique environmental conditions in the tomb had provided for the preservation of the cloth. To judge from the microscopic analysis, it consisted of two or more pieces and was made of two different materials: wool and linen.[2]

---

1. Photo:http://saltandlighttv.org/blogfeed/getpost.php?id=69058&language=en. Used by permission.
2. Radio-carbon dating placed it in the early first century; the same cannot be said of the famed Shroud of Turin, though debate over that relic continues. For discussion, see Gibson, 139-47.

After wrapping the body, it would be placed in the tomb, and a large stone would be rolled into place to protect the tomb from scavengers. The stone may have been round, but more commonly such a stone was rectangular, placed like a large plug into the tomb entrance. Whatever the shape of the stone, it would have been too heavy for a single person to lift, so it had to be rolled or tumbled into place.

When we put all the evidence together it is probable that, near the time of sunset, with Shabbat fast approaching, Joseph of Arimathea, a wealthy and well-connected Jewish aristocrat, approached Pilate and received permission to bury Jesus, in accordance with Roman law and cultural practices. Soldiers took down the body, handed it over to Joseph who, perhaps with some assistance (John says that Nicodemus helped him), carried it to his own newly-excavated rock-cut tomb. There he undertook his mournful tasks. After briefly washing off the grime and the blood, he wrapped the body properly in linen cloths.[1] Then, lifting the corpse into his tomb, he slid it into place in one of the *kokhim* or perhaps laid it on a carved bench or *arcosolium*. Departing the tomb, he rolled the heavy stone over the entrance and trudged back to his home. He may have been well-respected and well-connected, but this day likely drove a wedge between Joseph and the house of Annas. As the sun set, it was time to join in the festival but, strained by loss and stained by the pollution of death, it seems unlikely that he felt much like celebrating.

Meanwhile, the horrors of the day had had their way with Jesus's family and closest followers. Crucifixion had had its intended effect. They were frightened, they were confused, they were anguished, and they did not know where to turn, so they did the most natural thing in the world, holing up in private and mourning their loss. Qohelet, the wise teacher of Ecclesiastes, said that there is a time to weep and a time to laugh. This was a time to weep.

---

1. There is a discrepancy at this point in the sources. Mark 16.1, Luke 23.56 and John 19.40 all mention spices, but John has them applied in great quantity immediately upon his burial. For Mark and Luke, the motive of the women who went to the tomb early on Sunday morning was to bring spices with which to anoint the body of Jesus. In this case, John seems to have displaced the spices to an earlier place in his narrative, as he had probably done earlier with the purple robe and crown of thorns. Of course, it is possible that spices were involved at both points, but that seems like overkill unless, of course, the women did not know about the spices already applied by Joseph.

As the family of Annas celebrated the festival of Unleavened Bread, and went about the business of leading the grand gathering of the Jewish people in Shabbat worship on the Temple Mount, as Pilate kept a watchful eye, revelling in his newfound confidence, the followers of Jesus were reduced to a bedraggled and disheartened lot. Their leader had been condemned, abused, and executed in the most shameful manner. Their treasurer had betrayed Jesus and abandoned them. Their informal spokesman, Peter, had denied his association with Jesus. That Passover Shabbat was, for them, an ironic mockery of the deliverance of the Hebrew people. Jesus had given them hope that the Kingdom of God would fulfil the deepest aspirations of every Passover pilgrim. Rather than provide deliverance, he was himself delivered to the Roman executioner. For the men and women who gathered in shared mourning, this *Pesach* had little meaning. Their hopes had been dashed. All they could do to manage the grief was to get on with the necessary logistics.

When Shabbat was over, early on Sunday morning, some women among the disciples visited the tomb of Jesus to provide for a fuller preparation of the body. They thought they would do something special. The norm was to anoint the body of deceased loved ones with oil, but they also planned to add aromatic spices – to provide a burial fit for a king. When they arrived, they found the tomb empty. Thereafter, word got out, others visited the tomb, and all tried to make sense of what had happened. Some claimed that the risen Jesus had appeared among them. That combination of an empty tomb and stories of resurrection appearances seems to have transformed the fledgling community of Jesus followers, forming the impetus for one of the most significant movements in history.

Gospel Accounts of the Execution of Jesus

Mark 15	Matthew 27	Luke 23	John 19
15 So Pilate, wishing to satisfy the crowd, released Barabbas for them; and after flogging Jesus, he handed him over to be crucified.	26 So he released Barabbas for them; and after flogging Jesus, he handed him over to be crucified.	11 Even Herod with his soldiers treated him with contempt and mocked him; then he put an elegant robe on him, and sent him back to Pilate.	Then Pilate took Jesus and had him flogged.
16 Then the soldiers led him into the courtyard of the palace (that is, the governor's headquarters); and they called together the whole cohort.	27 Then the soldiers of the governor took Jesus into the governor's headquarters, and they gathered the whole cohort around him.	25 He released the man they asked for, the one who had been put in prison for insurrection and murder, and he handed Jesus over as they wished.	2 And the soldiers wove a crown of thorns and put it on his head, and they dressed him in a purple robe.

3 They kept coming up to him, saying, 'Hail, King of the Jews!' and striking him on the face. |
| 17 And they clothed him in a purple cloak; and after twisting some thorns into a crown, they put it on him. | 28 They stripped him and put a scarlet robe on him,

29 and after twisting some thorns into a crown, they put it on his head. They put a reed in his right hand and knelt before him and mocked him, saying, 'Hail, King of the Jews!' | 26 As they led him away, they seized a man, Simon of Cyrene, who was coming from the country, and they laid the cross on him, and made him carry it behind Jesus. | 5 So Jesus came out, wearing the crown of thorns and the purple robe. Pilate said to them, 'Here is the man!'

16 Then he handed him over to them to be crucified. So they took Jesus; |
| 18 And they began saluting him, 'Hail, King of the Jews!'

19 They struck his head with a reed, spat upon him, and knelt down in homage to him. | 30 They spat on him, and took the reed and struck him on the head. | 27 A great number of the people followed him, and among them were women who were beating their breasts and wailing for him. | 17 and carrying the cross by himself, he went out to what is called The Place of the Skull, which in Hebrew is called Golgotha. |

Mark 15	Matthew 27	Luke 23	John 19
20 After mocking him, they stripped him of the purple cloak and put his own clothes on him. Then they led him out to crucify him.	31 After mocking him, they stripped him of the robe and put his own clothes on him. Then they led him away to crucify him.	28 But Jesus turned to them and said, 'Daughters of Jerusalem, do not weep for me, but weep for yourselves and for your children.	18 There they crucified him, and with him two others, one on either side, with Jesus between them.
21 They compelled a passer-by, who was coming in from the country, to carry his cross; it was Simon of Cyrene, the father of Alexander and Rufus.	32 As they went out, they came upon a man from Cyrene named Simon; they compelled this man to carry his cross.	29 For the days are surely coming when they will say, "Blessed are the barren, and the wombs that never bore, and the breasts that never nursed."	19 Pilate also had an inscription written and put on the cross. It read, 'Jesus of Nazareth, the King of the Jews.'
22 Then they brought Jesus to the place called Golgotha (which means the place of a skull).	33 And when they came to a place called Golgotha (which means Place of a Skull),	30 Then they will begin to say to the mountains, "Fall on us"; and to the hills, "Cover us."	20 Many of the Jews read this inscription, because the place where Jesus was crucified was near the city; and it was written in Hebrew, in Latin, and in Greek.
23 And they offered him wine mixed with myrrh; but he did not take it.	34 they offered him wine to drink, mixed with gall; but when he tasted it, he would not drink it.	31 For if they do this when the wood is green, what will happen when it is dry?'	21 Then the chief priests of the Jews said to Pilate, 'Do not write, "The King of the Jews", but, "This man said, I am King of the Jews."'
24 And they crucified him, and divided his clothes among them, casting lots to decide what each should take.	35 And when they had crucified him, they divided his clothes among themselves by casting lots; 36 then they sat down there and kept watch over him.	32 Two others also, who were criminals, were led away to be put to death with him.	22 Pilate answered, 'What I have written I have written.'

Mark 15	Matthew 27	Luke 23	John 19
25 It was nine o'clock in the morning when they crucified him.	37 Over his head they put the charge against him, which read, 'This is Jesus, the King of the Jews.'	33 When they came to the place that is called The Skull, they crucified Jesus there with the criminals, one on his right and one on his left.	23 When the soldiers had crucified Jesus, they took his clothes and divided them into four parts, one for each soldier. They also took his tunic; now the tunic was seamless, woven in one piece from the top.
26 The inscription of the charge against him read, 'The King of the Jews.' 27 And with him they crucified two bandits, one on his right and one on his left.	38 Then two bandits were crucified with him, one on his right and one on his left.	34 Then Jesus said, 'Father, forgive them; for they do not know what they are doing.' And they cast lots to divide his clothing.	24 So they said to one another, 'Let us not tear it, but cast lots for it to see who will get it.' This was to fulfil what the scripture says, 'They divided my clothes among themselves, and for my clothing they cast lots.'
29 Those who passed by derided him, shaking their heads and saying, 'Aha! You who would destroy the temple and build it in three days, 30 save yourself, and come down from the cross!'	39 Those who passed by derided him, shaking their heads 40 and saying, 'You who would destroy the temple and build it in three days, save yourself! If you are the Son of God, come down from the cross.'	35 And the people stood by, watching; but the leaders scoffed at him, saying, 'He saved others; let him save himself if he is the Messiah of God, his chosen one!'	25 And that is what the soldiers did. Meanwhile, standing near the cross of Jesus were his mother, and his mother's sister, Mary the wife of Clopas, and Mary Magdalene.
31 In the same way the chief priests, along with the scribes, were also mocking him among themselves and saying, 'He saved others; he cannot save himself.	41 In the same way the chief priests also, along with the scribes and elders, were mocking him, saying,	36 The soldiers also mocked him, coming up and offering him sour wine, 37 and saying, 'If you are the King of the Jews, save yourself!'	

Mark 15	Matthew 27	Luke 23	John 19
32 Let the Messiah, the King of Israel, come down from the cross now, so that we may see and believe.' Those who were crucified with him also taunted him.

33 When it was noon, darkness came over the whole land until three in the afternoon.

34 At three o'clock Jesus cried out with a loud voice, 'Eloi, Eloi, lema sabachthani?' which means, 'My God, my God, why have you forsaken me?'

35 When some of the bystanders heard it, they said, 'Listen, he is calling for Elijah.' | 42 'He saved others; he cannot save himself. He is the King of Israel; let him come down from the cross now, and we will believe in him.

43 He trusts in God; let God deliver him now, if he wants to; for he said, "I am God's Son."'

44 The bandits who were crucified with him also taunted him in the same way.

45 From noon on, darkness came over the whole land until three in the afternoon.

46 And about three o'clock Jesus cried with a loud voice, 'Eli, Eli, lema sabachthani?' that is, 'My God, my God, why have you forsaken me?' | 38 There was also an inscription over him, 'This is the King of the Jews.'

39 One of the criminals who were hanged there kept deriding him and saying, 'Are you not the Messiah? Save yourself and us!'

40 But the other rebuked him, saying, 'Do you not fear God, since you are under the same sentence of condemnation?

41 And we indeed have been condemned justly, for we are getting what we deserve for our deeds, but this man has done nothing wrong.'

42 Then he said, 'Jesus, remember me when you come into your kingdom.' | 26 When Jesus saw his mother and the disciple whom he loved standing beside her, he said to his mother, 'Woman, here is your son.'

27 Then he said to the disciple, 'Here is your mother.' And from that hour the disciple took her into his own home.

28 After this, when Jesus knew that all was now finished, he said (in order to fulfil the scripture), 'I am thirsty.'

29 A jar full of sour wine was standing there. So they put a sponge full of the wine on a branch of hyssop and held it to his mouth.

30 When Jesus had received the wine, he said, 'It is finished.' Then he bowed his head and gave up his spirit. |

Mark 15	Matthew 27	Luke 23	John 19
36 And someone ran, filled a sponge with sour wine, put it on a stick, and gave it to him to drink, saying, 'Wait, let us see whether Elijah will come to take him down.' 37 Then Jesus gave a loud cry and breathed his last.	47 When some of the bystanders heard it, they said, 'This man is calling for Elijah.' 48 At once one of them ran and got a sponge, filled it with sour wine, put it on a stick, and gave it to him to drink. 49 But the others said, 'Wait, let us see whether Elijah will come to save him.' 50 Then Jesus cried again with a loud voice and breathed his last.	43 He replied, 'Truly I tell you, today you will be with me in Paradise.' 44 It was now about noon, and darkness came over the whole land until three in the afternoon, 45 while the sun's light failed; and the curtain of the temple was torn in two. 46 Then Jesus, crying with a loud voice, said, 'Father, into your hands I commend my spirit.' Having said this, he breathed his last. 47 When the centurion saw what had taken place, he praised God and said, 'Certainly this man was innocent.'	31 Since it was the day of Preparation, the Jews did not want the bodies left on the cross during the sabbath, especially because that sabbath was a day of great solemnity. So they asked Pilate to have the legs of the crucified men broken and the bodies removed. 32 Then the soldiers came and broke the legs of the first and of the other who had been crucified with him. 33 But when they came to Jesus and saw that he was already dead, they did not break his legs. 34 Instead, one of the soldiers pierced his side with a spear, and at once blood and water came out.

VIII

Ad Consummationem:
Conclusion

It is common, when grappling with the last days of Jesus, for people to ask the question: who killed Jesus? Let this question, then, draw our inquiry to an end. Thus far, I have tried to avoid theological issues, but it seems to me that this question requires an interdisciplinary response, both historical and theological.

Ever since that long-ago day when I took a course from an Orthodox rabbi, I have been concerned about the historical and rhetorical linkage between the execution of Jesus and Christian anti-Semitism. It is essential to be unequivocal. *Jews did not kill Jesus.* Moreover, although the high priestly family and their elite supporters were involved, the Jewish *people* had nothing to do with his trial or crucifixion. The history of Christian anti-Semitism is both shameful and ill-conceived, as I believe that this study consistently substantiates.

If my reconstruction is anywhere near correct, the answer to the question of who killed Jesus is complex. A small group of elite high priestly leaders arrested and prosecuted him; Pilate condemned him; Roman soldiers executed him. Thus far, few would disagree, but primitive Christian theology goes a step further, contending that responsibility for killing Jesus is a much more profound matter. According to what is likely the most ancient statement of Christian belief in existence, 'Christ died for our sins.'[1] Whatever the theology one might build upon that phrase, this most foundational of Christian beliefs suggests that all humans share responsibility for his death, that his suffering on a Roman cross transcends its historical context.

Jim McKay on ABC's *Wide World of Sports* captured a Roman perspective. The Romans exemplified the 'thrill of victory' while subjecting those who defied them to the 'agony of defeat'. In a sense, in

---

1. I Corinthians 15.3. This sentence is part of a primitive statement of faith quoted by Paul that probably dates from the 30s or 40s AD.

the trial of Jesus, the thrill of victory went to Pilate, though the house of Annas experienced a victory in its own right. Jesus was the loser, suffering the agony of defeat. Yet at the core of primitive Christian theology is an inversion of this basic Roman premise: Jesus, as he suffered agony, snatched away the victor's crown, conquering while hanging on a cross. Such inversions were Jesus's stock in trade: 'the last will be first'; 'the meek will inherit the earth'. By the same sort of logic, Jesus as victim became victor. Still, he was a different kind of victor, exchanging grace for vengeance – offering forgiveness, not only to his disciples, but to Annas and Caiaphas, to Pilate, to those who yelled 'crucify him', to those who flogged him, and even to those who drove the nails into his wrists. The theological paradox of forgiveness born of injustice, of healing born of suffering, draws us near to the beating heart of the history of Christianity. So it was, from the beginning, that Jesus's 'kingdom of heaven' made its presence felt in this world by inverting its *modus operandi*, embracing the thrill of defeat and the agony of victory.

Honoris Causa:[1]
Acknowledgments

The process of bringing a book into the world is never the work of one person. Its conception requires partnership, while its gestation and birth depend upon the support and nurture of many friends, family, doctors, and midwives. I am most grateful to my former Teaching Assistants: Mckayla Stevens undertook an initial investigation of *'synedrion'* in Greek literature; Katie Williams checked factual matters and documentation; and Jessica Hershey did preliminary research on Roman capital punishment and suggested the crucial distinction between times of peace and times of violence. My friend and former colleague at The College of Idaho, Denny Clark, gave graciously of his time and wisdom as I began to navigate the dynamic field of Historical Jesus studies. Alice Vinson provided several drawings of the Hidden Gate. Friends, family, and students offered many insights on the accessibility of this book to the 'educated popular reader'. In particular, I wish to express my appreciation to Dia Smith, Kai Matari, Gene Smith, Ione Larinan, Steve Hauge, Frank Powell, Paul Panther, Steve Penner, Mike Benton, Tom Walton, Bryan Appelt, K.J. Appelt, Charles and Mary Reed, Paula Schneider, Sarah Shoultz, Kenn Henman, Jeff Snyder-Reinke, Steven Maughan, Dori Johnson, Heather Vance, Fr. Thomas Rosica, Hailey Palmer, and Jesse Wilson. Dan Lewis, my colleague in Hawai'i, offered thoughtful and helpful input from a broad pastoral and Biblical perspective. Tim Vivian, fellow veteran of Isla Vista, provided a detailed critique from the field of Religious Studies, as did John Greene, my partner in the pits of Bethsaida and the caves of Nahal Hever. I would still be swimming in the shoreless sea of New Testament scholarship were it not for the learned counsel (not to mention lifeguarding skills) of Bob Gundry, whose guidance and support ever since my undergraduate days has earned my undying gratitude. Jeff Russell, eminent historian

---

1. *Honoris causa* is a term of esteem, commonly used at colleges and universities when they confer honorary degrees.

of Christianity, offered both moral support and incisive criticism on every level. Hal Drake, distinguished historian of the Roman Empire and *mein Doktorvater*, provided extraordinary prenatal care through every trimester of this project, including the careful reading of both the first and last drafts. Never was he lacking for an encouraging word or a humorous anecdote; I can never adequately express my appreciation.

I would like to thank The College of Idaho, especially the department of history, for the sabbatical that provided the space and time necessary to the concentrated task of writing and editing. Thanks also to the NEH for funding my research travel. To my colleagues in the Bethsaida Excavations Project, especially Rami Arav, Richard Freund, Nicolae Roddy, and Carl Savage: thank you for twenty-three years of friendship, exploration, camaraderie, and rigorous intellectual life together in the dirt. I would also like to express my appreciation to Philip Law, Adrian Brink, Angharad Thomas, and the editorial staff at the Lutterworth Press and James Clarke.

To everyone who has contributed, including the many teachers, colleagues, and students who have helped to inspire my efforts, to refine my perspective, and to curb my errant enthusiasms in more ways than I can ever acknowledge: you have my profound respect and affection. χάρις ὑμῖν καὶ εἰρήνη.

Appendix I:
The Chronology of Historical Jesus

The nature of our examination of the last days of Jesus requires firm grounding in chronology. In particular, when was Jesus born? When was he executed? Both of these are complex questions, but their answers boil down to two dates. The most probable conclusion to be drawn from the ancient evidence is that Jesus was born in Bethlehem in AD 6, and he was executed in Jerusalem on April 3, 33. Many would agree with the second, but most have never even considered the first. Both dates are the result of detailed historical analysis.

The Date of Jesus's Birth[1]

In many a Christmas pageant, the most regal character is Herod the Great, resplendent in his colourful robes and golden crown and usually possessed of a sonorous bass voice – the tyrant who presided over the birth of the child-messiah, who sought to deceive the Magi, and who decreed the destruction of dozens of defenceless children, causing Joseph, Mary and their baby to flee to Egypt. If my historical reconstruction is correct, however, Herod will in future need to be portrayed a little differently – wrapped in cloth and mouldering in a tomb – for Herod had already been dead some ten years when Jesus was born.

It was the sixth century monk, Dionysius Exiguus, who invented the BC/AD dating system. Unfortunately, his calculations seem to have missed their central mark, for few still believe that Jesus of Nazareth was born in the year one. Most scholars rather maintain that the first 'Christmas' occurred between 6 and 4 BC, during the waning years of the reign of Herod the Great, who died in 4 BC. This traditional view is

---

1. This appendix is based in part on my article, 'Of Jesus and Quirinius', *Catholic Biblical Quarterly* 62.2 (2000), 278-93.

based primarily on the infancy narrative unique to Matthew. A problem arises, however, when one compares Matthew's account with Luke's, for the latter, while mentioning Herod, claims also that the census which drew Joseph and the expectant Mary to Bethlehem was precipitated by the Roman legate of Syria: Publius Sulpicius Quirinius. The problem is that Quirinius attained jurisdiction over Judaea (and not Galilee) only after Herod Archelaus, son of the Great Herod, was deposed in AD 6.[1] There have been two attempts to overcome this difficulty, both of which are possible, but neither of which is wholly satisfactory. One approach argues that Quirinius must have served two terms as legate in Syria, the first during the reign of Herod the Great. The other contends that Luke was mistaken in his chronology.

Did Quirinius Serve Two Terms as Legate of Syria?

There is strong evidence that Quirinius served as legate of Syria in AD 6, but that is ten to twelve years after the date which most scholars assign to the birth of Jesus. In order to make Luke's account of Quirinius and his census square with the lifetime of Herod the Great, it is necessary to propose that Quirinius also served an earlier term as Legate of Syria, somewhere around 4-6 BC. It is theoretically possible that Quirinius could have served two terms in Syria, but there are three problems with this view.

First, it does not fit well with the information gleaned from other sources about the career of Quirinius. He was consul in 12 BC.[2] Sometime before 6 BC he led campaigns in Cyrenaica, and against the Homonadenses

---

1. Josephus variously describes the date as the tenth year of Archelaus (*Antiquities* 17.342; cf. *Life* 1.5), the thirty-seventh year after the battle of Actium, which took place in 31 BC (*Antiquities* 18.26) and, in the earlier *Jewish War* (2.111), as the ninth year of Archelaus' reign. The minor discrepancy between the *Jewish War* and the *Life* and *Antiquities* concerning whether the reign of Archelaus lasted nine or ten years may have to do with different starting points: perhaps it was ten years after Archelaus assumed the throne, but only nine if one discounts the several months it took before Archelaus's rule was officially recognised by Augustus. Dio places the end of Archelaus's rule in the year of the consulship of Aemilius Lepidus and Lucius Arruntius (AD 6) when, 'Herod of Palestine, who was accused of some wrongdoing by his brothers, was exiled beyond the Alps, and his part of the realm was confiscated'(55.27.6); cf. E. Schürer, *The History of the Jewish People in the Age of Jesus Christ*, revised ed. by G. Vermes, F. Millar, M. Black (Edinburgh: Clark, 1973), 1. 259; 399-427.
2. Tacitus, *Annals* 3.48, Dio 54.28.2.

in Asia Minor.[1] Between 1 and 4 AD he served as advisor (not legate) under Gaius Caesar in Syria and Armenia.[2] Two inscriptions mention Quirinius by name. One claims that he held a municipal office (*duumvir*) in Pisidian Antioch,[3] and the other, from Syria, mentions his name and his census, but neither offers any indication of date.[4] Finally, we have multiple references to his accession to the position of Legate of Syria in AD 6.[5] One intriguing piece of evidence is an inscription that mentions an unnamed Roman official who may have served twice as legate of Syria (but it could also be interpreted to mean that this person held the office of legate twice, the second term of which happened to be in Syria).[6] Although some have argued that this unnamed official may be Quirinius, a more probable identification is L. Calpurnius Piso.[7] For a Roman whose career is quite well-documented, it is at least remarkable that none of the sources mentions that Quirinius served as legate of Syria at any time before AD 6. Although this is an argument from silence, it is a fairly loud silence when one considers that Josephus spilt a great deal of ink on the last years of Herod, and he mentions many Roman officials, yet he knows nothing of an early *legatio* of Quirinius, who was certainly worthy of mention. Josephus does allude to Quirinius several times, but only when the latter comes to power in AD 6, and that in a portion of Josephus's text to which he devotes relatively little detailed narrative. It is therefore just possible to find room in Quirinius's career to fit an earlier stint governing Syria, but that glimmer of hope fades in light of another problem.

A second, and more significant, reason why Quirinius probably did not serve two terms as legate is that he does not fit into the well-documented chronology of legates of Syria known from other sources. Between 10/9 BC and 7/6 BC, C. Sentius Saturninus served as Legate.[8] He was succeeded by P. Quinctilius Varus, who governed from 7/6 BC to 4 BC.[9] What is important for our purposes is that Josephus narrates

---

1. During which he seems to have been based in Galatia; cf. R. E. Brown, *The Birth of the Messiah* (New York: Doubleday, 1993), 551; cf. Tacitus, *Annals* 3.48; Florus, *Epitome* 2.31; cf. A. N. Sherwin-White, 164-65.
2. Dio 55.10a.4-5; Velleius Paterculus, *Roman History* 2.102; cf. Brown, 550.
3. *Inscriptiones latinae selectae. Editio tertia lucis ope expressa* (ed. H. Dessau; Berolini: Apud Weidmannos, 1962), #9502.
4. *Inscriptiones latinae selectae* #2683.
5. E.g. Josephus, *Antiquities* 17.356; 18.1; 18.26; *Jewish War* 2.111.
6. *Inscriptiones latinae selectae* #918; cf. Schürer, 1. 258.
7. R. Syme, *The Roman Revolution* (Oxford: University, 1939), 398.
8. Josephus, *Antiquities* 16.277ff.; cf. Schürer, 1.257.
9. Josephus, *Antiquities* 17.89; 17.221-3; 17.250-99; cf. Schürer, 1.257-58.

in detail the actions of Varus both before and *after* the death of Herod the Great. It was he who had to put down all the revolts and riots that rocked the realm after the King's death and during the several negotiations surrounding the execution of his will and the establishment of his successors.[1] Varus was replaced in the latter part of 4 BC by L. Calpurnius Piso.[2] In order for an earlier term as legate for Quirinius to fit into this scheme in such a way as to alleviate the discrepancy between the infancy narratives of Matthew and Luke, it must have occurred before Herod's death in the spring of 4 BC.[3] In other words, the alleged first term must have fallen between 4 and 6 BC, precisely during the time Varus was legate. There is too much evidence for Varus's presence during the last years of Herod, as well as in the succeeding months, to invite any serious challenge. Saturninus's position is almost as well established. As a result, there is simply no room for an earlier term for Quirinius during the reign of Herod.[4]

A third reason why Quirinius and his census do not fit into the traditional chronology is that the legate of a Roman province would not have had the jurisdiction to impose a census (and the presumed taxation scheme that would go along with it) in the realm of a client king (*rex socius*) of Rome.[5] Indeed, the taxation system imposed by Herod the Great, as described by Josephus, is clearly his own creation, and administered without Roman interference.[6]

In short, it would be a welcome solution to the problem if Quirinius had undertaken his census during a first term as legate of Syria which coincided with the last years of Herod the Great.[7] Unfortunately,

---

1. Josephus, *Jewish War* 2.1-100; cf. *Antiquities* 17.206-99.
2. Schürer, 1.258.
3. To harmonise Luke with the story in Matthew would require both a census before the birth of Jesus and Herod to be still alive afterward, so he could meet the Magi, decree the death of the innocents, and precipitate the flight of Joseph and family into Egypt.
4. Brown, *Birth of the Messiah*, 550-51.
5. H. Hoehner's claims to the contrary cannot withstand careful scrutiny (*Chronological Aspects of the Life of Christ* [Grand Rapids: Zondervan, 1977], 16-17): Apamea was not 'autonomous', Cappadocia had been reduced to provincial status after the death of Archelaus the elder in 17 AD, and Petra was not explicitly subjected to a Roman census.
6. See the discussion in Schürer, 1.413-16.
7. Luke's description of the census as the 'first' has generated considerable discussion. Some interpret it to mean that this was the first census conducted by Quirinius, who then, presumably, conducted a second in AD 6. Others hold that 'first' should be interpreted as 'former' or 'prior to', with the result that

neither the concept nor the chronology lend themselves to such a solution.[1] The only way to make this theory work is to assume that the inscription mentioning an anonymous holder of two terms as legate of Syria refers to Quirinius (which is not the most likely interpretation). Then one must argue that Quirinius must have been given some special power (such as *maius imperium*) over Varus, which allowed him to direct the census-taking activities (a power rarely granted to any Roman officials and never attributed to him in any ancient source). Then one must assume that the Roman imperial administration adopted, in this special case, a policy it had historically avoided: the administration of a census in the realm of a client king. Finally, one must assume that Josephus either did not know about this extraordinary arrangement, or neglected to mention it in any of his accounts of the period. Such a reconstruction is possible, but just barely. Historians must evaluate the evidence in terms of probability, and for each of these assumptions, specific corroboration is lacking. We must therefore conclude that the probability of this reconstruction is quite low.

Was Luke Wrong about Quirinius?

Such arguments have given rise to a second attempt at solving the dilemma. On the assumption either that Matthew was right that Herod the Great was king when Jesus was born, or that neither Matthew nor Luke had any historical basis for their chronology, some recent interpreters have considered Luke's mention of Quirinius and his census to be erroneous – an anachronistic imposition. Once Quirinius is eliminated from the picture, the tension between the accounts of Matthew and Luke diminishes considerably. Luke claims that Herod was king at the time of John's conception, a few months before Jesus's birth, presumably in agreement with Matthew. Luke's note that Jesus was 'about thirty years old' in or soon after the fifteenth year of Tiberius's reign fits fairly well with this view.[2] In addition, Luke's theology which, at least in part, seeks to demonstrate that Jesus and

---

Luke refers to a census that occurred before Quirinius was legate in Syria, an interpretation that does not solve the most serious problems noted above. However, the most natural interpretation is that no Roman census had been held in Judaea before that of Quirinius, i.e. his is the first (K. Haacker, 'Erst unter Quirinius? Ein Übersetzungsvorschlag zu Lk 2,2', *Biblische Notizen* 38-39 [1987] 39-43; cf. Brown, *Birth of the Messiah*, 395, 668).

1. E.P. Sanders, *The Historical Figure of Jesus* (London: Penguin, 1993), 53.
2. 3.1, 23.

his family were loyal subjects of Rome, has been used to suggest why Luke might have chosen to include the reference to Quirinius in his narrative, despite the fact that it did not fit chronologically.[1]

Although this view succeeds in partially harmonising the accounts of Matthew and Luke, it fails to take into account the serious problems it raises concerning the nature of the evidence and the internal consistency of Luke's Gospel. If Luke was written during the late 50s or early 60s (as argued in Chapter II), there were still many people alive who remembered the cataclysmic events surrounding the misrule of Herod Archelaus, his deposition, the appointment of Quirinius, his commissioning of a census, and the ensuing Jewish rebellion fomented by Yehuda of Gamla.[2] These events loom large in Josephus's history, for according to his narrative, they were formative for the eventual birth of the Zealot movement which helped exacerbate the tensions between Jews and their Roman overlords. Because these events were so significant, there is little possibility that anyone who lived through them, or even anyone who knew anyone who lived through them, would confuse them with the last years of Herod the Great. Although there were Jewish riots both after the Great Herod's death and after the deposition of Archelaus, there was plenty of intervening time and the issues at stake were fundamentally different.[3] For first-century Jews to confuse these two events would be akin to late twentieth-century Americans confusing World War II and the Korean War.

The evidence provided by Luke is quite strong by historical standards, because it is falsifiable. If Luke talked to any Palestinian Jews in preparation for his writing, or consulted any traditions passed down by them (as he implies in his prologue), it is most probable that he would have been advised of any such chronological blunder. In addition, had he included such a chronological *non-sequitur*, his narrative would immediately forfeit the scrupulous tone which he sets up so carefully in

1. J.P. Meier (*A Marginal Jew: Rethinking the Historical Jesus* [New York: Doubleday, 1991], 213) sums up this attitude well as he summarily dismisses any questioning of this position: 'Attempts to reconcile Luke 2.1 with the facts of ancient history are hopelessly contrived.'
2. Josephus, *Antiquities* 18.23 and *Jewish War* 2.118. In *Antiquities* 18.4 he is called a Gaulonite, because he was from Gamla in Gaulanitis. That Luke was familiar with at least some details surrounding this period is evident from his reference to Judas and the census in Acts 5.37.
3. After Herod's death the primary problem was Archelaus's slaughter of Jews during the Passover; it had nothing to do with Roman government or a census.

the prologue.[1] Instead, before completing his second chapter, he would have revealed that he was not a careful researcher at all, and his audience would have little reason to take seriously the historical references in the remainder of his narrative. The fact that Luke's account is falsifiable and so easy for him to verify and correct, makes it most improbable that he made the error of which he has been accused.[2]

Not only is Luke's account of Quirinius and his census falsifiable as historical evidence, he had no good reason to invent this story. Two reasons have been offered, neither of which is compelling. The first is that Luke used Quirinius and his census to get Joseph and Mary to go to Bethlehem, as a form of 'prophecy historicised', fulfilling the prophecy in Micah 5.2.[3] This explanation fails on two counts: Luke makes no reference to the prophecy of Micah, so that can hardly be his purpose. He does mention a prophecy of Zechariah (which appears only in Luke 1.69) that God would raise up a 'horn of salvation' from the line of David,[4] but the fulfilment of that prophecy does not require a trip to Bethlehem or a Roman census, especially when Luke already devotes a lengthy genealogy to the point. In addition, Matthew places Joseph and Mary in Bethlehem without the elaborate ruse of a census – and he *does* make reference to the prophecy of Micah. This type of explanation therefore does not provide an adequate motive for Luke's allegedly anachronistic imposition of Quirinius and his census.

The second reason why Luke might have invented the Quirinius story, according to some, is his desire to portray the family of Jesus as model, submissive, Roman subjects who are not of the same spirit as those who rose in rebellion against Rome – perhaps part of a larger Christian strategy to distance themselves from Jews in the wake of the

---

1. Regardless of his literary context, and not neglecting the theological nature of his work, Luke does imply in his prologue that it was his purpose to produce an 'orderly account'. (See I.H. Marshall, *Luke: Historian and Theologian* [Grand Rapids: Academie, 1970], 217; cf. C.K. Barrett, *Luke the Historian in Recent Study* [London: Epworth, 1961], 36, 58, 61; cf. Sherwin-White). The precise nature of Luke's concern for historical accuracy relative to his theological aims has been the subject of considerable controversy. Even if one were to argue that his prologue is purely literary posturing, he would be unwise to subvert his position by including a simple, falsifiable chronological error so early in his text.

2. The term 'falsifiable' means that some people are still alive who could easily correct the mistake.

3. J.D. Crossan, *The Historical Jesus* (San Francisco: Harper, 1991), 371-72.

4. To which Sanders (87) points for his motive.

Jewish War.[1] That Luke concerns himself with making such a point throughout Luke-Acts is beyond question, but he certainly does not need Quirinius or his census to help him make it.[2] He could have sent the family to Bethlehem for any reason, or he could have begun his narrative in Bethlehem, as had Matthew, without damaging his theological point at all. Why would he make up a story with confused chronology, one which could easily be checked and falsified by his audience, when it offers him little advantage? In addition, Luke appears to have been remarkably well-informed about the geographical distribution and governmental structures and officials of the Roman provinces.[3] For example, despite the rapid changes that took place in the government of Cyprus, Luke correctly identifies Sergius Paulus as Proconsul. He rightly notes that Philippi was a Roman colony, governed by *strategoi*, the appropriate Greek equivalent of *duoviri iuri dicundo*. Epigraphic evidence has verified Luke's use of the unusual term 'politarchs' to describe the leaders of Thessalonica. The ruler of Malta is correctly styled 'First Citizen'. Both asiarchs and a proconsul appear in Luke's narrative of Paul in Ephesus, titles which are confirmed by Roman sources.[4] The point is, Luke could have used a general term like 'leaders' in each of these cases and saved himself considerable effort; he chose not to. Instead, he did his homework and, most importantly, in the cases where we can test him, he consistently got the details of chronology and terminology right. Here we get a glimpse into the mind of the author and his concerns. It is implausible that an author otherwise so familiar with the function and chronology of Roman provincial government, and so scrupulous on minor historical details, should be so careless on an historical issue of major import in order to make a minor theological point. In sum, this second view, though not

---

1. H.R. Moehring, 'The Census of Luke as an Apologetic Device', in *Studies in New Testament and Early Christian Literature: Essays in Honor of Allen P. Wikgren* ed. D.E. Aune (Leiden: E. J. Brill, 1972), 144-60; cf. Brown, 416-17. Note, however, that the most convincing date for Luke is before the Jewish War.

2. H. Conzelmann (*The Theology of St. Luke* [New York: Harper, 1960], 137-49) manages to discuss this theme in considerable depth without ever making reference to Luke 2.1-5.

3. R.P.C. Hanson, *The Acts* (Oxford: Clarendon, 1967), 2-3.

4. For many other examples, see the detailed discussions in Sherwin-White; cf. T.D. Barnes, 'An Apostle on Trial', *Journal of Theological Studies* N.S. 20.2 (1969), 407-19; cf. C.J. Hemer, *The Book of Acts in the Setting of Hellenistic History* (Tubingen : J.C.B. Mohr, 1989).

impossible, is not more probable than the former theory. As historians view probability, both of the common explanations for Luke's reference to Quirinius are less than convincing. Is there no other alternative?

Another Herod?

What if Luke believed that Jesus was born during the time Quirinius served as Legate? What if he thought Jesus was born in AD 6?[1] Can such a reconstruction do justice to the theology and internal consistency of Luke? If so, what are the implications for Matthew's account?

If Luke was right about Quirinius, a serious problem immediately raises its head. How can we explain the reference to 'Herod, King of Judaea', during whose reign Luke places the conception of John the Baptist, a few months before that of Jesus?[2] 'Herod, King of Judaea', could not, in this reconstruction, refer to the long deceased Herod the Great, but it could, at least chronologically, refer to Herod Archelaus, ethnarch of Judaea and son of the Great Herod. Can 'Herod, King of Judaea' refer to anyone other than the Great Herod? In fact, such an interpretation is entirely consistent with Luke's usage. The name 'Herod' occurs twenty-two times in Luke-Acts: fifteen times for Herod Antipas, son of Herod the Great and tetrarch of Galilee and Peraea;[3] six times for Herod Agrippa I, grandson of Herod the Great, and son of Aristobulus.[4] The title 'King of Judaea' would certainly be appropriate to Herod the Great, but if that is the correct interpretation, it is the only reference to him in Luke-Acts.

On the other hand, the title could just as well apply to Herod Archelaus. He certainly ruled Judaea. Although he is never called 'Herod' in Josephus or even elsewhere in the New Testament, he does use this name on his coins and Dio calls him 'Herod of Palestine'.[5] So, Archelaus was commonly referred to as Herod, but is there any evidence he was styled 'King' of Judaea? According to Josephus, his official title, as conferred by Augustus,

---

1. Although I came to this conclusion independently, some of my ideas were anticipated by the provocative article by J.D.M. Derrett, 'Further Light on the Narratives of the Nativity,' *Novum Testamentum* 17/2 (1975), 81-108, to which I am indebted – especially for the discussion of tax benefits.
2. 1.5.
3. Eleven times he is referred to as Herod (Luke 3.19; 8.3; 9.9; 13.31; 23.7[2x]; 23.8,11,12,15; Acts 4.27); four times as Herod the tetrarch (Luke 3.1; 3.19; 9.7; Acts 13.1).
4. Acts 12.1, 6, 11, 19, 21; 23.35.
5. 55.27.6; regarding coins see Y. Meshorer, *Ancient Jewish Coinage* (Dix Hills, New York: Amphora, 1982), 2. 31-34; 239-41; cf. Derrett, 84.

was 'ethnarch' – a title which, as one would expect, appears on virtually all his coins. There is, however, some evidence of confusion about his title (which is understandable since ethnarchs were quite rare in the Roman world). Josephus suggests that Herod had bequeathed to Archelaus the title of king in his last will, a title that was immediately acclaimed by many members of the royal family, as well as soldiers and citizens.[1] Even after Augustus had reviewed the Great Herod's will and demoted Archelaus and his brothers to the ranks of ethnarch and tetrarchs respectively, Josephus, apparently reflecting popular parlance, referred to Archelaus as 'King' in his later narrative.[2] The closest New Testament parallel (which is, intriguingly, the only explicit reference to Archelaus in the New Testament) appears in Matthew's claim that he was 'ruling over Judaea'.[3] There is ample evidence that Archelaus, who ruled over Judaea, was referred to as 'Herod' and 'King'. In the absence of further evidence, 'King of Judaea' in the context of Luke 1.5 must be considered equally applicable to either the Great Herod or to Archelaus, but the parallel in Matthew and the later reference to Quirinius in Luke, only a few months and a few verses later, makes it much more probable that Luke had in mind Archelaus. If we posit this identification, then the conception of John the Baptist would have taken place in the last few months of Archelaus's reign. By the time Jesus was born, Archelaus had been replaced by Quirinius who, as one would expect according to normal Roman procedure, had quickly commissioned a census so he could know the population and assets of the land he was to rule, not to mention his tax base. So far, Luke seems to be consistent.

There is, however, another problem with this view, namely the notice in Luke 3.1, 3.23 that Jesus 'was about thirty years old' when he began his ministry, during or just after the fifteenth year of the reign of

1. *Antiquities* 17.188-95; cf. *Jewish War* 1.665-2.13; cf. 2.93-95.
2. *Antiquities* 18.93; cf. Schürer, 1.354. Mark may reflect a similar popular usage when he refers to the Tetrarch Herod Antipas as 'King' (6.14). The only other Herod to whom Luke refers as 'King' is Agrippa I (Acts 12.1).
3. Matthew 2.22. The only difference between this phrase and the title attributed to 'Herod' by Luke is that Matthew uses the verb *basileuei* instead of the noun *basileus*. That Matthew chose to use *basileuei* (which could literally be translated as 'he is a King'), rather than a more generic verb such as *archō*, probably reflects his use of the popular language that referred to Archelaus as King. This is certainly the view of Schürer (1.354, n. 2): 'He (Archelaus) is inaccurately styled *basileus* in Mt. 2.22.' It is, however, somewhat problematic that Luke referred to Antipas as tetrarch (Luke 3.1, 19; 9.7; Acts 13.1), perhaps because this title was far more common than ethnarch. Matthew also refers to him as 'Archelaus', not as 'Herod', thus demonstrating that both names were in use at the time.

Tiberius. It is important to note that the chronological connection is not explicit between 3.1 and 3.23. According to Luke, John the Baptist began his public ministry in the fifteenth year of Tiberius. We cannot be sure, and Luke offers no help in determining, how long John's public ministry lasted or at what point in that ministry Jesus was baptised.[1] 3.23 claims only that Jesus began his work when he was about thirty, in context, after his baptism. If Tiberius began his reign in August of AD 14, his fifteenth year would extend from August 28 to August 29. If Jesus was born in AD 6, that would make him between twenty-four and twenty-five years old, depending on one's reckoning. If John's ministry lasted a year or two before Jesus was baptised, however, Jesus could have been as old as twenty-seven when he began his ministry. Is this close enough to be 'about thirty?' According to some, no.[2] If, however, we apply the same reckoning to the traditional view, and Jesus was born between 4 and 6 BC, then in 28/29 AD, he would be between thirty-two and thirty-six, and if we allow any intervening time for John's ministry, Jesus could even be thirty-seven or thirty-eight. In either case, 'about thirty' must be off by at least two years and possibly by as many as eight. Neither position is strongly supported or denied by 3.1 and 3.23. On both reckonings, there seems to be good reason for the 'about'.[3]

Once we have clarified the chronological issues, we have still to deal with the apparent confusion caused by the census, as perpetuated by the traditional view. It is commonly asserted that Quirinius's census was part of an empire-wide census that required citizens to go to their ancestral homes to register. The first assertion is demonstrably false, since Augustus could not commission a 'worldwide' census, nor does he appear to have commissioned an empire-wide census. Here the confusion is based upon a forced interpretation of Luke's statement that Augustus issued a decree that the 'whole world be registered'. Luke's statement is a simple case of hyperbole, akin to Matthew's 'all Judaea was going out' to be baptised by John.[4] No sensible ancient reader would

---

1. Luke is notoriously reluctant about Jesus's baptism, as is clear from his use of the passive voice in 3.21 and his narration of John's imprisonment before mentioning Jesus's baptism (see Meier, 1. 169; cf. E. Schweizer, *The Good News According to Luke* [Atlanta: John Knox, 1984], 75ff.).
2. Brown (548) considers this to be a fatal argument against the position here espoused, though he does not seem to notice the similar problems it raises for his own view.
3. For further discussion, see Hoehner, 29ff.
4. Matthew 3.5.

be bothered or surprised by such a statement. Perhaps Luke means to refer to the census of Judaea as part of a larger census-taking-strategy on the part of Augustus, but there is no way of being sure, and it would not have mattered to Luke or his audience.[1] Anyone living at that time would know that emperors at various times commissioned censuses, and might well do so in provinces other than their own. They would read nothing more into Luke's hyperbole. Rather, the description of the census in this way sets a tone of global proportions – that the events surrounding the birth of Jesus were of more than merely local significance.

The second dimension of the traditional view, that this census required people to register in their ancestral homes, is considerably more problematic, for such a practice would be an administrative nightmare and is patently absurd. As Sanders puts it:

> Luke's device is fantastic. According to Luke's own genealogy (3.23-38), David had lived forty-two generations before Joseph. Why should Joseph have had to register in the town of one of his ancestors forty-two generations earlier? What was Augustus – the most rational of Caesars – thinking of? The entirety of the Roman empire would have been uprooted by such a decree. Besides, how could any given man know where to go? No one could trace his genealogy for forty-two generations, but if he could, he would find that he had *millions* of ancestors (one million is passed at the twentieth generation). Further, David doubtless had tens of thousands of descendants who were alive at the time. Could they all identify themselves? If so, how would they all register in a little village? . . . It is not reasonable to think that there was ever a decree that required people to travel in order to be registered for tax purposes. . . . Ancient census-takers wanted to connect land and landowners for tax purposes. This meant that the census-takers, not those being taxed, would travel.[2]

Sanders's criticism is correct, providing one assumes the traditional interpretation of the text. The absurd implications of this interpretation have led many scholars to reject the historicity of Luke's account of the

---

1. For which there is considerable evidence. For details see F. Millar, *The Roman Near East: 31 BC-AD 337* (Cambridge: Harvard University Press, 1993), 46-7; cf. Brown, 549.
2. Sanders, 86-87.

census and Joseph's response to it, including the common belief that Jesus was born in Bethlehem. If one looks more closely at the text, however, it soon becomes evident that neither of these conclusions necessarily follows from the evidence.

A close reading of Luke reveals that the premise upon which Sanders bases his reconstruction is without foundation in the text. Nowhere does Luke say that the census of Quirinius required people to travel to the home of their ancestors. On the contrary, the text reads, 'the decree went out . . . that the whole world should be registered'. It does not say how or where. Sanders is correct about the issues with which Romans were concerned when administering a census and there is nothing in the narrative of Luke which departs from common practices. Rather, the text describes the perfectly normal response of the people to the decree: 'All went to their *own towns* to be registered.'

From what we know of Roman administration, a census required people to register where they lived and worked and owned property, for the objective of a Roman census was to ascertain the resources of a region so the government could provide suitable infrastructure and, of course, determine the potential for tax revenue and auxiliary troop recruitment. Indeed, it is the connection between census-taking and tax collection that lies beneath the subsequent riots.[1] Thus far, there is nothing curious in the text, certainly nothing that would lend credence to the idea that people had to go to the home of their ancestors. The problem emerges when one looks specifically at Joseph's response to the decree. Why did Joseph, who, according to Luke, was residing in Nazareth at the time (a region that was not required to register at all, since Galilee was under the jurisdiction of Herod Antipas and not directly ruled by the Roman Governor), respond to the decree at all, since it seems not to involve him; and why does Luke have him travel with his pregnant wife to Bethlehem? Luke says only that he went 'to register with Mary'. Note that it does not say he was required to go there, but simply that he went to Bethlehem to register because 'he was descended from the house and family of David' – it was his ancestral home.[2] It is important to emphasise at this point that he was not *required* to go to his ancestral home; the decree required people to register in their own towns; Joseph *chose* to go to his ancestral home. Why?

---

1. Especially the revolt precipitated by Yehuda of Gamla (Josephus, *Antiquities* 2.117-8). Cf. Millar, 46ff.
2. Brown, 396. Millar (46) seems to assume that Luke believes the census applied to Galilee as well as Judaea.

There are two good reasons why he may have done so and neither implies the absurdities of Sanders's reconstruction. First, we must acknowledge the fact that we have no evidence describing the property owned by Joseph or his family. The census required that all register in their 'own towns',[1] which Joseph considered to be Bethlehem. On the other hand, when Joseph, Mary and the newborn Jesus departed from the south, according to Luke, 'they went to their *own town* of Nazareth'.[2] How can Bethlehem be Joseph's 'own town', and Nazareth be 'their own town'? If Luke is correct that Bethlehem was Joseph's ancestral home, there is a strong possibility that he continued to own property there.[3] Joseph would then have needed to go to Bethlehem to maintain proper title to his property and to pay his taxes. This, of course, does not preclude his also owning a home in Nazareth.

Another possible reason why Joseph may have gone to Bethlehem grows out of studies of Hellenistic censuses in Egypt, which gave as much as a fifty percent tax reduction to those who resided in and around metropoleis.[4] Because of the proximity of Bethlehem to Jerusalem, Joseph may have been eligible for the reduced rate, which would never have been the case in Nazareth, and by registering his newborn child in the same place, he would be eligible for the same exemption when he came of age.[5] Perhaps both of these reasons worked together, so that

---

1. 2.3.
2. 2.39.
3. Brown (549) rejects the theory that Joseph owned property in Bethlehem, because he considers it a misguided attempt to harmonise Luke with the reference in Matthew 2.11 to a house in Bethlehem, in which Jesus and family were residing when the Magi visited. If one presses such a harmonisation, it founders on Luke 2.7. My reconstruction has no harmonising agenda. The property may have been something like farmland or a threshing floor. It may even have been a residence in which others resided, which would still cause Joseph and Mary to seek shelter in an 'inn' (*kataluma*). If, however, *kataluma* is used here as it is in Luke 22.11 to designate a sort of guest room, Joseph and Mary may have stayed in the main room of Joseph's own house, or that of a relative or friend – none of which has any significant bearing on the issue at stake; cf. I. H. Marshall, *The Gospel of* Luke (Grand Rapids: Eerdmans, 1978), 101.
4. For further discussion, see S.L. Wallace, *Taxation in Egypt* (Princeton: University, 1938); cf. N. Lewis, *Life in Egypt Under Roman Rule* (Oxford: Clarendon, 1983), 170; cf. Derrett, 90-94.
5. If, as most presume, Joseph and Mary owned a home in Nazareth, it may have been subject to a different taxation system altogether, under the jurisdiction of Herod Antipas.

Joseph went to Bethlehem to maintain the legal status of his property, as well as to take advantage of a tax loophole. Whatever the specific combination of motives, this reconstruction is far more probable than the administrative mare's nest implied by the traditional view. It also explains why Luke considered Quirinius and his census significant for his infancy narrative.

Now that we have grappled with the confusions created by the traditional interpretation of Luke's treatment of the census, it is no longer necessary or even probable to suggest, as many have done, that Jesus was not born in Bethlehem. We have already noted that there is no evidence within Luke of a prophetic theme that would motivate him to invent this story, and his theological and political motives could have been served just as well without the inclusion of this story. We have not, however, examined the nature of the historical evidence, which is significant. In the common parlance of historical Jesus scholars, the New Testament evidence for Jesus's birth in Bethlehem consists of triple attestation, from notably different sources and perspectives.[1] Few events or sayings of Jesus can boast such strong attestation. In addition, the testimony of patristic writings is unanimous in agreeing that Jesus was born in Bethlehem – there are no dissenting voices.[2] With such strong and consistent evidence, and the absence of compelling motives for the fabrication of the story, it is most probable that Luke believed that Jesus was born in Bethlehem, and that this belief rests upon a sound historical foundation.

To this point, we have shown only how Luke's Gospel is clearer and more consistent if we posit that he believed Jesus was born in AD 6, during the administration of Quirinius. It remains to examine the effects of such a reconstruction on the relationship between Luke's account and the infancy narrative of Matthew. As already noted, the traditional view

---

1. Matthew 2.1, 5, 6, 8, 16; Luke 2.4, 15; John 7.42. The absence of references to Bethlehem in Mark and Q do not pose any significant problem, since neither discusses the nativity of Jesus at all. The reference to Bethlehem in John hints (with appropriate irony typical of John) at it, but does not explicitly claim that Jesus was born there.

2. E.g. *Acts of Paul* 8.29; *Proteuangelion of James* 18.1, 21.1; *Ascension of Isaiah* 11.1-15; *Sibylline Oracles* 8.479; *Epistula Apostolorum* 3, *Acts of Pilate* 9.3 – as well as many references in the works of such fathers as Justin Martyr, Origen, Eusebius, and Athanasius. In saying that these are unanimous, I do not mean to imply that the discussion of the birth of Jesus was a major theme in the Early Church; it was not. Even the celebration of Christmas seems to have been a latecomer among early Christian festivals.

takes Matthew as its starting point, but it does so apparently without subjecting Matthew's reference to Herod to the same searching criticism that has been applied to Luke's reference to Quirinius. If Luke has as a minor theme the submission of Jesus's family to Roman authority, *the central theme* of the infancy narrative and early chapters of Matthew is a theological/typological parallel between Jesus and Moses, as is widely acknowledged.[1]

For example, in the first five chapters of Matthew, Jesus, as an infant, faces the threat of murder at the hands of a tyrant (causing him to flee to Egypt), undergoes his own exodus, wanders in the wilderness for forty days (cf. Moses's forty years), after which he ascends a mount and delivers the divine law to the people. Even though this literary parallel has been widely recognised, it has seldom been applied to discussions of the date of Jesus's birth. In order to make his parallel with Moses work, at least in his infancy narrative, Matthew needs a tyrannical king who is willing to kill babies. It is important to note that the presence of a baby-killing tyrant is *essential* to Matthew's version – his parallel will not work without it. The only such tyrant in the neighbourhood, both chronologically and geographically, was Herod the Great who, according to Josephus, even killed three of his own sons.[2] Matthew had every reason, therefore, to place the birth of Jesus in the reign of Herod the Great, whether or not he had any historical evidence on which to base it. Given Matthew's penchant for midrashic interpretation, this should occasion no surprise.[3]

I do not think that Matthew had any intention of offering a chronological account of Jesus's birth. His aim was not chronological but theological and literary. He may have taken his lead from a tradition that claimed Jesus's birth was around the time of an unspecified Herod; he may then have substituted Herod the Great for Herod Archelaus as a way of building his theological and literary edifice – but this is pure speculation. I do not think Matthew can be accused of falsifying the historical facts if he never intended to write an historical account. Rather, his infancy narrative should be judged upon its theological and literary merits. It is much more probable that Matthew would adopt a different chronology to fit his theological and literary scheme (or that he

---

1. Brown, 228ff.; cf. Sanders, 87; cf. R.H. Gundry, *Matthew: A Commentary on His Literary and Theological Art* (Grand Rapids: Eerdmans, 1982), 32-7; 54; 78ff; cf. D.C. Allison, *The New Moses: A Matthaean Typology* (Minneapolis: Fortress, 1993).
2. Not to mention his wife. *Jewish War* 1.438-551; 661-64.
3. Gundry, *Matthew*; cf. Brown, 557ff.

ignored chronological considerations altogether) than that Luke (who, in my opinion, did intend to maintain an historical framework for his narrative)[1] would make an easily falsified chronological blunder, which hurts his credibility as an author and contributes little if anything to his central theological or literary themes.

The historian must analyse the probabilities based on the available evidence. On this basis, the most probable reconstruction of the evidence at hand seems to me to be this: not only was Dionysius Exiguus wrong when he calculated the birth of Jesus in the year one, but most interpreters since have been even farther from the mark. Jesus was probably born in Bethlehem in AD 6. He was probably not born on December 25, at least if the shepherds in the fields, watching their flocks by night, have anything to say about it![2] Herod the Great's presence in the Christmas tradition makes for good pageantry but bad history. To my knowledge, no one has yet cast Quirinius in a Christmas play, but it might be worth a try.

The Date of Jesus's Execution

Given the nature of the evidence, any conclusions about the precise dating of the birth of Jesus are necessarily of modest probability. The date of his execution, however, is relatively straightforward: it was probably April 3, AD 33. There are a few chronological benchmarks that form the parameters for any discussion of the life of Jesus.

First and most important is Luke 3.1:

> In the fifteenth year of the reign of Emperor Tiberius, when Pontius Pilate was governor of Judaea, and Herod was ruler of Galilee, and his brother Philip ruler of the region of Ituraea

---

1. Luke's concern for historical detail does not exclude a concern for theology.
2. The custom of celebrating Christmas on December 25 appears to have begun around the time of Constantine, with Christmas serving as a substitute for the Roman festivals of Saturnalia and Compitalia. The coincidence between the celebration of the birth of the Christian saviour and the pagan celebration of the rebirth of *Sol* at the winter solstice, may well be Constantine's way of adapting Christian substance to pagan traditions, parallel with his proclamation of Sunday as a holiday. It may also reflect his own early attachment to *Sol Invictus* as celebrated on many issues of his coins dating from 310 until well after his conversion to Christianity. For further discussion, see O. Cullmann, 'The Origin of Christmas', *The Early Church* [Philadelphia: Westminster, 1956]), 21-36; Hoehner, 25-27; M. Salzman, *On Roman Time: The Codex Calendar of 354 and the Rhythms of Urban Life in Late Antiquity* (Berkeley: University of California, 1990).

and Trachonitis, and Lysanias ruler of Abilene, during the high priesthood of Annas and Caiaphas, the word of God came to John son of Zechariah in the wilderness.

All these synchronisms work together, but they rest on the meaning of the 'fifteenth year of Tiberius'. If one uses the same calculation Tacitus, Suetonius, and Dio employ, the fifteenth regnal year of Tiberius would run from August 19, 28 to August 18, 29. Since Romans usually considered regnal years based on the Julian calendar, they would normally count the first year as beginning on January 1, 14. According to the text of Luke, then, the beginning of the public ministry of John the Baptist started, at the earliest, in the autumn of 28 or, at the latest, in December of 29. John was active in public life long enough to make a significant impression before ever Jesus visited him and received baptism. If we give John a year before he baptised him, Jesus would have begun his public ministry in 30, but if we give John a longer period of public ministry or a start in late 29, then Jesus might have been baptised as late as early 31. In short, Jesus likely began his public ministry in 29 at the earliest but more realistically in 30, or even later still.

Then, the question becomes: how long was Jesus active in public ministry before he was executed? The synoptic Gospels mention only one Passover, while the Gospel of John mentions three.[1] This discrepancy is a problem only if we assume that the synoptics were making exclusive chronological references – that is, that Jesus celebrated *only* one Passover. Such an interpretation is possible, but is by no means necessary. The most natural interpretation of all the evidence suggests that the synoptics did not consider the other two Passovers worthy of mention or of interest to their literary objectives.

Many interpreters suggest a date of execution in 30. Even if Jesus celebrated only one Passover, it is very difficult to make that date work. The only way would be to have John begin his ministry in January of 29 (or maybe autumn of 28?), with Jesus receiving his baptism and launching his public ministry just after Passover in 29. This would give John only a very few months to launch his ministry and to make a substantial public impression before Jesus was baptised. Then, from that time, the entirety of Jesus's public ministry would last less than twelve months before 14 Nissan of 30. This kind of chronology may be plausible, but it is not very probable. Some who argue for a date of execution in 30 also argue that Jesus's ministry lasted something like a year and a half. It is difficult to make this chronology fit unless one allows for Jesus to be baptised in

1. John 2.13; 6.4; 11.55.

late 28 or early 29, before Passover (thus including more than the one Passover mentioned in the Synoptic Gospels). It is simpler and more probable to take an inclusive view of the evidence and allow for three Passovers, starting with the most common and natural reading of the 'fifteenth year of Tiberius'.[1]

If we allow for three Passovers, then the next issue concerns the day of the week on which Passover falls. According to all our sources, Jesus was executed on Passover, 14 Nissan, and that day fell on a Friday.[2] This combination narrows things down quite a bit for, based on astronomical calculations, there are only two dates during this period on which 14 Nissan fell on a Friday: April 7, 30 or April 3, 33.[3] Only April 3, 33 is possible when we allow for three Passovers, unless we posit that Jesus was baptised before Passover in 28.

There is one additional reason why 33 is to be preferred: the execution of Sejanus in 31. Philo's Affair of the Shields, discussed above, makes the most sense if placed just after Sejanus has been executed. After this date, Tiberius allowed Jews to return to Rome, which suggests that he had a more favourable attitude toward Jews than had his praetorian prefect (whom Philo accuses of anti-Jewish sentiments). Under the

---

1. For detailed discussion, see J.P. Meier, *A Marginal Jew: Rethinking the Historical Jesus* (New York: Doubleday, 1991), I, 372-433. His is one of the most thorough and persuasive arguments in favour of a date of 30 for the crucifixion but, in order to make his chronology work, he allows for virtually no time for the ministry of John the Baptist before the baptism of Jesus, placing the beginning of Jesus's ministry early in 28, both of which create a compressed and problematic reading of Luke's reference to the 'fifteenth year of Tiberius'.

2. See below, however, for the specific problems related to the Passover chronology in John, which does not include reference to the last supper as the Passover feast, has Jesus sacrificed along with the Passover lambs on Friday, and anticipates that the high priestly family will eat the Passover the evening after Jesus's execution.

3. For detailed discussion, see C.J. Humphreys, *The Mystery of the Last Supper: Reconstructing the Final Days of Jesus* (Cambridge: Cambridge University Press, 2011), who largely concurs with J.K. Fotheringham, 'The Evidence of Astronomy and Technical Chronology for the Date of the Crucifixion', *The Journal of Theological Studies* 35 (1943), 146-62, while also improving his astronomical modelling and answering some critiques of using astronomy as a means of determine ancient Passover chronology; cf. R.A. Parker and W.H. Dubberstein, *Babylonian Chronology, 626 BC-AD 75* (Providence: Brown University Press, 1956), 46 ff.; P.L. Maier, 'Sejanus, Pilate, and the Date of the Crucifixion', *Church History* 37 (1968), 3-13.

circumstances, it would make perfect sense for Pilate to have the shields made just after the execution of Sejanus, to demonstrate his loyalty to Tiberius at a crucial time in his career, when he knew he could be drawn into the treasonous accusations levied against many people loyal to Sejanus. This context would also explain why Pilate was so reluctant to move the shields once they were installed. Any such act could be viewed as a demonstration of disloyalty to the emperor at the worst possible moment. The issue was resolved, as we have seen, only when a Jewish delegation delivered a complaint to Rome, Tiberius received it, and issued a letter of rebuke to Pilate. Any such Jewish delegation before 31, at a time when Jews had been ousted from Rome, would not have received a warm reception from the emperor (indeed, he likely would not have known of its existence, since Sejanus was effectively administering the empire at that time). For such reasons, most scholars date the Affair of the Shields after the execution of Sejanus, in 31 or 32. The complaint of the delegation would have been a much riskier venture before 31.

Much the same can be said for the trial of Jesus. According to the Gospel of John, at a crucial moment, Annas made the argument, 'If you release this man, you are no friend of the emperor.'[1] This statement represents, in essence, the threat of another Jewish delegation sailing off to Rome to complain to Tiberius about Pilate. That threat would bear little weight in 30, for Pilate would be confident that the delegation would not receive a sympathetic hearing. After 31, however, that threat was potent and need hardly be voiced, for Pilate was still smarting from the latest rebuke from Tiberius, and he knew his career could not withstand another such blow. The timing of the execution of Sejanus, therefore, is one additional reason why it is less probable that Jesus was executed in 30, and more probable that the correct year was 33.[2] When put together, all the chronological markers point toward April 3, AD 33.[3]

---

1. John 19.12.
2. Maier, 8-13.
3. One additional chronological consideration comes from some of Paul's autobiographical references in the Epistle to the Galatians (1.18 and 2.1). These references seem to suggest that there needs to be time for at least fourteen years, and as many as seventeen, depending on whether one reads these references as additive or inclusive, from the time of Paul's conversion to his visit to Jerusalem. Most interpreters think that this particular visit can fit into Paul's chronology no later than 49, placing his conversion no later than 35. This chronology works, if just barely, for all agree that some time passed between the execution of Jesus and the conversion of Paul. For these reasons, Paul's chronological references seem to preclude any proposed

There remains one additional problem to be resolved, and that is the conflict between the synoptic Gospels and John concerning Passover. According to the synoptics, on Thursday evening before his arrest, Jesus ate the Passover with his disciples.[1] On the other hand, according to the Gospel of John, the high priestly family planned to eat the Passover on Friday, after the trial of Jesus.[2] Both, however, agree that Jesus was executed on Friday. So, when was 14 Nissan? How can we explain this chronological Passover impasse?

Historians focus on analysis and synthesis of ancient evidence. Synthesis, however, often turns into efforts at harmonisation, and efforts at harmonisation too often become more ingenious than faithful to the evidence. There have been a good many efforts to synthesise or harmonise this conflicting evidence, most of which have failed to persuade the scholarly community. Some have suggested that the Last Supper, on Thursday evening, was not the Passover. Others have suggested that the reference in John refers not to the Passover, but rather to the Feast of Unleavened Bread. Others still have proposed that Jesus held his own Passover a day early because he knew he would not be available Friday evening. Still others have suggested that, in Jesus's day, Passover was celebrated for two days because of the large number of lambs that needed to be sacrificed in the Temple. A variation on this theme is that there was a disagreement between Pharisees and Sadducees on when the Passover feast was to be held. None of these attempts has gained much traction. There are, however, two possibilities that are, in my judgment, more persuasive.

The first has to do with the reckoning of when a day begins. Some considered a day to last from sunrise to sunrise, while others, including modern Jews, consider it to last from sunset to sunset. Ancient Jewish writings are not consistent on this issue. Perhaps, then, there was in Jesus's day some confusion or disagreement or malleability on this issue. Indeed, perhaps there was a disagreement between Jesus and the high priestly family on this issue. Such a difference or disagreement is certainly plausible. With this distinction in mind, it is possible that Jesus and his disciples considered the day to begin at sunset. If so, they probably would have had their Passover lamb sacrificed in the late afternoon of 13 Nissan or early evening of 14 Nissan, so that they could eat the Passover feast

---

date for Jesus's execution after 33 (though of course, these references leave plenty of room for reconstructions that place Jesus's execution before 33). For further discussion, see Humphreys, 66.

1. Matthew 26.17; Mark 14.12; Luke 22.7.
2. John 18.28.

after sunset, on 14 Nissan. On this reckoning, Jesus would have been tried and executed, all on 14 Nissan, on Friday. Meanwhile, if the house of Annas reckoned the day to begin at sunrise, then the arrest of Jesus would be late on 13 Nissan, while the trial and execution would be on Friday, 14 Nissan, and they would sacrifice the lamb that same afternoon and eat the Passover feast Friday evening. This modest disagreement over when the day commences would provide a reasonable and plausible synthesis of the evidence.

C.J. Humphreys presents a fascinating variant on this kind of reasoning. He suggests, based on substantive if not abundant evidence, that some Jews adhered to a pre-exilic Hebrew calendar that was influenced by the early Egyptian lunar calendar.[1] This pre-exilic Hebrew calendar is largely reflected in the later Samaritan calendar. These calendars both considered the day to begin at sunrise.[2] Only later did some Jews from Judah, under the influence of the Babylonian lunar calendar, create the post-exilic calendar, which changed the reckoning of the beginning of the day from sunrise to sunset.[3] Jews who were not from Judah, however, did not necessarily accept this change. With just this difference in mind, perhaps some Jews considered 14 Nissan to begin at sunrise on Thursday, and thus sacrificed the Paschal lamb in the afternoon and ate the Passover meal on Thursday evening. The high priestly family, on the other hand, followed the 'official' post-exilic calendar, and thus considered 14 Nissan not to begin until sunset Thursday evening. They would therefore have waited until Friday afternoon to sacrifice the Paschal lamb and begin their Passover meal around sunset on Friday, extending into the new day, the evening of 15 Nissan. Such a disagreement over calendars would potentially alleviate key discrepancies among our texts if, indeed, there was some conflict over when the day began. Humphreys argues, however, that there was another difference between the pre- and post-exilic calendars: the reckoning of the beginning of the month. The pre-exilic Hebrew calendar may have considered, in line with its Egyptian model, that the month began at the time of conjunction, when the sun is in line with the moon, and therefore the new moon is not visible. The post-exilic calendar, by contrast, considered the new month to begin when the new moon is first visible, usually one or two days after the time

---

1. Humphreys, 115-20.
2. Humphreys further argues (140-46) that a similar calendar was employed as the Qumran Lunar Calendar (4Q321); cf. S. Stern, *Calendar and Community: A History of the Jewish Calendar: 2nd Century BCE- 10th Century CE* (Oxford: Oxford University Press, 2001).
3. Humphreys, 110-114.

of conjunction. According to Humphreys' astronomical calculations (in collaboration with the astrophysicist G. Waddington), if Jesus was using the pre-exilic calendar, he would have celebrated the Passover on Wednesday evening, not Thursday.[1]

One additional variation on this theory would be that John seems to calculate the hours of the day differently than the synoptic Gospels, beginning at midnight rather than 6 AM.[2] If, therefore, he considered 14 Nissan to begin at midnight, then on his calculation, Jesus was arrested at the end of 13 Nissan, the high priests' inquest took place in the wee hours of 14 Nissan, and Jesus's execution and the *Pesach* would take place before midnight on Friday. The primary problem with this view would be that Jesus and his disciples would then have eaten the Passover meal on 13 Nissan. Then again, John does not include a narrative of the Last Supper in his Gospel.[3]

A different approach comes from Pope Benedict XVI, who argued in his Holy Thursday Homily of 2007 that Jesus used the solar calendar of Qumran and, therefore, celebrated the Passover meal at least one day earlier than most Jews celebrated theirs. While this proposal solves some chronological problems, it creates others, especially when one considers the fact that we have no evidence of how those who created this alternative calendar attempted (or did not attempt) to square their solar calendar with the lunar calendar and the need for intercalary days to keep this three hundred and sixty-four day calendar from falling out of sync with agricultural seasons.[4]

Some scholars, after reviewing all of these explanations, fail to find any of them convincing, concluding instead that no synthesis between the synoptics and John on this issue is possible. Rather, they consider either John or the synoptic accounts to be historical and the other to be ahistorical or redacted for theological or literary reasons. If one opts for the 'no synthesis' position, there is relevant evidence as to why John might have changed the day of Passover for theological reasons. John alone includes the proclamation by John the Baptist that Jesus is the

---

1. Humphreys, 151-68.
2. John 1.39; 19.14; 20.19.
3. For a thoughtful review of the range of possible explanations, see Hoehner, 76-90.
4. Vatican City, April 6, 2007, as reported in zenit.org. Pope Benedict based his argument on the research of A. Jaubert, *The Date of the Last Supper* (Staten Island, NY: Alba House, 1965). Jaubert places Jesus's Last Supper on Tuesday evening, before his execution on Friday. For detailed discussion, see Humphreys, 95ff.

'lamb of God who takes away the sin of the world'.[1] John alone, moreover, makes a point of the fact that none of the bones of Jesus were broken, thus fulfilling the Hebrew Bible qualification to be the unblemished Passover lamb.[2] This theological theme would provide a good reason to have Jesus executed at the very same time that the Passover lambs were being sacrificed in the Temple.

While the Passover issue continues to generate scholarly consternation, the chronology of the life of Jesus otherwise rests on reasonably probable ground. Jesus was probably born in AD 6. John's ministry, meanwhile, probably began in early 29, maturing for a bit over a year before Jesus was baptised after Passover in 30. His first two Passovers as a public figure took place in 31 and 32. In AD 33, on 14 Nissan, he ate the Passover with his disciples, was arrested, and was then subjected to the high priests' inquest. The next morning, Friday, April 3, he was executed. This, in my judgment, represents the chronology of the life of Jesus that does justice to all the evidence with the highest level of probability permitted by the nature of the evidence.

---

1. John 1.29, 36.
2. John 19.36; cf. Exodus 12.46; Numbers 9.12; Psalms 34.20; cf. Revelation 5.6, 8, 12, 13; 6.1, 16, *et passim*.

Appendix II:
New Testament References to *Synedrion*

Matthew 5.22 But I say to you that if you are angry with a brother or sister, you will be liable to judgment; and if you insult a brother or sister, you will be liable to the council; and if you say, 'You fool,' you will be liable to the hell of fire.

Matthew 10.17 Beware of them, for they will hand you over to councils and flog you in their synagogues. . . .
Matthew 26.59 Now the chief priests and the whole council were looking for false testimony against Jesus so that they might put him to death. . . .

Mark 13.9 'As for yourselves, beware; for they will hand you over to councils; and you will be beaten in synagogues; and you will stand before governors and kings because of me, as a testimony to them.

Mark 14.55 Now the chief priests and the whole council were looking for testimony against Jesus to put him to death; but they found none.
Mark 15.1 As soon as it was morning, the chief priests held a consultation with the elders and scribes and the whole council. They bound Jesus, led him away, and handed him over to Pilate.
Luke 22.66 When day came, the assembly of the elders of the people, both chief priests and scribes, gathered together, and they brought him to their council.
John 11.47 So the chief priests and the Pharisees called a meeting of the council, and said, 'What are we to do? This man is performing many signs. . . .

Acts 4.15 So they ordered them to leave the council while they discussed the matter with one another.

Acts 5.21 When they heard this, they entered the temple at daybreak and went on with their teaching. When the high priest and those with him arrived, they called together the council and the whole body of the elders of Israel, and sent to the prison to have them brought.

Acts 5.27 When they had brought them, they had them stand before the council. The high priest questioned them . . .

Acts 5.34 But a Pharisee in the council named Gamaliel, a teacher of the law, respected by all the people, stood up and ordered the men to be put outside for a short time.

Acts 5.41 As they left the council, they rejoiced that they were considered worthy to suffer dishonour for the sake of the name.

Acts 6.12 They stirred up the people as well as the elders and the scribes; then they suddenly confronted him, seized him, and brought him before the council.

Acts 6.15 And all who sat in the council looked intently at him, and they saw that his face was like the face of an angel.

Acts 22.30 Since he wanted to find out what Paul was being accused of by the Jews, the next day he released him and ordered the chief priests and the entire council to meet. He brought Paul down and had him stand before them.

Acts 23.1 While Paul was looking intently at the council he said, 'Brothers, up to this day I have lived my life with a clear conscience before God.'

Acts 23.6 When Paul noticed that some were Sadducees and others were Pharisees, he called out in the council, 'Brothers, I am a Pharisee, a son of Pharisees. I am on trial concerning the hope of the resurrection of the dead.'

Acts 23.15 Now then, you and the council must notify the tribune to bring him down to you, on the pretext that you want to make a more thorough examination of his case. And we are ready to do away with him before he arrives.'

Acts 23.20 He answered, 'The Jews have agreed to ask you to bring Paul down to the council tomorrow, as though they were going to inquire more thoroughly into his case. . . .'

Acts 23.28 Since I wanted to know the charge for which they accused him, I had him brought to their council.

Acts 24.20 Or let these men here [Jews from Asia] tell what crime they had found when I stood before the council. . . .

Auctoritates:
Secondary Sources for Further Reading

Allison, D. *Constructing Jesus: Memory, Imagination, and History*. Grand
    Rapids: Baker, 2010.
—— *The New Moses: A Matthaean Typology*. Minneapolis: Fortress, 1993.
Arav, R. and Freund, R. *Bethsaida: A City by the North Shore of the Sea of Galilee*,
    Vol. II. Kirksville: Truman State University Press, 1999.
Avigad, N. 'How the Wealthy Lived in Herodian Jerusalem.' *Biblical
    Archaeology Review* 2, no. 4 (1976): 1, 23–32, 34–35.
Bammel, E., ed. *The Trial of Jesus*. London: SCM, 1970.
Bammel, E. and Moule, C.F.D., eds. *Jesus and the Politics of his Day*.
    Cambridge: Cambridge University Press, 1984.
Bauckham, R. *Jesus and the Eyewitnesses: The Gospels as Eyewitness Testimony*.
    Grand Rapids: Eerdmans, 2006.
—— 'Jesus' Demonstration in the Temple' in *Law and Religion: Essays on the
    Place of the Law in Israel and Early Christianity*, edited by B. Lindars and
    R. Bauckham, 72-89; 171-6. Cambridge: James Clarke, 1988.
Bauman, R.A. *Impietas in Principem: A Study of Treason against the Roman
    Emperor with Special Reference to the First Century AD*. Munich: C.H. Beck,
    1974.
Blinzler, J. *The Trial of Jesus*. Translated by Isabel and Florence McHugh.
    Westminster, Maryland: Newman Press, 1959.
Bodel, J. 'Graveyards and Groves: A Study of the *Lex Lucerina*.' *American
    Journal of Ancient History* 11 (1994): 1-117.
Bond, H.K. *Caiaphas: Friend of Rome and Judge of Jesus?* Louisville:
    Westminster John Knox, 2004.
—— *Pontius Pilate in History and Interpretation*. Cambridge: Cambridge
    University Press, 1998.
Borg, M. and Crossan, J.D. *The Last Week: What the Gospels Really Teach about
    Jesus's Final Days in Jerusalem*. New York: HarperOne, 2006.
Brown, R.E. *The Birth of the Messiah*. New York: Doubleday, 1993.
—— *The Death of the Messiah*. New York: Bantam, Doubleday, Dell, 1994.
Bruce, F.F. *New Testament History*. New York: Doubleday-Galilee, 1969.
Charlesworth, J.H., ed. *Jesus and the Temple: Textual and Archaeological
    Explorations*. Minneapolis: Fortress, 2014.

Crossan, J.D. *The Historical Jesus: The Life of a Mediterranean Jewish Peasant.* San Francisco: HarperCollins, 1991.

—— *Who Killed Jesus? Exposing the Roots of Anti-Semitism in the Gospel Story of the Death of Jesus.* San Francisco: HarperCollins, 1995.

Drake, H.A. *Constantine and the Bishops: The Politics of Intolerance.* Baltimore: Johns Hopkins University Press, 2000.

Evans, C.A. 'Jesus' Action in the Temple: Cleansing or Portent of Destruction?' *Catholic Biblical Quarterly* 51 (1989): 237-70.

—— *Jesus and the Ossuaries: What Jewish Burial Practices Reveal about the Beginning of Christianity.* Waco: Baylor University Press, 2003.

Evans, C.A. and Wright, N.T. *Jesus, the Final Days: What Really Happened?* Edited by T.A. Miller. Louisville: Westminster, John Knox, 2008.

Eck, W. *The Age of Augustus.* Oxford: Blackwell, 2007.

Fiensy, D.A. *Christian Origins and the Ancient Economy.* Cambridge: James Clarke, 2014.

Finley, M.I. *Ancient History: Evidence and Models.* New York: Penguin, 1985.

Funk, R.W. and Hoover, R.W., eds. *The Five Gospels.* New York: Macmillan, 1993.

Fuhrmann, C.J. *Policing the Roman Empire: Soldiers, Administration, and Public Order.* Oxford: Oxford University Press, 2012.

Garnsey, P.D.A. and Saller, R.P. *The Roman Empire: Economy, Society, and Culture.* Berkeley: University of California Press, 1987.

Geva, H. *Ancient Jerusalem Revealed.* Jerusalem: Israel Exploration Society, 1994.

Gibson, S. *The Final Days of Jesus: The Archaeological Evidence.* New York: HarperCollins, 2009.

Goodacre, M. 'Scripturalization in Mark's Crucifixion Narrative' in *The Trial and Death of Jesus: Essays on the Passion Narrative in Mark,* edited by G. Van Oyen and T. Shepherd, 33-47. Leuven: Peeters, 2006.

Goodman, M. *Rome and Jerusalem: The Clash of Ancient Civilizations.* New York: Vantage, 2007.

—— *The Ruling Class of Judaea: The Origins of the Jewish Revolt against Rome A.D. 66-70.* Cambridge: Cambridge University Press, 1987.

Gundry, R.H. *Mark: A Commentary on His Apology for the Cross.* Grand Rapids: Eerdmans, 1993.

—— *Matthew: A Commentary on His Handbook for a Mixed Church under Persecution.* Grand Rapids: Eerdmans, 1995.

—— *The Old is Better: New Testament Essays in Support of Traditional Interpretations.* Eugene: Wipf and Stock, 2005.

—— *A Survey of the New Testament.* Grand Rapids: Zondervan, 2012.

Hammond, N.G.L. *Sources for Alexander the Great.* Cambridge: Cambridge University Press, 1993.

Hendin, D. *Guide to Biblical Coins: Fifth Edition.* New York: Amphora, 2010.

Hengel, M. *Crucifixion.* London: SCM, 1977.

—— *Zealots.* London: Bloomsbury T&T Clark, 2000.

Horbury, W. 'The Messianic Associations of the "The Son of Man."' *Journal of Theological Studies* 36 (1985): 34-55.

Horsley, R.A. *Jesus and the Politics of Roman Palestine.* Columbia: University of South Carolina Press, 2014.

Horsley, R.A. and Hanson, J.S. *Bandits, Prophets, and Messiahs: Popular Movements in the Time of Jesus.* Minneapolis: Winston Press, 1985.

Horst, P.W. van der. *Philo's Flaccus: The First Pogrom.* Atlanta: Society for Biblical Literature, 2003.

Humphreys, C.J. *The Mystery of the Last Supper: Reconstructing the Final Days of Jesus.* Cambridge: Cambridge University Press, 2011.

Hurtado, L.W. *Lord Jesus Christ: Devotion to Jesus in Earliest Christianity.* Grand Rapids: Eerdmans, 2003.

Jeremias, J. *Jerusalem in the Time of Jesus.* Philadelphia: Fortress, 1969.

Jones, A.H.M. *Studies in Roman Government and Law.* New York: Praeger, 1960.

Judge, E.A. *Social Distinctives of the Christians in the First Century: Pivotal Essays by E.A. Judge.* Edited by D.M. Scholer. Peabody: Hendrickson, 2008.

Kloppenborg, J.S. 'The Growth and Impact of Agricultural Tenancy in Jewish Palestine.' *Journal of Economic and Social History of the Orient* 51 (2008): 33-66.

Kyle, D.G. *Spectacles of Death in Ancient Rome.* London: Routledge, 1998.

Lanciani, R. *Ancient Rome in the Light of Recent Discoveries.* London: MacMillan, 1888.

Leclercq, H. 'Supplice de la flagellation' in *Dictionnaire d'archéologie chrétienne et de liturgie*, Vol. 5, 1637-44. Paris: Letouzey et Ané, 1923.

Lendon, J.E. *Empire of Honour.* Oxford: Clarendon, 1997.

Levine, A-J. *The Misunderstood Jew: The Church and the Scandal of the Jewish Jesus.* New York: HarperOne, 2006.

Levine, L.I. *Judaism & Hellenism in Antiquity: Conflict or Confluence?* Seattle: University of Washington Press, 1998.

Lintott, A. Imperium Romanum: *Politics and Administration.* New York: Routledge, 1993.

MacMullan, R. *Roman Social Relations: 50 B.C. to A.D. 284.* New Haven: Yale University Press, 1974.

Magness, J. *The Archaeology of the Holy Land: From the Destruction of Solomon's Temple to the Muslim Conquest.* Cambridge: Cambridge University Press, 2012.

—— *Stone and Dung, Oil and Spit: Jewish Daily Life in the Time of Jesus.* Grand Rapids: Eerdmans, 2011.

Maier, P.L. *Pontius Pilate.* New York: Doubleday, 1968.

—— 'The Episode of the Golden Roman Shields at Jerusalem.' *Harvard Theological Review* 62 (1969): 109-21.

—— 'Sejanus, Pilate, and the Date of the Crucifixion.' *Church History* 37 (1968): 3-13.

Mason, S. *Josephus and the New Testament*. Peabody: Hendrickson, 2003.

Mazar, A. 'The Aqueducts of Jerusalem' in *Jerusalem Revealed: Archaeology in the Holy City 1968-1974*, edited by Y. Yadin, 79-84. Jerusalem: Israel Exploration Society, 1975.

McCane, B.R. *Roll Back the Stone: Death and Burial in the World of Jesus*. Harrisburg: Trinity Press International, 2003.

McLaren, J. *Power and Politics in Palestine: The Jews and the Governing of their Land 100 BC-AD 70*. London: Bloomsbury, 2015.

Meier, J.P. *A Marginal Jew: Rethinking the Historical Jesus*. New York: Doubleday, 1991. Vol. I.

Meshorer, Y. *Ancient Jewish Coinage*. New York: Amphora, 1982.

Millar, F. *The Emperor in the Roman World*. Ithaca: Cornell University Press, 1977.

— *The Roman Near East, 31 BC-AD 337*. Cambridge: Harvard University Press, 1993.

Mommsen, T. *The Provinces of the Roman Empire*. New York: Barnes and Noble, 1885, 1996.

Nineham, D.E., ed. *Historicity and Chronology in the New Testament*. London: SPCK, 1965.

Parchami, A. *Hegemonic Peace and Empire: The Pax Romana, Britannica, and Americana*. London: Routledge, 2009.

Reed, J.L. *The HarperCollins Visual Guide to the New Testament: What Archaeology Reveals about the First Christians*. New York: HarperCollins, 2007.

Reinhartz, A. *Caiaphas the High Priest*. Minneapolis: Fortress, 2013.

Richardson, J. *Roman Provincial Administration*. Bristol: Bristol Classical Press, 1976.

Richardson, P. *Herod: King of the Jews and Friend of the Romans*. Minneapolis: Fortress, 1996.

Ritmeyer, L. *The Quest: Revealing the Temple Mount in Jerusalem*. Jerusalem: Carta, 2006.

Ritmeyer, K. and Ritmeyer, L. 'Akeldama: Potter's Field or High Priest's Tomb?' *Biblical Archaeology Review*, Nov/Dec 1994, 22-35, 76, 78.

Rogan, J. *Roman Provincial Administration*. Chalford: Amberley, 2011.

Rousseau, J.J. and Arav, R. *Jesus and His World: An Archaeological and Cultural Dictionary*. Minneapolis: Fortress, 1995.

Russell, J.B. *The Devil: Perceptions of Evil from Antiquity to Primitive Christianity*. Ithaca: Cornell University Press, 1977.

Saldarini, J.S. *Pharisees, Scribes, and Sadducees in Palestinian Society*. Grand Rapids: Eerdmans, 1988.

Saller, R.P. *Personal Patronage under the Roman Empire*. Cambridge: Cambridge University Press, 1982.

Sanders, E.P. *The Historical Figure of Jesus*. London: Penguin, 1993.

— *Judaism Practice and Belief 63 BCE-66 CE*. London: SCM, 1992.

Schäfer, P. *The History of the Jews in the Greco-Roman World*. London: Routledge, 1995.

Schenck, K. *A Brief Guide to Philo.* Louisville: Westminster John Knox, 2005.

Schürer, E. *The History of the Jewish People in the Age of Jesus Christ.* Revised and edited by G. Vermes, F. Millar, M. Black, and P. Vermes. Bloomsbury: T & T Clark, 2014.

Shanks, H. *Partings: How Judaism and Christianity Became Two.* Washington D.C.: Biblical Archaeological Society, 2013.

Shaw, B.D. 'Bandits in the Roman Empire.' *Past and Present,* 105 (November, 1984), 3-52.

—— 'Roman Taxation' in *Civilization of the Ancient Mediterranean: Greece and Rome,* edited by M. Grant and R. Kitzinger, Vol. 2, 809-27. New York: Scribner, 1988.

Sherwin-White, A.N. *Roman Society and Roman Law in the New Testament.* Oxford: Oxford University Press, 1963.

Smallwood, E.M. *The Jews under Roman Rule: From Pompey to Diocletian, A Study in Political Relations.* Leiden: Brill, 1976.

Smith, M. 'Capital Punishment and Burial in the Roman Empire' in *Bethsaida in Archaeology, History, and Ancient Culture: A Festschrift in Honor of John T. Greene,* edited by J. Harold Ellens, 381-422. Newcastle: Cambridge Scholars, 2014.

—— 'Of Jesus and Quirinius.' *Catholic Biblical Quarterly* 62.3 (2000), 278-93.

Stambaugh J. and Balch, D. *The Social World of the First Christians.* London: SPCK, 1986.

Strickert, F. *Philip's City: From Bethsaida to Julias.* Collegeville, MN: Liturgical Press, 2011.

Tabor, J. *The Jesus Dynasty: The Hidden History of Jesus, His Royal Family, and the Birth of Christianity.* New York: Simon and Schuster, 2007.

Tarn, W.W. *Alexander the Great: Sources and Studies.* Cambridge: Cambridge University Press, 1950.

Toynbee, J.M.C. *Death and Burial in the Roman World.* Baltimore: Johns Hopkins University Press, 1996.

VanderKam, J.C. *From Joshua to Caiaphas: High Priests After the Exile.* Minneapolis: Fortress, 2004.

Wallace-Hadrill, A., ed. *Patronage in Ancient Society.* London: Routledge, 1989.

Wright, N.T. *Jesus and the Victory of God.* Minneapolis: Fortress, 1996.

—— *The New Testament and the People of God.* Minneapolis: Fortress, 1992.

—— *The Resurrection of the Son of God.* Minneapolis: Fortress, 2003.

Woods, D. 'Tiberius, Tacfarinas, and the Jews.' *Arctos Acta Philologica Fennica* 42 (2008): 267-284.

Zugibe, F.T., *The Crucifixion of Jesus: A Forensic Inquiry.* New York: M. Evans and Company, 2005.

Index

If you liked this book, why not try. . .

The Destruction of Sodom
A Scientific Commentary
Graham J. Harris

ISBN: 9780718893682
PDF ISBN: 9780718843144
ePub ISBN: 9780718843151
Kindle ISBN: 9780718843168

In *The Destruction of Sodom*, the Biblical account of the destruction of Sodom and Gomorrah is examined under the spotlight of modern science against a cultural backdrop of history and archaeology. In this scientific reconstruction, the account of events described in the book of Genesis is verified and it is established that the destruction occurred at about 2350 BC as a result of an earthquake-induced landslide transporting Sodom to the depths of the Dead Sea. Strands of geography, geology, and engineering science are drawn together to provide comprehensive treatment of all relevant scientific aspects pertinent to a rational understanding of the mechanics of the disaster. The detailed scientific argument follows a discussion of the Genesis account and considerations of Canaanite culture and commerce, with specific attention to the trade in bitumen. On this point, Graham Harris provides evidence that the mainstay of Canaanite commerce was the exploitation of the bitumen resources of the Dead Sea, that the Sodomites were among the world's first chemical engineers, and from the resources of the region a large number of processed materials also would have been exported to Egypt.

The Destruction of Sodom is an example of the application of science to a fuller understanding of one of the most intriguing events of the Old Testament, and will be of direct interest to scholars as well as to the wider public.

Available now with more excellent titles in Paperback, Hardback, PDF and Epub formats from the Lutterworth Press.

#0030 - 210218 - C0 - 234/156/15 - PB - 9780718895105